UNDERSTANDING WRITING

UNDERSTANDING WRITING

James Kinney
Virginia Commonwealth University

David E. Jones
Los Angeles Valley College

John Scally
Lewis-Clark State College

RANDOM HOUSE  NEW YORK

First Edition
987654321
Copyright © 1983 by Random House, Inc.

All rights reserved under International and Pan-American Copyright Conventions. No part of this book may be reproduced in any form or by any means, electronic or mechanical, including photocopying, without permission in writing from the publisher. All inquiries should be addressed to Random House, Inc., 201 East 50th Street, New York, N.Y. 10022. Published in the United States by Random House, Inc., and simultaneously in Canada by Random House of Canada Limited, Toronto.

Library of Congress Cataloging in Publication Data

Kinney, James, 1942–
Understanding writing.

1. English language—Rhetoric. I. Jones, David E., 1939–
II. Scally, John. III. Title.
PE1408.K667   1982   808'.042   82-23090
ISBN 0-394-33149-4

Manufactured in the United States of America

Text design: Karin Gerdes Kincheloe
Painting and cover design: Maria Epes
Production: Laura Lamorte

Permissions and Acknowledgments

Chapter One   P. 14. Excerpt from pp. 19–20 from *The Peter Principle* by Dr. Laurence J. Peter and Raymond Hull. Copyright © 1969 by William Morrow and Company, Inc. By permission of the publishers.

P. 19. "The Righting of Writing," *Time* (May 19, 1980), p. 92. Copyright © 1980 by Time Inc. All rights reserved. Reprinted by permission of *Time*.

Chapter Two   P. 29. "Seeing the Light: A Blackout Tale," from *New York Magazine* 10, No. 30, July 25, 1977, p. 6. Copyright © 1977 by News Group Publications, Inc. Reprinted with the permission of *New York Magazine*.

Pp. 29–30. Council on Environmental Equality, *Solar Energy: Progress and Promise* (Washington, D.C.: U.S. Government Printing Office, 1978), p. 8.

P. 30. Excerpted from "Living with Less Oil" by William B. Mead, *Money*, March 1975, by special permission; © 1975, Time Inc.

P. 31. From an advertisement in *Sports Illustrated* 46 (April 18, 1977), pp. 60–61. Reprinted by permission of the Piper Aircraft Corporation.

P. 32. "Can Anybody Clean Up the Teamsters?" November 7, 1976, by A.H. Raskin. Copyright © 1976 by The New York Times Company. Reprinted by permission.

P. 35. James O'Toole, *Work in America* (Subcommittee on Employment, Manpower, and Poverty of the Commission on Labor and Public Welfare, U.S. Senate; Washington, D.C.: U.S. Government Printing Office, 1973), p. 28.

P. 37. From "New Day at Black Rock," *Time*, December 31, 1973, p. 49. Copyright © 1973 Time Inc. All rights reserved. Reprinted by permission from *Time*.

Pp. 37–38. "Preparing Soil Like My Father Did—By Hand," Warren C. Goodwin, April, 1973, *Organic Gardening*. Reprinted from *Organic Gardening*, Emmaus, PA 18049, with permission of Rodale Press, Inc., copyright 1973.

P. 38. From "Building an Outdoor Deck," from *Popular Science,* June 1977, p. 138. Reprinted with permission from *Popular Science* © 1977, Times Mirror Magazines, Inc.

P. 39. "A Profound Lesson for the Living" by Loudon Wainwright, *Life* Magazine, © 1969 Time Inc. Reprinted with permission.

P. 42. From "Pumping Fuel Under Water," *Time*, March 14, 1977, p. 47. Copyright 1977 Time Inc. All rights reserved. Reprinted by permission from *Time*.

P. 44. "Crazy Over Cats," *Time*, December 7, 1981, p. 72. Copyright © 1981 Time Inc. All rights reserved. Reprinted by permission from *Time*.

Chapter Three P. 55. From *The Little Prince* by Antoine de Saint-Exupéry, copyright 1943, 1971 by Harcourt Brace Jovanovich, Inc. Reprinted and reproduced by permission of the publisher.

Chapter Four P. 66. From *The Poverty of Power,* by Barry Commoner. Copyright © 1976 by Barry Commoner. Reprinted by permission of Alfred A. Knopf, Inc.

P. 72. From "A Different Dose for Different Folks," Thomas Szasz, *Skeptic*, Number 17, January/February, 1977, p. 48. Reprinted by permission.

P. 75. From "The Search for Work Is a Discouraging One for Jimmy Richardson," *The Wall Street Journal*, August 20, 1975, p. 1. Reprinted by permission of *The Wall Street Journal*, © Dow Jones & Company, Inc. 1975. All Rights Reserved.

Chapter Five P. 79. Advertisement from *Bell System Yellow Pages* (The Pacific Telephone and Telegraph Co., 1977), p. 374; Los Angeles, Northwestern Area.

P. 88. From "This Mantle of Charity," Stovall-Mathis-Elliott-Hagler-Poole: *Composition: Skills and Models*, Second Edition. Copyright © 1978 by Houghton Mifflin Company. Used by permission.

Pp. 89–90. Excerpts from *How Does It Work?* by Richard M. Koff. Copyright © 1961 by Richard M. Koff. Reprinted by permission of Doubleday & Company, Inc.

P. 90. From Sylvia Rabiner, "Daytime TV: What You're Missing (or Not Missing)," *Working Woman*, Volume 2, February 1977, p. 29. Reprinted with permission from *Working Woman*. Copyright © 1977 by HAL Publications, Inc.

Pp. 92–93. From Phelps, Stanlee, and Austin, Nancy, *The Assertive Woman*. Copyright © 1975. Impact Publishers, Inc., San Luis Obispo, California. Reprinted by permission of the publisher.

P. 96. From *How You Can Get Better Medical Care for Less Money* by Dr. Morris Placers and Charles Marwick. Copyright © 1973 by Walker and Company. Used with the permission of the publisher, Walker and Company.

P. 101. From *Good Health: Personal and Community,* by Zelma Miller and Benjamin F. Miller. Copyright © 1960, by W.B. Saunders Company. Reprinted by permission of Holt, Rinehart and Winston, CBS College Publishing.

Pp. 105–106. Excepts from *How Does It Work?* by Richard M. Koff. Copyright © 1961 by Richard M. Koff. Reprinted by permission of Doubleday & Company, Inc.

Pp. 108–109. From William H. Whyte, Jr., *The Organization Man,* p. 3. Copyright © 1956 by William H. Whyte, Jr. Reprinted by permission of Simon & Schuster, a Division of Gulf & Western Corporation.

Chapter Seven   P. 123. *Noise—The Third Pollution* by Theodore Berland, Public Affairs Pamphlet No. 449. Copyright © 1970, by the Public Affairs Committee, Inc. Used with permission.

Chapter Eight   Pp. 131–132. Wayne C. Booth, " 'Now Don't Try to Reason With Me!': Rhetoric Today, Left, Right, and Center." Reprinted from *The University of Chicago Magazine,* November-December 1967. © The University of Chicago.

P. 134. From "Math Mystique: Fear of Figuring," *Time,* March 14, 1977, p. 36. Copyright 1977 Time Inc. All rights reserved. Reprinted by permission of *Time.*

Pp. 134–135. From Morton J. Schussheim, "Why We Have Not Built More Houses." Reprinted with permission of the author from *The Public Interest,* No. 19 (Spring, 1970), pp. 20–22. © 1970 by National Affairs Inc.

P. 137. From "Is This Any Way to Make a Living?" by Myra Friedman. *Esquire* (July 1977). Copyright © 1977 by Esquire Publishing Inc.

Pp. 139–140. From William E. Blundell, "Confused, Overstuffed Corporate Writing Often Costs Firms Much Time—And Money," *The Wall Street Journal,* August 28, 1980. Reprinted by permission of *The Wall Street Journal,* © Dow Jones & Company, Inc. 1980. All Rights Reserved.

P. 142. From "Hell No, We Won't Glow," from *Time,* May 21, 1979, p. 17. Copyright 1979 Time Inc. All rights reserved. Reprinted by permission from *Time.*

Pp. 145–147. Herrick Neal, "Who's Unhappy at Work and Why" from *Manpower,* Employment and Training Administration, U.S. Dept. of Labor.

Chapter Nine   P. 150. From Isaac Asimov, "The Nightmare Life Without Fuel," *Time,* April 25, 1977, p. 33. Copyright 1977 Time Inc. All rights reserved. Reprinted by permission from *Time.*

Pp. 155–156. From *Does It Matter?* by Alan Watts. Copyright © 1968, 1969, 1970 by Alan Watts. Reprinted by permission of Pantheon Books, a Division of Random House, Inc.

P. 163. Robert Cary, "The Life and Death Struggle of a Miracle Child," *The Boston Globe* (May 29, 1977), p. A–1. Reprinted by permission of United Press International.

Chapter Ten   Pp. 180–181. From "Industrial Robots Seem Ready to Roll," *Richmond Times-Dispatch,* Nov. 9, 1980. Reprinted by permission of United Press International.

Pp. 182–183. From "Foreigners Rap U.S. Campaigns," *Richmond Times-Dispatch,* Nov. 10, 1980. Reprinted by permission of United Press International.

Pp. 184–185. "Your Future in Accounting Careers," by Lawrence Rosenthal, reviewed by Kristina Kendall. Reprinted by permission of Kristina Kendall.

Chapter Eleven   P. 197. Adapted from "Nuts, Bolts and Directions," *Esquire* (July 1977). Copyright © 1977 by Esquire Publishing Inc.

Chapter Twelve   P. 231. From *Television Production Handbook,* Third Edition, by Herbert Zettl. Copyright © 1976 by Wadsworth Publishing Company, Inc. Reprinted by permission of Wadsworth Publishing Company, Belmont, California 94002.

PREFACE

Most students who enroll in college want to develop skills that will lead to professional success. The practical use of your writing skills will be to write reports, proposals, memos, and business correspondence, but all writing grows from basic ways of thinking about the world and relies on some basic principles. The first two sections of the text introduce you to these principles and give you practice in developing those ways of thinking that lie behind all successful writing. The third section is devoted to explaining and illustrating the main types of writing required by many different professions.

To begin with, it helps to think of writing as a process that takes time. In the process of writing, there is time to change and develop what you say and how you say it. The traditional way to think about writing says that you first get your main idea perfectly clear, that you then make an outline you must follow, and that you finally write out in a perfectly correct manner the details to fill in the outline. But research about writing shows us that very few people actually follow this rigid, step-by-step pattern. Instead, recent ideas about the writing process suggest that first you need to explore a subject, to write out information and ideas about it before trying to organize a possible outline. Then, with this rough outline in mind, you write out a draft, but don't necessarily stick to the outline if some good ideas come along while writing. Next you go over the draft to revise and improve both the organization and development of your ideas. Only at the end of the process do you worry about getting everything correct—that is, after you have finished all your major revisions you proofread carefully to make sure that spelling, grammar, punctuation, and other mechanical concerns are handled properly.

SUMMARY OF THE WRITING PROCESS

1. Explore a subject to generate written information and ideas.
2. Sort through this material to group as much as possible into blocks of related items and to set up a possible organization (outline) for these blocks.
3. Write out a draft.
4. Revise extensively to rearrange and improve the organization where necessary, to fill in needed material, or to cut out unnecessary and unrelated information.
5. Proofread carefully to correct any problem in spelling, grammar, punctuation, and so forth.

In Part One, "Basic Concepts," we discuss the important differences between speaking and writing, then examine some *general* ways to explore subjects and to group the generated material into paragraphs. In Part Two, "Strategies for Writing," we examine in detail more *specific* strategies that can be used both to think about a subject in exploring it and to organize a paragraph, a group of paragraphs in a longer piece of writing, or even a whole paper. These strategies are artificially separated into individual chapters, but when writing in the business world you most often use combinations of these strategies, depending upon your actual audience, purpose, and subject.

The strategies in Part Two are based on common ways people think and organize their thoughts. We begin each chapter by seeing the strategy first as a way of understanding the world around us—and thus of exploring the subjects we are called upon to write about—and, second, as a way of organizing written material in a pattern that other people, our audience, will find familiar and easy to follow. The organization of chapters in Part Two follows a clear progression, but it is not necessary to study them in this order nor to study all of them. While each chapter is clearly related to the others, each one is also a self-contained unit.

We organized the strategies in Part Two according to the developmental relationship among the thinking processes called for in each one:

1. Describing: observing physical details of a person, place, or thing
2. Comparing: noting likenesses and differences between observed persons, places, or things
3. Classifying: grouping individual items according to observed likenesses, then subdividing large groups into smaller ones according to differences
4. Defining: classifying, then separating out an individual item from other members of the same class
5. Analyzing: dividing an individual item into parts, functions, processes, causes and/or effects
6. Persuading: using various strategies to bring about desired effects on an audience

In Part Three, "Practical Applications," we present the fixed kinds of writing you will be asked to do in college and the business world. You will have the opportunity to become familiar with these forms, and to practice applying the strategies learned in Part Two within the limits imposed by the kinds of writing found in Part Three.

Finally, the appendixes treat common writing problems and provide exercises for you to improve your ability to proofread and correct your papers.

During more than five years of development, *Understanding Writing* has benefited from the generous advice of colleagues around the country, and we would like to acknowledge their thorough readings and helpful suggestions. Michelle Loris at Sacred Heart University, Paul G. Kreuzer at Northeastern University, Maurine Magliocco at Western Illinois University, Gerard O'Connor at University of Lowell, and John Bell at New York City Technical College, City University of New York, helped us revise and strengthen the final draft of *Understanding Writing*. Lois Cundiff, the late Gregory Cowan, C. Jeriel Howard, Roberta S. Matthews, David Skwire, Kathleen O. Sterns, and Richard Sterling reviewed the manuscript in its early stages and provided valuable advice. We are particularly indebted to Richard Larson of the City University of New York and to Elisabeth McPherson, who both provided invaluable aid in revising early versions of the book.

Understanding Writing also reflects the influence of innumerable friends and colleagues who have affected our thinking about the nature of written composition. To single out one source of inspiration is not to slight the many others, but Frank D'Angelo's *A Conceptual Theory of Rhetoric* has been at the core of our belief that traditional rhetorical patterns are first of all ways of understanding the world.

In addition, we are indebted to the former Random House editorial team of Richard Garretson and Christine Pellicano, who shepherded the project through difficult times. Our special thanks go to the people at Random House responsible for guiding *Understanding Writing* into print: Steven Pensinger, for his crucial faith and support; Dorchen Leidholdt, for her generous and intelligent work as project editor; Barbara Zimmerman, for securing permissions; Sheila Steinberg, for excellent copyediting; Laura Lamorte, for supervising the production process; and Karin Kincheloe, for creating an attractive and functional design.

We also thank Irene Weiner, Toros Yetenekian, and Cheryl Jones for their most generous research assistance, and Carol Hunter, our typist, for her speed, accuracy, and unflagging spirit.

Finally, we want to acknowledge the support of The National Endowment for the Humanities, which brought us together and gave us time to begin, and to thank Judy and Chris for their patience throughout.

CONTENTS

PREFACE vii

part one / BASIC CONCEPTS — 1

1 / SPEAKING, WRITING, and EXPLORING — 3

Speaking and Writing — 3
Two-Way Communication — 3
Exercises — 4
Written Communication — 5
Summary — 6
Exercises — 6

Writing to an Audience 7

Attitude Toward the Subject 8
Identifying the Audience 8
Attitude Toward the Audience 8
Effect on the Audience 9
Appropriate Voice 11
Exercise 14
Summary 15
Writing Assignment 15

Exploring the Subject 15

Observe and Note Details 16
Free Association Lists 16
Free Writing 17
Brainstorm 18
Interview People 18
Research and Read 18
Exercise 19
Writing Assignment 19

2 / PARAGRAPHING 21

Building Paragraphs 21

Exercise 22
Grouping Material 23
Exercises 24
Seeing the General and the Specific 25
Exercises 26
Forming the Topic Sentence 26
Exercises 28
Checking for Unity 29
Exercise 30
Finding a Pattern for Development 31
Setting an Order 35
Making Transitions 44
Summary 46
Writing Assignment 46

part two / STRATEGIES for WRITING   49

3 / DESCRIBING   51

Understanding Description   51
Seeing the Whole First   52
Paying Attention to Detail   53
Summary   54

Writing Description   54
Words   56
Exercise   57
Steps in Writing Description   57
Exercise   58
Summary   59
Writing Assignments   59

4 / COMPARING   61

Understanding Comparison   61
Comparison and Contrast   61
Summary   62
Exercises   63
Types of Comparison   63
Exercises   66
Standards of Comparison   67
Exercises   68

Writing Comparisons   69
Whole-by-Whole Method   69
Summary   71

Exercise	72
Point-by-Point Method	72
Exercises	74
Combination of Methods	74
Summary	74
Writing Assignments	75

5/CLASSIFYING 77

Understanding Classification 77

Classifying and Dividing	77
Exercise	78
Finding a Principle	78
Exercises	82
Summary	83
Exercises	84

Writing Classification 85

Getting Started	85
Exercise	86
Making Transitions	87
Exercise	87
Another Exercise	91
Summary	91
Writing Assignments	91

6/DEFINING 95

Understanding Definition 95

Relationship of Definition to Classification and Division	95
Exercises	96
Simple Definitions	97

Exercise	98
Problems in Definition	98
Exercises	100

Writing Extended Definitions 100

Placing the Term in a Class	102
Exercises	103
Distinguishing the Term from Others in the Class	103
Exercises	104
Comparing a Term to a Commonly Known Thing	105
Exercise	106
Using an Example	107
Exercise	107
Using a Negative Example	108
Exercises	109
Summary	110
Writing Assignments	110

7 / ANALYZING: PARTS, FUNCTIONS, and PROCESSES 113

Understanding Analysis 113

Analytic Thinking	113
Exercises	114
Types of Analysis	115
Exercises	117

Writing Analysis 118

Analysis of Parts and Component Assemblies	118
Exercises	119
Analysis of Functions	120
Exercise	122
Analysis of Steps in a Process	123
Exercises	126
Summary	126
Writing Assignments	127

8 / ANALYZING CAUSES and EFFECTS — 129

Understanding Cause-Effect Analysis — 129
Sequence Versus Causality — 129
Exercise — 130
Immediate and Remote Causes — 131
Exercises — 132
Uses for Cause-Effect Analysis — 133
Exercises — 135
Evaluating Cause-Effect Analysis — 136
Exercise — 137
Summary — 138

Writing about Cause and Effect — 138
From Cause to Effect — 138
Exercises — 140
From Effect to Cause — 141
Exercises — 142
Combination: Effect-Cause-Effect — 143
Exercise — 144
Organizing a Cause-Effect Analysis — 144
Summary — 147
Writing Assignments — 148

9 / PERSUADING — 149

Understanding Persuasion — 149
Subjects for Persuasion — 151
Exercise — 152
Evidence — 152
Sources of Evidence — 154
Exercises — 154
Use of Examples — 155
Exercises — 156

Writing to Persuade — 157
- Logical Persuasion — 157
- *Exercises* — 160
- *Exercises* — 162
- Emotional Persuasion — 162
- *Exercises* — 165
- Personal Persuasion — 166
- *Exercises* — 168
- *Summary* — 169
- *Writing Assignments* — 169

part three / PRACTICAL APPLICATIONS — 171

10 / WRITING in COLLEGE — 173

Writing about What You Know — 173
- Essay Exams — 174
- *Exercise* — 175
- General Essays — 175
- *Exercise* — 176

Writing about What You Read — 177
- Summaries — 177
- Sample Summaries — 180
- *Exercise* — 184
- Critical Reviews — 185
- *Exercise* — 191
- *Summary* — 191
- *Writing Assignments* — 192

11 / FINDING a JOB — 193

Understanding the Job Search — 193
- The Job Market — 194
- Journals — 195
- *Exercises* — 195

Steps in the Job Search — 196

The Résumé — 197
Exercise — 201
The Cover Letter — 201
Exercise — 204
The Interview Appointment Letter — 204
The Interview — 204
The Follow-Up Letter — 205
Summary — 206
Writing Assignment — 207

12 / WRITING LETTERS, MEMOS, and INSTRUCTIONS — 209

Letters — 210

Format — 210
Claim and Adjustment Letters — 215
Exercises — 217
Inquiry Letters and Responses — 217
Exercises — 218
Order Letters — 218
Exercise — 219
Summary — 219

Memos — 219

Memos That Inform — 219
Memos That Explain — 220
Exercises — 222
Memos That Persuade — 223
Exercises — 224
Memos That Instruct — 225
Exercise — 226
Summary — 227

Giving Instructions — 227

Guidelines — 228
Exercises — 231
Summary — 232
Writing Assignments — 232

13 / WRITING REPORTS and PROPOSALS — 235

Reports — 235

Purpose and Audience — 235
Reports That Inform — 237
Exercises — 240
Exercises — 242
Reports That Interpret and Evaluate — 242
Exercise — 246
Reports That Recommend — 246
Exercises — 250

Proposals — 251

Format — 251
Exercises — 254
Summary — 255
Writing Assignments — 255

appendixes / BASIC SKILLS — 257

A / UNDERSTANDING SENTENCES — 259

Exercises — 259

Word Groups — 260

Phrases and Clauses — 260
What Is a Sentence? — 261
Subject Groups and Verb Groups — 262
Adverbials — 263
Exercise — 264
Review Exercises — 265

Nouns and Verbs — 266

Finding Nouns — 266
Exercises — 267

CONTENTS

Exercise	267
Exercise	268
Exercise	268
Exercises on Finding Nouns	269
Finding Verbs	269
Exercise	270
Finding Main Verbs	271
Exercises	273
Exercise	274
Finding the Subject	275
Exercise	276
Prepositional Phrases	276
Exercise	277
Agreement	278
Exercise	279
Review Exercises	279

B / COMBINING SENTENCES — 281

Why Combine Sentences? — 281

Economy	282
Clarity	282
Variety	283
Emphasis	284

Ways to Combine Sentences — 285

Combining Independent (Coordinate) Groups	285
Exercise	287
Exercises	288
Combining Sentences with Prepositional Groups (Phrases)	288
Exercises	290
Combining Sentences by Using *Wh-* Groups	290
Exercises	292
Combining Sentences by Using *-ing* and *-ed* Groups	293
Exercises	294
Exercises	296
Combining Sentences by Using Dependent (Subordinate) Groups	296
Exercise	298

C / IMPROVING USAGE 299

Subject-Verb Agreement 299
-s and -es Endings 300
Exercise 301
Words Between the Subject and the Verb 301
Exercises 302
Subjects—Singular or Plural? 302
Compound Subjects 302
Exercise 303
"Either/Or"; "Neither/Nor" 303
Exercise 304
"There Is"/"There Are" 304
Exercises 304
"You"/"I" 305
Exercises 305
Verbs: Mainly in the Present Tense 306
The Verb "To Be" 306
Exercise 306
"Have/Has"; "Do/Does" 307
Exercise 307
All Other Verbs in the Present Tense 308
Exercise 308

Verbs: Past Forms 309
Forming the Past Tense 309
List of Irregular Verbs 310
Exercises 314

Pronoun Problems 314
Pronoun Agreement 314
Exercise 315
Indefinite References 316
Exercise 316
Vague Pronouns 317
Exercise 318
Exercise 318
Review Exercise 319

part one

BASIC CONCEPTS

1

SPEAKING, WRITING, and EXPLORING

Speaking and Writing

Two-Way Communication

Most of us feel we can communicate fairly well in speech. Nearly every writing instructor has heard students say, "I can explain what I mean but I can't write it down." Talking gives us many more communication tools than writing does. Face to face with a listener, we get feedback that tells us how well the message is being received. A nod of the head tells us we're doing okay; a puzzled look says we'd better go back over that point again to explain, or use an example. In fact, we often form our ideas in the process of expressing them—we "talk it out."

Many communication tools do not involve words or sounds at all. The importance of "body language" in interpersonal communication is well known. A handshake says, "I'm glad to meet you." Leaning forward slightly in your chair tells the other person, "I'm listening to what you say." Looking into someone's eyes shows you mean what you say or that you care about what he or she is saying. A business person who looks at his or her watch at the start of an interview says, "You are not important. I have little time for you."

4 BASIC CONCEPTS

In general, our facial expression reveals much about our attitude or feelings toward what we are saying (our *subject*), while our overall posture and gestures indicate our attitude toward the person(s) we are speaking to (our *audience*). A pained expression indicates a friend might not have had a good time, despite her saying she enjoyed herself; standing with your head down, looking at the floor, and making nervous hand-movements suggest you feel intimidated by the person you're talking to. We also send messages to others through the clothes we choose to wear, the style of our hair, even the car we choose to drive. The teacher who wears a suit and tie or a tailored dress is sending you a message; the teacher who wears jeans and T-shirts is sending you another.

EXERCISES

1. Pick two or three people you see every day and write down how their choice of clothing matches (or doesn't match) what you know about their personalities and life styles.

2. Consider you own way of dressing, moving, and gesturing. Write out brief responses to:
   A. What message does your clothing send about you?
   B. What impression do people you are just meeting form about you?
   C. Do you think they see you as shy? Or outgoing? Or friendly? Or aggressive?

3. Find a place where people meet and talk—a restaurant, for example. Watch people talking, then:
   A. Make a list of different expressions and gestures they make.
   B. Note your impression of them. Can you discern the attitude of a person you are observing toward the subject he or she is discussing and toward his or her audience? What clues help you?

Clothes, hair style, body language, gestures all help us communicate face to face. What happens when these message senders can't operate? When we have to rely on spoken words alone? Have you ever found yourself talking on the phone and smiling? Or holding the phone in one hand while walking around the room gesturing with the other hand to the empty air? The person you're talking with can't see your smile or your gestures. But those expressions and gestures are such a total part of our communication package that we can't give them up.

How do we control our spoken voices to project the message we want to communicate even when we aren't with our audience? We do it through a constant, flowing pattern of changes in the stress or emphasis we put on words, in the pitch of our voice, and in the pauses we use. These three things by themselves sound simple, but taken together in all their possible combinations and variations, they add up to a highly complex system of signals. How does the listener know what the signals mean? How did we learn to send them out? We, and our listeners, learned to use and understand these signals while we learned to speak. We never become consciously aware of all these signals, but learning to speak means mastering the signal system along with learning how to pronounce words. Let's look at a very simple example of this complex system, just to illustrate how it works.

> We ask questions all the time. We often signal the kind of answer we want back, and the person being asked the question understands the signal—even though neither one of us is consciously aware that this signal is being sent and received. A friend stops by your house. After you've greeted your friend, you ask, "Do you want a beer or a coke?" Ask this question aloud. Notice what your voice does when it gets to the word "coke." If your voice goes up in pitch on "coke," you are signaling that you want a *yes or no* answer, and your friend will get that message. If you keep your voice at the same pitch for both "beer" and "coke," you signal that you expect your friend to respond by *choosing* one or the other.

Our spoken language is filled with these subtle signals. We control these signals without having to think about them, and when we want to communicate with our voices, we automatically direct this complex signal system to do the job for us.

Written Communication

At first most of us feel frustrated when we try to put down on paper what we know we can say to someone else, because words alone don't communicate very well. Dress, body language, facial expressions, gestures, stress, pitch, and pause are all active parts of communicating, and they carry more than half of the message that we're trying to get across. When we write, we lose everything except words, and we get no feedback at all from our audience. We try, however, to hang on to some of our signal system—that's what punctuation is for. Commas (,), periods (.), and semicolons (;)—along with dashes (—) or colons (:)—are used to indicate on paper where and how we pause in speech. Exclamation points (!) and question marks (?) try to hint at changes in stress and pitch. We also try to indicate stress by underlining or even CAPITALIZING a word, but most of the complex signal system of speech is lost forever on the silent page. In the following passage the author, Tom Wolfe, uses a variety of visual signals—punctuation marks—to get his message across. Wolfe is trying to close the gap between speaking and writing.

> Something will pan out. It's a magic economy—yes!—all up and down the coast from Los Angeles to Baja California kids can go to one of these beach towns and live the complete surfing life. They take off from home and get to the beach, and if they need a place to stay, well, somebody rents a garage for twenty bucks a month and everybody moves in, girls and boys. Furniture—it's like, one means, you know, one *appropriates* furniture from here and there. (Tom Wolfe, *The Pump House Gang*)

SUMMARY

The basic differences between speaking and writing are as follows:

1. Speaking is two-way communication; you receive feedback from your audience as you are communicating. Writing is one-way communication. You receive no audience feedback and have no way of knowing how effectively you are getting your message across.

2. In face-to-face communication in contrast to writing you have many more communication tools to use: dress, facial expression, gesture, stance, pause, pitch, and stress. In written communication all of these are lost, except for a limited number of punctuation marks to indicate some of the pauses or changes in pitch and stress that occur when speaking.

EXERCISES

1. List the devices Tom Wolfe uses to make his written "voice" more like a spoken one.

2. Look through some issues of magazines such as *Time, Newsweek, Ebony,* or *People* for pictures of people that accompany stories and ads. Make notes describing what their expressions, gestures, clothing, or any other factors tell you about each person at that moment.

3. Read the sentence "Maria bought that house" to show astonishment (A) that Maria was the one who bought it; (B) that she bought it rather than rented it; (C) that she bought that house rather than another. Read the question "Are we going to that again?" in different ways, showing pleasure, boredom, annoyance, and anger.

4. Make a tape recording of your side of a telephone conversation.

A. Transcribe the conversation into writing.
B. Punctuate and add any other signals you can to get across the message you tried to communicate on the phone.
C. Have someone else read it aloud to see if it communicates everything you intended.

5. Watch some television commercials with the sound off.
   A. Observe the setting, gestures, and expressions.
   B. Jot down what messages you get about attitude toward both the subject and the audiences.

6. Select an object you are quite familiar with, but most other people might not be (e.g., a particular chair in your living room at home).
   A. Create a nonsense name for this object (e.g., "filig" or "whorp") and using this name write a detailed description of the object. Try to make the description a clear and precise piece of one-way communication, so that someone else will be able to picture the object on the basis of your description alone.
   B. Now exchange your description with someone else in class, and both of you try to draw a picture of the object the other person has described. It's no fair asking questions.

Writing to an Audience

Knowing the differences between speaking and writing points the way to a basic principle for effective written communication:

PAY CAREFUL ATTENTION TO YOUR AUDIENCE

In other words, when your audience is not immediately present, you must work at overcoming the problems built into one-way communication. Here are five guidelines:

1. Know your own attitude toward the subject.
2. Clearly identify your audience.
3. Know your attitude toward your audience.
4. Know how you want to affect your audience—your *purpose* for writing.
5. Create a written "voice" appropriate to your subject, audience, and purpose.

Attitude Toward the Subject

Understanding the subject you are writing about is, of course, crucial to good writing. But the writer must also be aware of personal feelings and attitudes he or she might have toward the subject. Strong personal feelings can influence the way we see a subject and influence what facts we choose to include or leave out of our discussion. For example, Sarah has strong personal feelings against drugs and dislikes a colleague because she smokes marijuana, but the woman asks Sarah to write a letter of recommendation for her. Sarah's feelings about the subject—her colleague—could influence the kind of letter she will write. For another example, people in some cultures believe that the cow is a holy animal; they do not see cattle as a potential source of food. Anyone from such a culture would write about cows with a different attitude and voice from a rancher who raises beef cattle for those who like to eat meat.

Identifying the Audience

Writers for mass media publications have more problems than most people when it comes to identifying their audience, but even in this situation one can be more specific than just calling the readers the "general public." Which portion of the public makes up the largest part of the readership? Old, young, middle-aged? High income, low income, middle income? Educated through grade school, through high school, through college? Urban dwellers, suburban, rural? Business persons or skilled workers? Northerners, southerners, or westerners? Men or women?

Answering questions such as these can help you identify the values, prejudices, political views, and other characteristics of your audience.

In most work-related situations you will know who your audience is. You will be writing to someone within the same organization or to someone with shared business interests. You will be writing to people who buy or sell products, receive or provide services. You address people above you, below you, or on the same level in the organizational hierarchy. Moreover, the work they are doing probably has a defined relationship with your work; for example, if you are in production, you will deal with people in purchasing on one hand and those in marketing on the other.

Attitude Toward the Audience

Once you have identified the audience you are addressing, try to define your relationship with that audience. Do you know them at all? Are they outsiders who would not understand what you are saying as easily as someone inside would? Do you see them as people you must instruct in the basics of the situation? If co-workers, for how long, and how well do you know them? Do they share a common base of knowledge with you on this subject? Do you have to be careful not to irritate them by explaining something they already know more about than you do? Is this a superior you are addressing? Do you have a personal, friendly relationship anyway, or is it formal? Finally, you must decide which you are most concerned about, the subject itself or the impression on the audience.

Draw yourself a mental picture of your audience or of a typical member of your audience. Then write as if you were speaking directly to that person. Readers respond most positively to a piece of writing that speaks directly to them.

Which of the following shows the greatest understanding of the audience to which the letter is written? Which is most likely to get results?

Dear Mr. Grimes:

This is the second time we have to warn you that your time payment on your television set is overdue. If we don't get the payment within a week, we will make court action.

Sincerely,
Ace Credit Union

Dear Mr. Grimes:

We have enjoyed working with you in the past and your fine payment record makes us wonder if you are experiencing financial difficulties. Your payments on your television set are overdue. If you are having financial troubles, perhaps we can help you work them out. Please let us know when we can expect a payment.

Sincerely,
Ace Credit Union

Effect on the Audience

Obviously, the attitude you have toward your audience is influenced by the effect you want to have on them—your purpose for writing. Are you trying to draw attention to something you've done well, or to distract attention from some problem? Are you trying to buy something or to sell something? Are to trying to encourage, or intimidate, or praise, or blame? Do you want to please them or make them angry enough to get going? Until you know what effect you want, you can't construct an appropriate voice.

All writing has a purpose. In general, most writing intends to achieve one or more of the following:

>To express the writer's feelings
>To inform
>To explain
>To persuade

Very seldom will any writing be a pure example of only one of these purposes. Most writing blends them all to some degree, but it is common for one purpose or the other to dominate.

To Express

We have strong feelings on certain subjects and sometimes write just to get those feelings out. Personal diaries or journals contain expressive writing, as do angry letters to the editor where the sole purpose is to express the writer's annoyance at the newspaper's coverage of some story. We will not be concerned in this textbook with purely expressive writing, although most writing to some degree expresses the writer's attitude toward both his or her subject and audience.

To Inform

Often writing intends simply to provide information of interest or need to a given audience. School personnel, for example, might be interested in the following information:

> Today, proportionately more American teenagers are working while still in school than at any other time in the past quarter century. Between 1940 and 1970, the proportion of 16 year old males attending high school and working part time increased from 4 percent to 27 percent. For females the same age, the increase was from 1 percent in 1940 to 16 percent in 1970. Current estimates indicate that at some given time during the school year, about 50 percent of all high school juniors and seniors and about 30 percent of all 9th and 10th graders are employed. (Sheila Cole, "Send Our Children to Work?" *Psychology Today*)

To Explain

One of the most common purposes for writing in the business world is to explain the various elements involved in a situation or to explain how something is done. This textbook is an example of writing intended to explain.

To Persuade

More than anything else, we write to convince others to accept our view of things. We have a point to make and want our audience to consider it. Here is an example of persuasive writing:

> Sexuality has for too long been denied its proper place among other human activities. Physical eroticism has been either shrouded in mystery and surrounded by taboos or heralded far beyond its capacity, by itself, to contribute to the fullness of life. Human sexuality grows increasingly satisfying as life itself becomes more meaningful. The time has come to enhance the quality of sexuality by emphasizing its contribution to a significant life. ("A New Bill of Sexual Rights and Responsibilities," *The Humanist*)

Appropriate Voice

Just as your tone of voice changes when you talk with different people about different subjects, each piece of writing projects a different "voice" for the writer. Knowing your subject, your audience, and your attitude toward each, you should be able to determine whether a distant, formal voice or an involved, casual voice is most suitable. Generally, if you are on good terms with someone, even your boss, you shouldn't adopt a very formal, even stuffy, voice just because you are writing. On the other hand, a chatty, casual voice might be inappropriate when addressing someone you do not know personally. Your purpose will also affect your choice. Persuasion, for example, more often speaks directly to readers than instruction does.

How do you make your written voice distant or involved? One way to make it distant is to use long words, long sentences, and long paragraphs, but even these don't always produce a formal voice. The real key lies in how much attention you pay to your audience; that is, how much attention you let them see you paying. If you concentrate solely on the subject and do not give the audience cues that you are aware of them as readers, the voice will be distant and formal:

> Foremost among iatrogenic (doctor-induced) diseases was the pretense of doctors that they provided their clients with superior health. First, social planners and doctors became its victims. Soon this epidemic aberration spread to society at large. Then, during the last fifteen years, professional medicine became a major threat to health. Huge amounts of money were spent to stem immeasurable damage caused by medical treatments. The cost of extending sick life? More and more people survived longer months with their lives hanging on a plastic tube, imprisoned in iron lungs, or hooked onto kidney machines. New sickness was defined and institutionalized; the cost of enabling people to survive in unhealthy cities and in sickening jobs skyrocketed. The monopoly of the medical profession was extended over an increasing range of everyday occurrences in every man's life. (Ivan Illich, *Tools for Conviviality*)

The informal voice gets the reader involved. The writer often speaks in the first person ("I") and talks directly to the reader, as in this example:

> But . . . I think we are looking for more, much more. First, we want to find ourselves; to become more fully human. That single goal pervades a great deal of the highly desperate kind of searching we are witnessing today. We seek a moral purpose to life, a vision, idealism, truth, love, excitement. Second, we want a return to old values—not necessarily of our parents, but of our grandparents. All about us—in furniture, clothes, entertainment, the return to nature—we see the nostalgic looking back to a simpler life. We are coming to reject the very corporate life style being sold by the major corporate contributors to both parties. And I think any party, or candidate, who fails to recognize these facts will have little political influence. (Nicholas Johnson, *Test Pattern for Living*)

Involved Voice

If your written voice sticks strictly to the subject and never acknowledges that it is addressing an audience, it will be distant. But if your voice keeps reminding the audience that you are aware of them and are trying to consider their reaction, you will create an involved effect. Here are some ways of creating an informal, involved tone:

1. Address the audience directly; let them know that you know they are there. Don't be afraid to use the word "you." *Example*: "By now you should be aware that the authors of this book have been addressing you directly throughout it."
2. Use the pronoun "I." Address the reader as one person speaking directly to another. *Example*: "I hope that you will agree with my suggestions in this memo."
3. Use "we" frequently. Draw the audience into a relationship with you as the author. Create a sense of shared concerns and common problems. *Example*: "Assuming that you do agree with my suggestions, we need to begin thinking about how to implement them."
4. Keep people active in your writing. Make it clear *who* is taking action. *Example*: "You and I have got to support each other on this issue" instead of "It is necessary that a united front be presented on this issue."
5. Use contractions and less "standard" punctuation marks such as dashes and exclamation points. *Example*: "Look—we may as well hang together on this one, because if the project manager doesn't buy it, we'll hang separately for sure!"

Obviously, using all these devices in a piece of writing could make it very informal indeed. Don't overwhelm your reader with chattiness.

SPEAKING, WRITING, AND EXPLORING 13

These are just tools, and you should practice their use, practice mixing them in various combinations, until you learn how to vary the degree of informality. When in doubt, don't be afraid to be a little less formal than you might think is necessary. Most of the time people err on the side of being too formal, and a touch of informality is usually a welcome change.

Distant Voice

The trouble with being formal and objective is that your writing can start sounding a little pompous and "stuffy." But here are some hints for writing in a distant, objective voice without sounding stuffy:

1. Try to begin sentences with the subject (underlined).
   Stuffy: In the event that the quotas are not met, sales <u>personnel</u> will not receive bonuses.
   Better: Sales <u>personnel</u> will not receive bonuses if the quotas are not met.

2. Avoid deadwood and empty phrases. Eliminate unnecessary words.
   Stuffy: The School of Education is committed to offering services in the field of instructional development.
   Better: The School of Education offers instructional development services.

3. Use active verbs. Avoid relying too much on forms of "be" (is, are, was, were).
   Stuffy: The purpose of this memo is to outline our new promotion program.
   Better: This memo outlines our new promotion program.

4. Vary the length of your sentences. A series of long sentences creates a stuffy tone. If you have to write a long sentence, try to follow it with a short, emphatic one.

Long sentence: I watched the recent Frost-Nixon interviews with great interest, curious to see what three years of seclusion had done to Richard Nixon's posing and affectation.
Short sentence: They had done little.
Long sentence: But watching one interview shortly after reading a number of freshman essays, I was struck by how consistently Nixon's response to pressure was to strike a dramatic pose.
Long sentence: Faced with an audience he could not see and with the need to impress them with the quality of his thought, which even he could sense was inadequate, he chose again and again to use

14 BASIC CONCEPTS

Short summary sentence: posturing to draw his listeners away from the substance of his remarks. This seemed the perfect analogue for my freshman writers. (Daniel Shanahan, "Why Johnny Can't Think," *Change*)

EXERCISE

Read the following passage, then describe the voice speaking in it:

1. Do you like (are you attracted to) this voice?
2. What kind of audience is the writer speaking to?
3. What is the writer's purpose?
4. Is this voice formal or informal?
5. Rewrite the first paragraph to create a new voice while keeping the message the same.

When I was a boy I was taught that the men upstairs knew what they were doing. I was told, "Peter, the more you know, the further you go." So I stayed in school until I graduated from college and then went forth into the world clutching firmly these ideas and my new teaching certificate. During the first year of teaching I was upset to find that a number of teachers, school principals, supervisors and superintendents appeared to be unaware of their professional responsibilities and incompetent in executing their duties. For example my principal's main concerns were that all window shades be at the same level, that classrooms should be quiet and that no one step on or near the rose beds. The superintendent's main concerns were that no minority group, no matter how fanatical, should ever be offended and that all official forms be submitted on time. The children's education appeared farthest from the administrator's mind.

At first I thought this was a special weakness of the school system in which I taught so I applied for certification in another province. I filled out the special forms, enclosed the required documents and complied willingly with all the red tape. Several weeks later, back came my application and all the documents!

No, there was nothing wrong with my credentials; the forms were correctly filled out; an official departmental stamp showed that they had been received in good order. But an accompanying letter said, "The new regulations require that such forms cannot be accepted by the Department of Education unless they have been registered at the Post Office to ensure safe delivery. Will you please remail the forms to the Department, making sure to register them this time?"

I began to suspect that the local school system did not have a monopoly on incompetence.

As I looked further afield, I saw that every organization contained a number of persons who could not do their jobs. (Dr. Lawrence J. Peter and Raymond Huall, *The Peter Principle*)

SPEAKING, WRITING, AND EXPLORING | 15

SUMMARY

The basic concepts necessary for writing effectively are:

1. Pay attention to your audience. This means you must recognize the readers' needs because readers are not present to give you feedback. You must consider your attitude toward both subject and audience; clearly identify your purpose and your audience. Ordinarily, one purpose will dominate a single piece of writing: to express, to inform, to explain, or to persuade.

2. Create a "voice" in writing appropriate to your particular subject, purpose, and audience, as the spoken tone you use is appropriate when addressing different people in different situations. Depending on subject, purpose, and audience your voice may be distant or involved, that is, tending to be formal and objective, or informal and personal.

WRITING ASSIGNMENT

Here's an assignment calculated to challenge your ability to handle the problems of audience, purpose, and voice: The editors of *Seventeen* magazine are publishing a special issue devoted to careers. They have invited you, among several other people, to write a 300 to 400 word open letter to their readers about the career field you are preparing for. The purpose of your letter should be to get the readers thinking about your field, whether welding or law, as a possibility for them to consider. The letter should not try to be a "hard sell," but simply to open the reader's mind to a career possibility. NOTE: The average readers of *Seventeen* are thirteen- to fourteen-year-old girls.

Exploring the Subject

To begin with, we established that speaking and writing differ in significant ways, and, because of these differences, that you must pay careful attention to the needs of your audience when writing. In school many writing assignments exist in a vacuum—the textbook or teacher gives you a topic and you write to the teacher to fulfill the assignment. You have no "real" audience or purpose. Outside of school, however, almost all writing takes place in a very specific context. You start with the subject, audience, and purpose given to you. For example, a typical kind of writing called for in a work situation is a progress report: The subject is the project you are responsible for, the audience is your supervisor, and your purpose is to inform him or her about the state of the project. You may have an additional purpose, such as persuading the supervisor that you have been doing an excellent job under difficult circumstances, or that the project would come along better if an additional person could be assigned to it. In short, most writing in business begins with an audience and purpose, and you should begin with them too—explore audience and purpose in the ways suggested earlier in the chapter; making notes to yourself about both should be your first step in writing anything.

Having completed this first step, you need to explore in some systematic way the subject before you. In this section, we will examine six ways to do this:

1. Observe and note sensory details.
2. Make free association lists.
3. Do free writing.
4. Brainstorm.
5. Interview people.
6. Research and read.

Let's assume that your subject is your English class and see how each of these methods could be applied.

Observe and Note Details

Whatever the subject, if it is at all possible, spend some time observing it—in this case the place and people involved. Take notes on the physical details—sights, sounds, smells, and other sensory facts. Observe and note details, for example, of the room and its furnishings, and the dress and behavior of the teacher and other students in the class.

Free Association Lists

Write the subject—English class—at the top of a sheet of paper and jot down any words or phrases that come to mind. Usually these will come in bursts, one leading to another. When the flow stops, read back over your list to start the association process again. A very short example of such a list might look something like this:

SPEAKING, WRITING, AND EXPLORING | 17

ENGLISH CLASS

books	escape	degree
paper	lunch	job
pen	friends	application
writing	work	resume
hard	reports	letter
boring	assignments	money
important	pass	car

In going back over this list, you should look for relationships among the items and what ideas those relationships suggest for further development. You might, for example, see a pattern here suggesting that the hard work you put into an English class now may pay off later when you are applying for jobs.

Free Writing

A very similar exploration technique is to start writing and keep writing without stopping for a set time, say ten or fifteen minutes. Again, begin with the subject at the top of the page and just write. If you can't think of anything more to write, keep going by writing "I can't think of anything more" over and over, or just keep writing the last word repetitiously until something new comes along. Once you've finished your free writing, go back and underline words and phrases that seem interesting or important. Pay absolutely no attention to grammar, spelling, or punctuation while you are doing this free writing. It's not intended for anyone else to see.

ENGLISH CLASS

The only reason I'm takin English is because I have to because <u>I cant get a degree here without it</u> [emphasis added] but sometimes I wonder if it matters whether I learn to write will I really have to do any of theis stuff as a <u>computer programer</u> I know I'll have to <u>write programs</u> but thats in Fortran or Cobol not English and won't there be secretaries to write the letters I dictate but I suppose I need to know something about <u>organizing the stuff in the letter just like you have to organize—flow chart—a program</u> that's really hard to do. Programming is harder than organizing a letter, a letter, letter, I'm really stuck, I cant think of anything more to write, to write, to write is not much fun but everyone says that <u>its necessary on the job</u> to write <u>memos</u> and <u>reports</u> and stuff if you really <u>want to get ahead</u>, like people who can write well <u>even if there not better at the job</u> like programming still sometimes <u>get promoted</u> because they can <u>impress the boss</u> or somebody by their reports even if somebody else may actually be a better programmer.

Further thought about the underlined parts of this free writing might lead to developing the connection between your English class and the kind of advantage a skill like writing may have on the job, even an advantage over simply being skilled at doing the job itself. Another line of thought suggested by the free writing might be the similarities in the process of flow charting and in the process of writing.

Brainstorm

Brainstorming is very similar to free writing, except that you do it out loud with some other people. Essentially, it's a way of getting thoughts flowing and picking up a variety of ideas, possibilities, and perspectives on the subject that might never have occurred to you by yourself. Get together with several members of your English class and have an open-ended discussion about it. People can bounce things off one another—one person's remark may spontaneously suggest a whole new way of looking at the subject to you. Be sure to take notes.

Interview People

One of the best ways to explore a subject is to talk with people who know something about it. If you were writing a progress report, if at all possible you should talk to each person working on the project. If you want to write a proposal for a new project, you should talk to someone who has had experience in a similar one. To write about your English class, discuss the subject with your teacher. Having done some free writing and other explorations, you should be able to focus the interview somewhat, perhaps on what real connections the teacher can see between the class he or she is conducting and the career you have chosen. Try to prepare the questions you are sure you want to ask ahead of time so that you will not waste time unnecessarily during the interview. One key question should be to find out the name of at least one book or article you should read on the subject.

Research and Read

An advantage of interviewing knowledgeable people is that they can direct you to some good initial reading about a subject. Rather than spending hours poking through the card catalogue under the subject heading "English," you could go directly to a source that will be useful. Moreover, most sources will mention other books and articles that you can then look up, until you gather as much information as you need.

Perhaps your English teacher will refer you to an article making the connection between writing and the world of work, such as a *Time* magazine piece called "The Righting of Writing," where you would learn that:

> Behind the push by business to improve employee writing is a recognition that bad writing costs money. "We can't do anything with their engineering if they can't explain it to us," says an Amoco supervisor in Wyoming. "I don't have time to fiddle around with their ideas unless they've worked them into shape." As Gene Cartwright, a manager at Standard Oil of Indiana, puts it, "Companies are built around reports." Robert L. Craig, an official for the American Society for Training and Development, goes further. Poor writing, he insists, is a significant "factor in the whole drop in the growth of American productivity." (*Time*)

EXERCISE

Select another class, this time in your career field, as a subject. Spend two or three days in which you go through all six exploration techniques to develop material about the class. Keep all your notes in a folder.

WRITING ASSIGNMENT

Using the material you gathered in the preceding exercise, write a letter of 300 to 400 words to a friend interested in the same career. The purpose of the letter is to advise your friend whether the class is valuable. Remember to keep your "voice" appropriate to the subject, audience, and purpose.

2

PARAGRAPHING

Building Paragraphs

In Chapter 1, we discussed the purposes of writing and the ways to generate material. After you have explored your subject, you need to put the material you have generated into some reasonable order. You need to decide which ideas belong together because they are closely related and then, after that decision is made, how one group relates to another. The method used in writing to show these relationships is the paragraph. A *paragraph* is a group of sentences that:

1. relate to one idea
2. are arranged in a certain order

Paragraphs are basic devices. Whole essays, reports, memos, and so forth are made up of an organized series of paragraphs.

Imagine for a moment a small piece of land on which a mound of junk has been tossed—several hundred pieces of wood, long strands of wire, some pipe of various sizes and shapes, some glass, a few doors, a sink or two, and some nails and screws—all this thrown together. Make a strong mental picture of this scene and take note of your responses. Can you *name* what you're looking at? Can you describe the size? Does it seem to have a purpose as it is there on the ground?

Now imagine watching that same material being arranged to form a house. The carpenter begins with an idea: to build a house. He or she follows a plan: Each piece of wood and wire and pipe belongs in a particular place. If any pieces are left out, the house is incomplete. But if all the materials are arranged in a fairly standard order, anyone looking at the structure sees that it's a house. Now the materials have meaning that observers understand. The difference between the formless, meaningless material and the easily perceived house is the *organization of material to make a specific form*. Nothing else has been added to the "heap" or "pile" of material except the *idea* of a house and the *order* in which material was arranged.

EXERCISE

Groups of sentences follow that need to be placed in a logical order before their message becomes clear.

1. Write the sentences in a logical order.
2. Note *why* you organized the sentences as you did.
3. Compare your organization with that of several classmates. Are several ways of organizing this material equally valid?

   A. (1) When everybody else is done taking advantage of them, old people are turned over to sometimes unscrupulous nursing home operators.
   (2) The elderly are among our society's habitual economic victims.
   (3) The term "golden years" suggests the money to be made by selling things to old people.

   B. (1) In football, for example, only one player, the quarterback, must have the ability to throw the ball.
   (2) Whether a player is a pitcher, catcher, infielder, or outfielder, the ability to throw is essential to the game.
   (3) Many other sports don't require this ability.
   (4) In the game of baseball, every player must have the ability to throw.

   C. (1) She prepared carefully for the follow-up interview.
   (2) When he called and told her, she was pleased.
   (3) Among other things, she read the company's annual report.
   (4) After the first interview, the personnel director decided to ask Sharon to come back.

PARAGRAPHING 23

The preceding exercise asked you to put into a sensible order material that had already been selected and grouped. When you explore a subject yourself, however, you should have pages of notes and lists that you must run through and find a way to select and group material into paragraphs on your own. Building paragraphs, that is, pulling related material together and organizing it, involves seven elements:

1. grouping material
2. seeing the general and the specific
3. forming the topic sentence
4. checking for unity
5. finding a pattern for development
6. setting an order
7. making transitions

Grouping Material

As a writer, your task is to discover order in apparently random facts and ideas. Any task that requires analyzing a problem, writing memos, instructions, reports, and so forth is much like looking at that random heap of boards, pipe, and wire. There is no meaning until you analyze the material, name the items, and order them.

Analyzing data means discovering what a group of objects or ideas has in common. For example, if you look at a fish and then a potato, you would *see* nothing in common; they don't look alike. By thinking about it, of course, you can say that both are food. "Food" is the *name* you have given to what both have in common. Grouping and naming things in this way is essential to clear thinking and writing.

What do the items in the following list have in common?

Nurse
X-ray technician
Dental assistant
Mental health technician
Physical therapist
Optometric technician
Emergency paramedic

At first you might have recognized that a dental assistant has something to do with teeth and that an optometric technician has something to do with eyes. Eyes and teeth aren't in themselves at all similar. Studying the list again, however, you discover that each item names a job people do every day. So if you say that "jobs" is the name of this group, you have given order to what at first seemed unrelated items.

But before you move on to the next step, reexamine your data to see if you have given the most specific name possible. Our minds are often too quick in finding easy answers to confusion. Notice that the list didn't include, say, auto mechanic, teacher, or truck driver. These are jobs too. A truck driver and a mental health technician share the common characteristic of "jobs." Yet each of the jobs on the list is more closely related than this. They are "jobs in allied health."

To start organizing the material you gathered while exploring a subject, sort through your lists, underlined free writing, brainstorming notes, and research data to see which items can be pulled out and given a common name. Any group you can create may be the basis for a single paragraph. If you can create three or four clear groups out of your material, it may indicate that your complete paper will have three or four paragraphs in it. Obviously, much of the material may not go into one group or another and may have to be put aside.

EXERCISES

1. Name, as specifically as possible, the groups to which the following objects belong:
   A. comb   deodorant   toothbrush   nail file   hair spray   razor   make-up   hairbrush
   B. canned vegetables   knapsack   dehydrated soup   hatchet   waterproof matchbox   smoked meat   compass   canteen   first-aid kit   socks   shirts   tin cup   frying pan

2. Divide the following objects into two groups and name each group. Discard items that fit in neither group.

   automatic switchboards   computers that understand spoken English   birth-control pills   airbags for automobiles   two-way television   space shuttles   calculators   nuclear submarines   solar hot-water heaters   automatic typewriters   automatic subway trains.

3. From the following list of characteristics, sort out four personality types. Each personality type is made up of four aspects: speech, writing, dress, and surroundings.
   A. First organize the material below into these four categories.
   B. Now select from each category (speech, writing, dress, and surroundings) the appropriate descriptions that go together to make up one personality type.
   C. Having regrouped the material into four personality types, make up a name to describe each type.

Speaks abruptly and to the point; writes highly personalized letters and memos; shows a mixed, unpredictable choice of clothing; too busy to be neat so surroundings are often cluttered; wordy but aloof and impersonal in speech; clothes are colorful, tailored to mood; prefers work area to be correct, tasteful, nondistracting; writes in intellectual, often abstract terms; wears informal, simple, functional clothes; writes in briefest of terms, with sense of urgency; businesslike, ordered, and specific in speech; likes to personalize surroundings in warm colors, informal objects, mementos, snapshots; speech is warm, friendly, humorous, abundant; dresses conservatively, unassumingly, understated. (Dudley Lynch, "In Sync With the Other Guy," *TWA Ambassador*)

Seeing the General and the Specific

This section builds on the practice you have just had in naming groups. To give a name to a large number of items requires you to go from your analysis of individual items to a general term that includes all of them. This is thinking from the specific to the general. Naming groups, however, is only a two-step process; you jumped from the lowest level of specifics to a much higher term that included all of them. This section develops your skill in determining more than two levels. Facts and ideas can be specific or general on more than two levels.

Suppose, for instance, that you have a sister Sue who owns a 1965 Ford Mustang. You could put her car into a group named "cars." But there are more specific groups between her particular car and cars in general that you could have used. There are also more general groups beyond the group of cars. Here's the way it would look on a generalization ladder:

> Transportation
> Vehicles
> Motor vehicles
> Cars
> Fords
> Mustangs
> Sue's 1965 Ford Mustang

"Transportation" is the most general term in this group because it *includes* all the other groups. "Transportation" is broader than any term below it on our ladder. Transportation is so broad that it includes not only vehicles but animals or anything else that can carry things. The group "vehicles" is *part* of the larger group of things that can transport or carry things. The group of vehicles, in turn, includes any device for carrying that is on wheels or runners, but generally does not include other forms of transportation such as animals or even surfboards. The further down the ladder, the smaller the group. The size of the group in comparison to another is a good test of how specific it is. When you get down to a single item, you have a *specific example* of the group. Remember, most things are neither general nor specific by themselves, but are only general or specific in relation to other things on the ladder. "Car" is more *general* than "Mustang," but more *specific* than "vehicle."

EXERCISES

Rearrange the following terms on ladders like the one on transportation to show order from general to specific.

1. apple; food; fruit; organic matter
2. truck; vehicle; machine; conveyance
3. United States; countries; the world; continents
4. domestic animals; cats; animals
5. World War II; conflict; violence; war
6. shelter; the Winslows' house at 3288 Pattyann Drive, Stow, Ohio; property; house
7. invasion of Normandy; war; the death of Corporal Gomez; the loss of the fifth platoon; human conflict; Company C's storming of the beach; World War II
8. nurse interviews patient; conversation; communication between a professional person and patients; communication

Forming the Topic Sentence

After analyzing your data and determining the appropriate group name, you are ready to say something about the data. You will state a number of specific things about the data, but there is always a reason you are doing all this in the first place. There is something you're trying to prove, a question you're trying to answer.

This main idea you want to communicate is usually a generalization that requires other more specific sentences to explain it. This generalization is the *controlling idea* in the paragraph. If you begin a paragraph with a clear statement of your main idea, that sentence, called a *topic sentence*, provides a control or check on the sentences that follow. A topic sentence at the beginning not only helps you control the logic and order of each of your sentences, but it also helps the reader understand the meaning of each following sentence. The topic sentence usually is the first sentence in a paragraph, but does not have to be first. Sometimes an introductory sentence may precede the topic sentence. Often the topic sentence will be placed last, so that the specific details lead up to the statement of the general idea controlling the paragraph.

You can discover the importance of topic sentences by reading a paragraph from which the topic sentence has been omitted. How far into this paragraph do you have to read before figuring what it's about?

> For some people, going to the beach is the way. The vastness of the ocean and the rhythmic breaking of the waves have the desired effect. For others, it's the quiet power of the mountains, the sense of total isolation that can be found there. But not everyone needs a radical change of environment. Some people can simply spend a few hours alone, reading favorite poetry or escaping into a fantasy world of science fiction.

By now you probably have supplied a topic sentence for that paragraph. Compare yours with the original: "Life in our complex society hammers us until we need a way to relax completely or we'll break." Notice how the topic sentence in the following paragraph summarizes the meaning of a number of facts and statistics:

> *The most glaringly visible effects of job hatred on the workers have been the increase in absenteeism and in turnover* [emphasis added]. These are simple solutions to the worker's dilemma: he or she doesn't like the job, so he or she doesn't show up. In a quite different situation, in the politics of East versus West, involving escapees from Communist countries seeking refuge in western nations, this behavior has aptly been called "voting with the feet." The worst jobs, predictably, were those with the highest rates of absenteeism and turnover, so it has been in the automobile industry that the problem first was brought to national attention. Absenteeism doubled over the years between 1960 and 1970 at General Motors and at Ford, with the rate of increase at its highest in the last year of that period. It reached the point where an average of 5 percent of GM's hourly workers were missing from work without explanation every day. On some days, notably Fridays and Mondays, the figure went as high as 10 percent. Tardiness increased too; it sounds like a trivial matter, but where production requires the concerted efforts of all the men on the line, just one late worker can delay the start of the entire process. (Judson Gooding, *The Job Revolution*)

Effective communication of ideas in a paragraph depends on the clarity of its topic sentence, which differs from other sentences that develop from it and support it. The basic difference is the level of generalization. The topic sentence is the highest level in the paragraph. It's at the top of the ladder for the material in that paragraph.

A topic sentence sums up all the rest of the sentences in the paragraph, giving the reader the gist of your message. Like the headlines in a newspaper, the topic sentence says, "This is what you will find here."

To be sure that your topic sentence says just what you want it to, keep in mind that most sentences contain two basic parts: (1) the subject (which *names* what you're talking about) and (2) a statement *about* that subject. The controlling idea is found in those few words that tell *about* your subject. In this sentence, for example, "John studies more than anyone in the class," John is the subject. Without the rest of the sentence you could write anything about John in the rest of your paragraph. But once you add the statement "studies more than anyone in the class," you have *limited* or *focused* what you will say about John. The rest of the paragraph must develop this point only. If you mention how friendly he is, where he works, how much money his parents have, or anything else, your paragraph will probably lack *unity* because these details seem to have nothing to do with your claim that he studies harder than others.

EXERCISES

1. Notice how the following sentences indicate what you would find in the paragraphs that develop them. Supply facts and examples that could be used to develop a paragraph that begins with one of these sentences.
   A. Workers in America complain that their jobs are too repetitive.
   B. Older workers are difficult to train for new jobs.
   C. This country should reinstitute the draft.
   D. Instances of violence on television have declined in the past five years.
2. Write a topic sentence for each of the following paragraphs.
   A. Read the information carefully before making a decision.
   B. Decide whether your topic sentence should go at the beginning or end of the paragraph.

These people usually act very friendly and nice when they talk with me. Behind my back, however, they tell tales and lies about me. I know they do this because these people usually gossip about others to me. These people seem very unhappy about themselves and their relationships with others. The lies they tell are an attempt to break up other people's friendships. A person who lies about others becomes very unhappy, because lies are always discovered and his or her offers of friendship are rejected.

Joe makes $800 a month, but his take-home paycheck is only $635. Grocery bills amount to about $200 a month. From the remaining $435, mortgage, telephone, electricity, and gas bills claim $210, life insurance $12, and car expenses including insurance and payments $75. Their church receives $2 a Sunday, or $8 a month. Joe spends $20 out-of-pocket a month, Mary about the same. Clothing, personal care, and other family expenses take up as much as $50. They stubbornly save $30 a month whenever possible. Therefore, if they are lucky—if the sink doesn't stop up, if the children don't catch the flu, and if everything else works okay—the Taylors end up each month with about $10 to spare. (Abraham Ribicoff, "The Alienation of the American Worker," *Saturday Review*)

A major indicator of this need is the unavailability of health insurance programs to many. As of 1975, approximately 25 percent of the poor and near poor were not covered by either Medicaid or Medicare. An estimate that includes 1978 statistics indicates that less than half of the population is protected against catastrophic illness expenses. In addition, most private and public insurance companies do not cover ambulatory or health maintenance types of expenses, or drugs. The overall insurance picture is a dim one for individuals who are not fortunate enough to have coverage through a unique plan or rich enough to afford one. *(American Journal of Nursing)*

A friend of ours who lives in New Jersey awoke on the morning of July 14, dressed quietly in the dark for fear of waking her husband, walked to the bus stop, and got on a Manhattan-bound bus. There were four other passengers on the bus. Surprisingly few, she thought. At 9:30 A.M., she arrived at Port Authority, which was dark and virtually deserted. Strange, she thought—a fuse must have blown. Noting that it was after 9:40 on the P.A. clock, she hurried to catch the 42nd Street crosstown bus. At Third Avenue, she got off and walked to her office in the East Thirties. She rang for the elevator. It did not come. Very annoying, she muttered as she walked up the seven flights to her office. Tired and thirsty, she went to pour herself a glass of water. No water. Just as she was beginning to think that this simply wasn't her day, someone mentioned the blackout. (Joseph A. Page and Mary-Win O'Brian, *New York*)

Checking for Unity

Unity means oneness. The *United* States is one country made up of fifty states. A *uni*body construction on automobiles means that all the smaller parts are welded solidly together to form *one* whole body. Your paragraph is *unified* if it develops *one* and only one idea. *Each sentence must relate to that one idea.* To check for unity in your own writing, focus your attention on the controlling idea, those few words that state something about your subject. Be certain that each sentence adds information about the controlling idea.

The following paragraph lacks unity because we have added a sentence to it that isn't related to the controlling idea. We have put parentheses around the topic sentence and underlined the sentence that does not belong.

(Recent advances in solar power offer increased hope for a solution to the energy crisis.) There has been particular progress in solar hot-water and space heating. Optimism also has grown regarding other small-scale, on-site solar energy devices, such as those capable of providing both electrical energy and heat for a building or mechanical power for an irrigation pump. <u>Nuclear power plants will solve our energy problems.</u> Within the last year alone, there have been many other encouraging signs: the number of solar-heated houses has increased dramatically; the cost of photovoltaic cells has dropped sharply; and

BASIC CONCEPTS

the development of small, solar-actuated engines has progressed substantially. (Adapted from the Council on Environmental Quality, *Solar Energy: Progress and Promise*)

Here is a positive example. The words in italics all relate back to the paragraph's controlling idea. Repetition of the controlling idea throughout emphasizes the unity of the paragraph. Again, we have put parentheses around the topic sentence.

(Electricity rates will rise sharply as a result of Ford's boost in the price of oil.) Utilities that burn oil will *pay more* for it, and those that burn coal will *pay more*, too. The price of coal is not regulated, and coal, like gas, tends to *move up* in price toward parity with oil on a penny-per-unit-of-energy basis. Coal prices have been *climbing fast* but still have a long way to go. Last June, the most recent month for which figures are available, utilities were paying 70¢ for coal generating the same amount of electricity as $1.95 worth of oil. As with gas, the speed of coal price *increases* is tempered by long-term contracts at low prices; as with gas, the more successful the Administration's program to *increase* coal production, the more new coal at high prices, and the more electric rates *will climb*. A doubling of a utility's fuel costs *increases* its rates by about 30 percent. In figuring that Ford's program would *increase* electric rates only 6 percent, the Administration conveniently left out any *increase* in the price of coal, which is used to generate 44 percent of U.S. electricity. (William B. Mead, "Living with Less Oil," *Money*)

EXERCISE

In the following paragraphs:

1. Put parentheses ( ), around the topic sentence.
2. Underline the key word or words in the other sentences, those words that point back to the controlling idea.
3. Check each paragraph for sentences that violate its unity and eliminate any you find.

The concord grape is the most widely grown grape in America for a good variety of reasons. For juice and jelly, it is unsurpassed in flavor. We find the concord a good-keeping grape as well as an excellent eating grape, whether eaten raw or baked in a pie. The concord is also suited to culture in a wide variety of climates and soils, is extremely hardy even where winters are severe, and is also disease-resistant and highly productive. The fruit is large and grows in nice-sized bunches containing medium amounts of sugar and acid. *(Organic Gardening)*

A study of 120 medical nurse-practitioner students and 31 physicians at the University of Rochester also lends support to the assertion that in this neofeminist period nurses are overcoming ingrained psychological barriers.

(Sullivan, 1978) When tested, using the Edwards Personal Preference Schedule, these nurses showed a noteworthy shift in identified needs. Whereas nurses had traditionally scored high on "order," "deference," and "endurance," they scored highest in the needs of "heterosexuality," "dominance," "change," and "achievement." These findings of the shift in needs of nurses and the high degree of similarity between the needs of nurses and physicians suggest an emerging assertiveness on the part of nurses and a trend toward similarity of need patterns with primary care physicians. There is no question but that this period of neo-feminism affords nursing the opportune environment in which to realize a bid for increased status as a practice profession. *(Nursing Forum)*

It is barely 16 years since Rachel Carson's *Silent Spring* initiated a serious concern for the environmental impact of our commercial and industrial activities. The immediate response in most quarters was that this book overstated a relatively small problem. A large problem in American society has been the integration of public education. We have come to learn, however, that the warning was correct. The late 1960s saw the development of a popular national effort, culminating in Earth Day, which called attention to the need for a public commitment to a safe and healthy environment. Although some saw this as a passing phase, the reemergence of popular protest against nuclear power and even high power transmission lines has gained a growing coalition of young and old, liberal and conservative calling for the preservation of the environment. (Adapted from David H. Wegman, "The Environmentalist Challenge," *American Journal of Public Health*)

Finding a Pattern for Development

Having settled on a general topic for your paragraph, and having selected a related group of specifics, you need to find a basic pattern or structure for relating the specific material to the general, controlling idea. Most paragraphs use one of three structures for relating general and specific material:

>general question/specific response
>general assertion/specific support
>general topic/specific illustration

General Question/Specific Response

This device is used effectively if not overused. The idea is to put the question in our mind in case it wasn't there before. Beginning with a question has psychological appeal and creates a sense of neatness and clarity:

>Where's the best place to learn to fly? At your local participating Piper Flite Center, where you'll learn to fly in a modern Piper Cherokee, the best learn-to-fly aircraft for several good reasons. (Piper Aircraft ad, *Sports Illustrated*)

Notice how this advertisement uses a question to catch our attention. Notice, too, how it attempts to answer the question. Why do we say "attempts?" Do you think this ad could be improved? The problem, of course, is that the response fails to answer the question adequately. In addition to having an adequate response, to be most effective, your question should be one that your reader would naturally ask—usually growing from the context of the writing in which it appears. The following paragraph comes after a complaint about corruption among leaders of the Teamsters Union.

> And where in industry or politics is there a shining light to which the rank and file might repair for inspiration? Certainly not among the trucking employers. The Central States Pension Fund records indicate that some of the most venal conflict-of-interest loans involved employer trustees. Collusion between company and union representatives has often turned the Teamster grievance machinery into an instrument for destroying, rather than protecting individual rights and job security. The master agreement between the union and the trucking industry is in many respects a device for helping big transcontinental fleets squeeze out small independent truckers. Not that the general ethical standards of the rest of industry are higher. Each day brings fresh revelations of illegal payoffs by arms contractors or oil companies or others in the biggest of big business to foreign officials or domestic politicians. A Federal judge expresses dismay at his inability to halt graft at an aircraft company despite persistent punishment of the officials who parade before him. The impression that comes through to the rank and file is that everyone is on the take. (A. H. Raskin, "Can Anybody Clean Up the Teamsters?" *The New York Times Magazine*)

EXERCISES

1. Using your personal experience, develop a short paragraph as an answer to each of these opening questions.
    A. What effect will 15,000 hours of television viewing have on high school age youngsters? (Pretend you are writing for parents of preschoolers who will have watched that much television by the time they are in high school.)
    B. What are we doing about the energy crisis?
2. Use the following information to develop a general question/specific response paragraph. You will have to formulate the question.
    A. Meat quality is determined by fat content.
    B. Present standards for USDA beef grades emphasize the amount of fat in the meat.
    C. The highest grade (Prime) has more fat in the muscle than Choice.
    D. The higher the grade, the more calories and less protein there is per gram of meat.

E. Marbling (fat within the muscle) is one of the major considerations in grading beef.
F. Current beef grades are based on the calorie value of beef.
G. Good has less fat than Choice.
H. Higher fat content has little nutritive value except as a source of calories.

General Assertion/Specific Support

Paragraphs developed by assertion and support demand solid supporting evidence. An assertion states the writer's opinion or judgment; the reader then looks for convincing evidence to support the opinion. We all hold many beliefs; persuading others to accept those beliefs requires evidence or reasonable argument. Whenever you speak your mind, that is, assert your opinion about something, you leave yourself open to challenge. If you assert that "all these shortages we're having are created by big business to raise prices," the response may be: "Prove it." You would then try to support your assertion by naming some specific examples as evidence.

The following paragraph uses the assertion/support structure to explain the advantages of air patrols to detect forest fires:

Assertion: Daily air patrols have numerous advantages. For one, aircraft look down on the terrain instead of across it. Every valley and ravine can be observed. The fire lookout in a tower is very restricted in range of vision. Aircraft can also observe
Support: a great deal more territory than a lookout. One airplane can cover in two hours an area that requires six lookout towers to cover adequately. While the cost of air patrols creates objections to their use, these costs are much less than the expense of salaries, transportation, energy, and maintenance for six lookouts in their towers.

EXERCISES

Here are some sayings you have probably heard many times in one or another form. These sayings are actually unsupported assertions.

1. Write a paragraph for each, supplying the kind of reasoned evidence these assertions need to support them.
2. Begin by stating precisely what is being asserted in each case.
   A. Winning isn't the most important thing; it's the only thing.
   B. A rolling stone gathers no moss.

C. Religion is the opium of the masses.
D. A penny saved is a penny earned.
E. People in glass houses shouldn't throw stones.
F. Nice guys finish last.

General Topic/Specific Illustration

One of the most common ways we have of explaining ourselves to someone is to give an example of what we are talking about. "For instance," or "for example" are phrases we use constantly. Examples allow us to "show" someone what we mean, and that is why this technique is called "illustration." The example we create with words serves the same purpose as a picture or drawing. Often the best way to explain a complicated idea is with an example. That's why technical and scientific books use so many illustrations. Throughout this textbook, we have been using many examples to help you understand the ideas being presented. The next two selections show examples being used to explain the controlling idea in a paragraph. The use of a well-developed example to illustrate a general topic is the most common form of paragraph.

> While skilled workers dislike a lazy worker, *they do enjoy a monumental rip-off of the company* [emphasis added]. There is usually a lull in work just prior to a model changeover. Major changes are in the offing and things are generally in good shape. Supervision tends to get sloppy, and the atmosphere is relaxed and easygoing. Two millwrights had found an old time clock and, being good mechanics, they got it in working order. For a month they came in late and left early, setting the clock to the time they wanted, punching their time cards and leaving them in the rack. This required considerable ingenuity because they had to know when the timekeeper was going to pick up their cards. The rest of the crew admired their audacity because they beat the company at its own game. They used the resented clock, the worst of the surveillance mechanisms, to defeat the company. (Bill Goode, "The Skilled Trades," in *Auto Work and Its Discontents*)

EXERCISES

Study the following paragraph.

1. What is the *controlling idea*? The *topic* of the paragraph?
2. What example illustrates it?

> We must recognize that manual work has become increasingly denigrated by the upper middle class of this nation. The problems of self-esteem inherent in these changing attitudes are further compounded by the impact of the communication media. For example, the images of blue-collar

workers that are presented by the media (including school textbooks) are often negative. Workers are presented as "hard-hats" (racists or authoritarians) or "fat cats" (lazy plumbers who work only twenty-hour weeks yet earn $400.00 a week). The view of the worker in the mass media is that he is the problem, not that he *has* problems. (James O'Toole, *Work in America*)

Write a paragraph about how the American people behave.

1. From the following data, use the specific example of the American attitude toward pets to illustrate your controlling idea.
2. State your general topic and construct a paragraph using the details provided to develop your example.
3. In writing this paragraph remember what would happen if you just let the example stand by itself without pointing out to the reader how the example relates to the controlling idea. (An example can be misinterpreted unless you make sure the reader understands what it is intended to illustrate.)

Americans spend 2.5 billion dollars per year to feed pets. "Good Breath" toothpaste is available for dogs. Pet boutiques from coast to coast carry the latest in pet fashions, jewelry, and perfumes. People crackers for dogs sell well. Special butcher shops deal only in meats for pets. A special limousine service in Los Angeles delivers pets to the hair dresser or training classes. The rich invest in lions, tigers, and other large animals as pets. Special graveyards and burial ceremonies have been designed for pets. Wrist watches, contact lenses, and dentures for pets are available on the market. Pet food manufacturers spend 165 million dollars per year on advertising. Every year it costs 100 million dollars to exterminate unwanted pets. Cats and dogs eat at the family dinner table.

Select one of the following topics and develop a specific example to illustrate it.

1. Many career fields are getting overcrowded.
2. Well-educated people may be underemployed.
3. Salaries sometimes bear little relation to the social value of the work done.

Setting an Order

In the preceding section, we said that the basic relationship between general and specific sets the pattern or structure of the whole paragraph—a general topic is stated, for example, and is developed by a specific illustration. But the example you use to illustrate your topic may itself contain a number of specific details. How do you arrange details within the paragraph in the best possible order? Whatever the overall structure of the paragraph may be, there are four common ways to set the details in order:

> by time (from the past to the present or vice versa)
> by space (from left to right, top to bottom, front to back)
> by most general to most specific (or vice versa)
> by least important to most important

In most cases, the material you are working with will suggest the best order.

By Time

Order is so basic to clear thinking and writing that without it there is no understanding, no communication. Think, for example, of all the experiences you have on any day of the week. These events follow each other in time—first one thing happens, then another, then another. If you were to try to tell someone everything you did last Friday, you would likely begin with the first event and follow the time order until you had finished your account of the day. Obviously, your listener would be confused (and probably amused) if you didn't follow a reasonable time order:

> First I ate breakfast, went to Chemistry class, got dressed, got out of bed, and woke up.

Careful attention to time order is essential for several important types of writing: reports and the description of processes, such as the process of conducting a lab or field experiment and any process telling someone how to do something. In each of these writing assignments, be certain that you use words and phrases that make clear to your reader exactly what is first, second, and so on.

All writing indicates time by the tense of the verbs. So it's important to attend to your choice of verbs and the time sequence they indicate. But time can also be indicated by common words and phrases that either specify time or show relationship of time. You specify time by telling when something happened:

now	last week	1979
then	two years ago	a year from now
yesterday	March 4	never

You state *relationships* between events by words and phrases such as:

before	after	for some time
until	as soon as	as long as
when	prior to	since

Notice in the following example how easy it is to follow the sequence of events and, because of that, to understand the point the author is making; that is, Lieberson's influence in the recording industry:

> The success of the original-cast album of *South Pacific*, produced by Lieberson *in 1949*, gave Columbia's new long-playing record the commercial push it badly needed. It also paved the way for a hugely profitable succession of similar ventures, such as *My Fair Lady* and *Sound of Music. In the 1950's*, he kept up a steady reissue of such jazz greats as Louis Armstrong, Bix Beiderbecke and Bessie Smith, and brought in Mitch Miller to manage the company's middle-of-road pop line. *In the early 1960's*, as Lieberson is fond of pointing out, he helped usher in the rock era by signing Dylan, Simon and Garfunkel, and the Byrds. *(Time)*

Explaining a process also requires clear time reference so the reader knows exactly when to do the next step. A process is simply a number of events in a particular sequence required for some activity. Baking a pie is a process. And if you've ever cooked at all, you know the importance of doing each step when it should be done: The *crust* must be placed in the pan *before* the apples. Similarly, in repairing a car: The axle nut *must* be tightened *before* popping on the hubcap. Notice the clear time references in the next two examples that give directions.

> Registering as a special student can get rather involved. *First of all,* go to the department offering the course you want to see if the instructor will give permission. *Then* go to the dean's office, where you must file the permission slip. *After that,* you go to the registrar's office to be put on the roll. *Finally,* go to the cashier's office to pay for the course.

> (Notice that the following example is actually a short essay. Each paragraph is arranged in time order, and the series of paragraphs is arranged in time order as well. Emphasis has been added.)

> I leave a fall-planted crop of brome-grass kale or winter wheat *until spring* to be tilled under. A spring tilled crop is left *until* plants and soil are chopped and mixed. This is allowed to rest undisturbed *until spring rains settle it. Then* I till again with my new riding tiller-tractor—a 12 h.p. Simplicity that has replaced the two wheel model.

> *Next,* I test the soil, and if it is not quite in perfect balance, I add more nutrients to bring it to the point I want. *Then* the soil bed is tilled again, rolled and planted. Blood meal is a good source of nitrogen with small amounts of phosphorus and potash. I apply this at the rate of 265 pounds to the acre, or ten ounces to 100 square feet, which provides about two percent of the nitrogen needed. For a major source of phosphorus, I use steamed bone meal which supplies 28 percent phosphorus and four percent nitrogen.

> *As seedlings appear,* I break up the soil lightly with an iron garden rake; *then as they become firmly established,* I start my program of a twice-monthly thorough tilling to a shallow depth. This controls weed growth and aerates the soil, giving the sun and moisture the opportunity to speed early plant growth. *As the season gets into full swing,* I mulch with peat moss, wood chips, sawdust and grass clippings.

> Potatoes are planted *the second week of May* in my area, on new ground that

has been turned over the fall before and is loose and workable to a depth of six inches. *As soon as* the potato crop is harvested, this area is tilled thoroughly and sown to winter rye or some other cover crop. This is left to grow in the *spring* until it is about time to plant this area to strawberries. *(Organic Gardening and Farming)*

EXERCISES

1. Underline all the references to time and to time relationships in the following:

    ### BUILDING AN OUTDOOR DECK
    We first lowered the dirt grade and paved it with rocks to speed evaporation. Next, we rebuilt the underframing, making it as moistureproof as possible. Preparation was complicated by the fact that the steel I-beams had to be thoroughly scraped clean and given a protective coating to retard rust.

    All the wood-framing members were replaced with LP Wolmanized Southern Pine from the Koppers Co. According to Koppers, the 2½-lb.-per-cubic-foot of CCA preservative should extend the life of this deck well over 20 years.

    We bolted on a trim edge that provides space for planters or box benches, then laid the decking. Again, we used Wolmanized Southern Pine. To cut down on the number of debris-catching cracks, we chose 2×8 planks.

    Before nailing, we drilled holes one size smaller and ¾" shallower than the stainless-steel ring nails used. The tip of a crowbar served to space each plank properly. The joint between planks should be no less than ³⁄₁₆" but no more than ½" wide.

    Painting the trim was the final step. Though the Wolmanized decking can be stained, we left it natural; it will weather to a silvery gray. *(Popular Science)*

2. The following paragraph uses time order to record and describe the typical childhood of a girl in Samoa. Use this paragraph as a model and write a paragraph describing a girl's or boy's childhood in the United States.

    The first attitude which a little girl learns towards boys is one of avoidance and antagonism. She learns to observe the brother and sister taboo towards the boys of her relationship group and household, and together with the other small girls of her age group she treats all other small boys as enemies elect. After a little girl is eight or nine years of age she has learned never to approach a group of older boys. This feeling of antagonism towards younger boys and shamed avoidance of older ones continues up to the age of thirteen or fourteen, to the group of girls who are just reaching puberty and the group of boys who have just been circumcised. These children are growing away from the age-group life and the age-group antagonisms.

They are not yet actively sex-conscious. And it is at this time that the relationships between the sexes are least emotionally charged. (Margaret Mead, *Coming of Age in Samoa*)

3. Arrange the sentences in the following paragraph into a sequence that accurately describes the order of events in the birth of kittens.

She also becomes restless, meows a great deal, and demands a lot of attention. She is looking for a quiet place to have her kittens. When a kitten is ready to be born, the mother cat contracts her stomach muscles and squeezes. As the sixty-three days near an end, the mother cat becomes interested in snug corners. Each kitten is born one at a time in this way. She does this several times, pushing the unborn baby down the uterus toward the enlarged vagina. It is usually well away from activity in a dark place, and here she makes her nest. The average number of kittens in a litter is four, and there may be twenty minutes to an hour between each birth. Presently the head of the kitten appears through the vagina and a moment later the whole kitten appears. Then she will disappear altogether into her nest for a long spell.

4. Use the preceding paragraph as a model and describe some other natural process that takes place over time.

5. The following passage has no time signals. Write appropriate time signals for each blank.

The basic findings of Dr. Ross and her seminar are that the very ill proceed through five emotional stages along the way to death. [1]_____ is denial, and at this point, which often occurs following the person's initial awareness of his sickness, the patient is unwilling or even unable to accept the real nature of his predicament. [2]_____ —when physical indications such as loss of weight or increasing pain make further denial impossible—is anger. [3]_____ the patient, enraged at his illness, may become angry with his family or his doctor, berate the nurses, insist on continuous attention and never find it satisfactory, and generally behave in ways that may provoke in return the anger of his targets.
[4]_____ is often a stage of "bargaining." [5]_____ the patient attempts to stave off the inevitable by striking a bargain for an extension of life or a short period without pain. Many promises made "to live a life dedicated to God" or to the church, or offers to give the body or parts of it to science, are made with the silent additional clause that the Lord or the doctors must live up to their part of the bargain. Yet the bargaining does little but provide a temporary respite in the progress toward dying.
[6]_____ is a period of increasing depression in which he realizes what is happening to him, that denial, anger, bargaining are of no real use any longer. [7]_____ the dying quite literally grieve for themselves, for the fact that they are going to be separated from all they have known and loved. [8]_____ does the patient usually arrive at the final stage before death, the stage of acceptance. [9]_____ even though the smallest glimmer of hope will remain, he is ready to let go. (Adapted from London Wainwright, "A Profound Lesson for the Living," *Life*)

By Space

The order of space arranges the details of an object or scene. Most things have a shape or take up space, and an effective ordering technique follows the shape of the object being described. Begin at one end or the other to fill in details. Describing your new stereo to someone who knows little about stereo sets, you likely would describe the walnut casings for the speakers and the external appearance of the amplifier (how it looks from the outside). Then you might move in and describe some of the internal components (first in the amplifier, then move out to the speakers). To describe a building, take the reader up to and through the front door, showing what the eye would see on such a tour. In the following example, notice how Studs Terkel takes us from outside to inside and back out again:

> Outside the rooming house: It is twilight. Red neon cuts through the grayness. The window of the manager's office is open. It is a furnished room itself; the presence of a desk rather than a bed differentiates it from the others. There is, too, a slightly tattered divan and a TV set. The matronly woman in charge is watching a television program. Her manner is catatonic. Two guests saunter into the office; blond young men. Their manner is desultory. Across the street is a large sign above a building entrance: Montrose Urban Progress Center, Chicago Committee on Urban Opportunity. Mayor Richard J. Daley, Chairman. (Studs Terkel, *Division Street: America*)

Using space order allows the reader to follow easily the relationship of the details you are presenting. It's like using a movie camera—if someone filmed the inside of a room by showing first a shot of the ceiling, then a shot looking out a window, followed by a jump cut to a shot of one corner where two walls meet the floor, and so on, the effect might be cinematically dramatic, but it would be hard for the viewer to form a clear concept of the room. Instead, we expect that the camera will pan slowly around the room, moving directly from one wall to an adjoining one until we have a clear image in mind.

Space order is the natural order to follow in describing people, places, and things, just as time order is the natural order to follow in retelling a story or outlining the steps in a process. Sometimes space order can also be used when organizing material other than descriptions. The idea of geographic space, of things being near or far from us, can be used to organize details. For example, in writing a paragraph that summarizes the unemployment situation in the United States, you might divide the country into geographic areas and move from the farthest away to your own area (or vice versa).

> Unemployment statistics released by the Department of Labor today show that the number of people unable to find work seems to be holding steady at about 6 percent in the Far West. The Southwest is doing much better, with an

unemployment rate hovering around 4.5 percent. The industrial areas of the Midwest have been hard hit by the recent recession and unemployment there has soared past 7 percent, while the Northeast seems to be permanently burdened with a rate of 7.5 percent. Here at home in the Southeast, our current 4.8 percent unemployment looks good by comparison.

EXERCISES

1. Arrange the details in space order to complete the following paragraph describing a house:

   The front of my home faces the lake. An entire wall of glass reflects the sunlight and water. From the beach, we enter the living room through sliding glass doors.

   A. The carpeting is brown and beige, matching the color of the sand on the beach.
   B. The north wall of the living room is entirely glass, offering an uninterrupted view of the lake.
   C. The brown tweed couch, matching tweed armchair, and leather easy chair cluster around the fireplace.
   D. The west wall is dominated by a natural stone fireplace big enough to receive four-foot logs.
   E. Ceiling-high bookcases frame the fireplace.
   F. The south wall and east wall are covered with soft, gray barn wood.
   G. Swinging louvered doors provide entry through the south wall to the kitchen.
   H. The high cathedral ceiling is supported by beams stained walnut brown.

2. Imagine someone has given you $100,000 to build your ideal home. Write a paragraph organized by space order to describe the home you would build.

3. Use the order of space to arrange the following sentences into a paragraph.

   A. Giant beams crisscross to form towers rising twenty-three stories above the waves.
   B. The most remote are exploring for gas 110 miles off the coast of Texas and Louisiana.
   C. A helicopter whirls 1,000 feet overhead.
   D. Some offshore rigs are pushing their steel drilling bits down through 1,800 feet of water and then through 23,000 feet of mud, shale, and rock.
   E. The gas and oil rigs look like pieces of some monster Erector Set.

F. In the swampy bayous near the coast, production and drilling equipment stands in tight clusters at the older drilling sites.

G. As the mud-brown waters turn to green and finally blue, the rigs thin out. (Adapted from "Pumping Fuel Under Water," *Time*)

4. Use the idea of geographic space, of near and far, to organize the details of a paragraph outlining the housing and industrial patterns in your town or city.

By Most General to Most Specific

Time order and space order are built into some subjects naturally, but often facts and details do not lend themselves to being ordered in either of those ways. In these cases, the general to specific order often proves useful. This order is like climbing down the generalization ladder, leading the reader deeper and deeper into details that are increasingly specific. Recalling our discussion of the generalization ladder (p. 25), let's look at how a paragraph arranged by moving from the most general to the most specific might look (we've italicized the different "rungs" moving down the ladder):

> *Saving money* is a problem for everyone today. As a major expense for most of us, *housing costs* are one area where we can try to cut back. *Utilities* make up a large part of housing costs each month, and if we live in a house rather then an apartment, cutting down on the *heat bill* alone can lead to significant savings. Perhaps the best way to reduce the cost of heating without freezing ourselves is to *reduce heat loss*. According to all the studies I've seen, *caulking* the siding joints and around all windows and doors is the simplest, cheapest, and most cost-effective way to save money by cutting heat loss.

Ordering details in this manner is like using the zoom lens on a camera; first you survey the scene, then move in closer and closer until you focus on a single detail. Obviously, the process can be reversed. In the following paragraph, the attention moves from specific instances—the death of a father and uncle—to a general statement about the fate of chemical workers.

> And, well, my father worked in a chemical plant right next door to the one I work for; about twenty years. He's dead now. I had an uncle; he also worked in a chemical plant, the same plant right next door to me. He died of cancer, this cancer in the throat. He had a tube in his troat, and it was result of working in this chemical plant; he didn't have it before he went there. But a certain chemical that he inhaled got in his throat, and his throat was a mess and he died. I mean, I don't use the expression—he died like a dog. We're a small bunch but we've got a problem. These chemicals are going to kill us all. (Joseph A. Page and Mary-Win O'Brian, *Bitter Wages*)

PARAGRAPHING | 43

EXERCISES

1. Arrange the following sentences in the general to specific order:
   A. Today's computers can add one million two digit numbers in seconds.
   B. With the help of a computer, a business person can check inventory and monthly sales in a matter of seconds.
   C. The computer makes many business operations quick and easy to perform.
   D. Operations that once required a number of personnel now require only one programmer, one secretary, and a computer.

2. The following paragraph is arranged to some degree in time order, but it is also arranged from general to specific information. Rewrite the paragraph, making changes where necessary, so that the first sentence—the most general statement—is placed last.

   A science which orders its thought too early is stifled. For example, the ideas of the Epicureans about atoms two thousand years ago were quite reasonable; but they did only harm to a physics which could not measure temperature and pressure and learn the simpler laws which relate to them. Or again, the hope of the medieval alchemists that the elements might be changed was not as fanciful as we once thought. But it was merely damaging to chemistry which did not yet understand the composition of water and common salt. (Jacob Bronowski, *The Common Sense of Science*)

By Least Important to Most Important

The information you have gathered for a paragraph may not move from general to specific; much of the detail may be equally specific or equally general. In this case, you may organize your details by beginning with the least important one and progressing to the most important one. This order is commonly found in assertion/support paragraphs in which you build to a climax by ending with your strongest piece of support. There is little reason to reverse this ordering of details, that is, to begin with the most important and end with the least. To do so creates the impression in the reader's mind that your case is getting weaker as you go along.

Notice how the following paragraph works up to the most impressive statistic:

Thirty-four million cats—often in multiples—inhabit 24 percent of American households, an increase of 55 percent in the past decade. The dog population, meanwhile, has stabilized in recent years at some 48 million. In Washington, D.C., and New York, feline adoptions from animal shelters have zoomed 30 percent in the past three or four years. Cats are also becoming a factor in the

American economy. Owners will shell out $1.4 billion for 1 million tons of cat food that carry such whisker-licking names as Meow Mix and Tender Vittles. ("Crazy Over Cats," *Time*)

EXERCISES

1. Arrange the following sentences to form a paragraph using the order of importance.
   A. With the help of an X-ray, a doctor can remove the appendix before it ruptures, preventing possible death or violent illness.
   B. X-ray examinations ensure that the patient will receive the correct medical treatment.
   C. Without X-ray examinations the doctor could make the wrong diagnosis and prescribe the wrong treatment.
   D. Without X-rays a patient with the symptoms of appendicitis might be treated for a stomach ache.
   E. Good X-ray examinations are important in medical care.

2. The following information needs a topic sentence and a principle of order, which may be either general to specific or the order of importance. Provide a topic sentence and organize the details into a paragraph.
   A. Women represent 4.9 percent of those in skilled crafts.
   B. The percentage of female faculty members in universities and colleges fell by almost a full point from 22.5 to 21.7 in the last academic year.
   C. Sixty of every 100 women workers in 1976 were clerks, saleswomen, waitresses, or hairdressers according to the Department of Labor.

Making Transitions

As you develop your ideas in a paragraph, you will find that certain relationships exist between the sentences. A sentence may add something to what you have said in the previous one, or it may take off in a new direction entirely. Another sentence may state what resulted from the actions described in the one before it. Helping words or phrases aid the reader in seeing these relationships. If something adds to what you have just said, you might begin the new sentence with "moreover" or "in addition." A sentence that gives the reader an illustration might include "for example." The chart given here names the most common kinds of relationships possible between sentences and gives you a number of alternative words and phrases to indicate these relationships so that you can avoid repeating the same "transitional" words too often.

ADDITION	EXPLANATION	CAUSE & EFFECT
in addition	namely	because
moreover	for example	consequently
furthermore	that is	in order that
too	such as	so that
also	for instance	for
besides	in other words	for that reason
likewise	as I have said	thus
similarly	for instance	as a result
in like manner		

SEQUENCE	CONTRAST	
first	however	notwithstanding
secondly	but	nonetheless
then	nevertheless	nevertheless
next	still	all the same
finally	yet	after all
	rather	for all that
	on the other hand	at the same time
	on the contrary	conversely
	by contrast	despite this

CONCLUSION

therefore
hence
so
thus
in conclusion

We have italicized the transition signals in the following paragraph.

These findings may suggest some of the practical limitations of past and present studies of causes of addiction. It is not too difficult to summarize these findings in a very general way. *To begin with*, it is now known that there is no single "type" among addicts—the physician who succumbs to addiction, *for instance*, is a quite different type sociologically (and perhaps psychologically) from the poverty-stricken minority-group member enmeshed in a delinquent and addict subculture. *However*, individuals in certain socioeconomic categories run a relatively greater risk of encountering and using narcotics than do those in other categories. *Also,* it seems likely that of those individuals in the high-risk categories it is the more troubled or the more disadvantaged, situationally, who are especially likely to take up drugs. (*Although in another sense* they could be viewed simply as those most fully socialized into the prevailing, if deviant, pattern.) The specific policy implications stemming from conclusions of this sort are not very clear. *On the one hand* it seems that addiction is partly caused by other general social disorders and that one way to deal with it is to attack the various socioeconomic ills which constitute the breeding ground of drug use. *Similarly,* various types of family life are highlighted as being detrimental, and presumably measures should be taken (assuming it could be determined just how this might be done) to improve the quality of interparent and parent-child relations. *And* if those individuals who do become addicted have certain personality problems, some kind of therapy or counselling should be aimed at treating the addicts themselves. (Edwin Schur, *Crimes Without Victims*)

SUMMARY

1. Paragraphs are the basic device used in writing to organize into reasonably sized blocks the material gathered while exploring a subject. These blocks help the reader follow your ideas.

2. Sort through your notes, selecting and grouping related items. Within each group, look for the relationship between *general* and *specific*. State your controlling general idea in a topic sentence, check for unity, and look for a basic structure such as question/answer, assertion/support, or topic/illustration. Within your basic structure, organize details by time, space, general/specific, or order of importance.

3. Use transitions where appropriate to show the relationship between one sentence and the next. The same transitional words and phrases can be used to start a new paragraph.

WRITING ASSIGNMENT

1. In one paragraph, tell about some funny, embarrassing, or confusing event you have experienced at work or at school. For example, you may have been blamed or praised for some other person's act. Use time order to arrange the details.

2. In a second paragraph, describe a person or place involved in the preceding incident. Use space order to arrange the details of this description.

3. In a paragraph structured by topic/illustration, use the event as a specific example illustrating a more general topic. Organize the details by most general to most specific.

4. Pose a question about the meaning of this event, and provide a response in which the details are arranged from specific to general.

5. Make an assertion about the meaning of this event, and write a paragraph supporting that assertion by moving from the least important to the most important facts.

part two

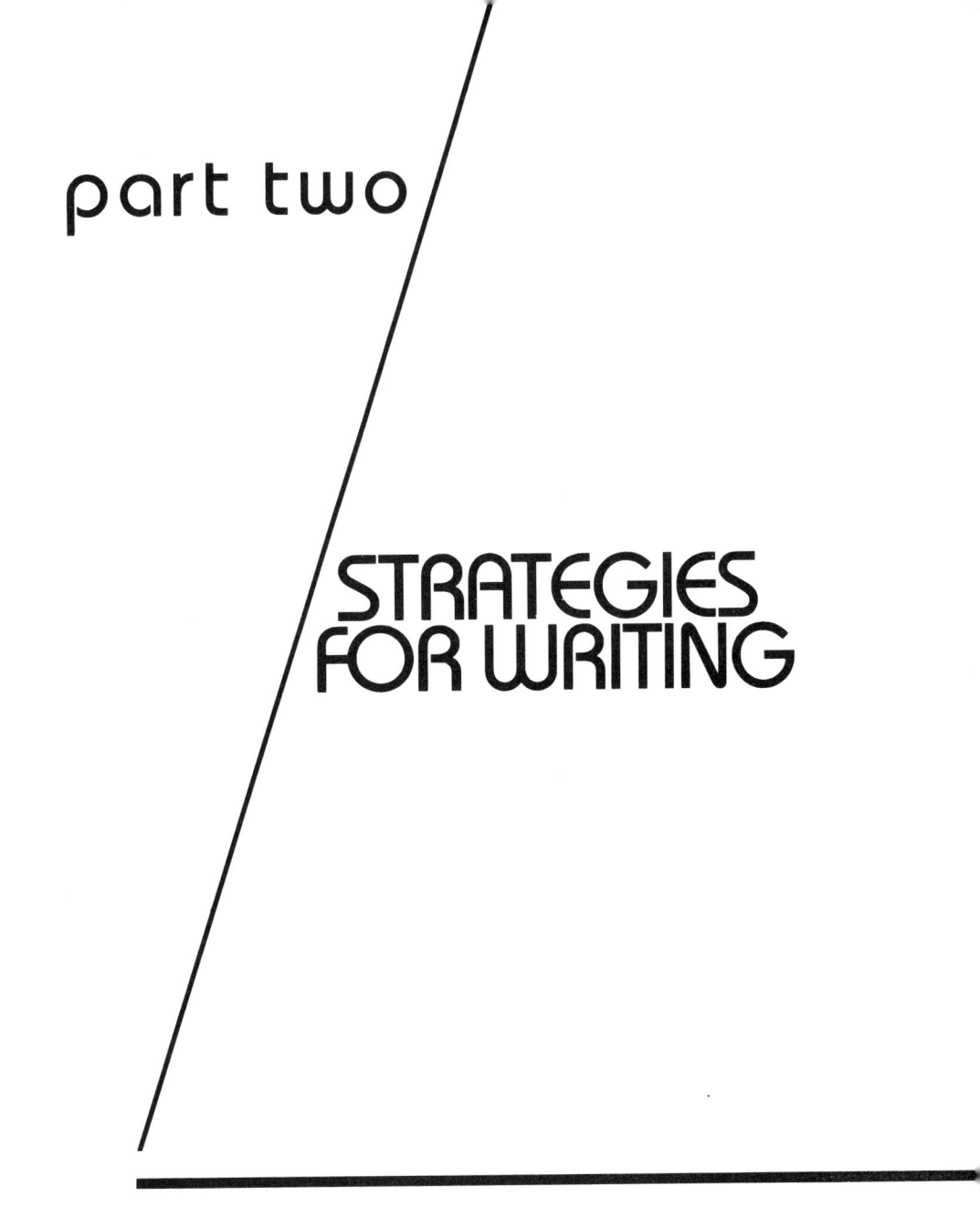

STRATEGIES FOR WRITING

3

DESCRIBING

Understanding Description

Of the various purposes for writing discussed in Chapter 1—to express, to inform, to explain, to persuade—expressive writing is seldom used in college and almost never on the job. We will begin, therefore, with writing intended to inform. Physical description is a basic kind of information. We often discuss or write about persons, places, and things. When we do, the details of what the subject looks like, sounds like, smells like, tastes like, or feels like are important and must be communicated if we want our listener or reader to "see" what we are talking about. Description is the general name for communication that supplies these physical details about an object, a place, or a person.

Every day we have direct experience with things other people want to know about. Friends ask you to "describe it" when you tell them you are about to buy a new car or a dress you are excited about. Police officers write reports describing accident scenes; real-estate agents describe property they have listed for sale; nurses describe the physical appearance of patients; advertisers describe products; carpenters describe types of wood, cuts, and joints.

Description is obviously a familiar activity, and describing something seems simple enough until we try it. Sometimes it goes well, especially if our audience or readers already know about the object, person, or place we are describing. When you write to a friend that you have just bought a German shepherd, he or she has a pretty good start on knowing what you are talking about. You fill in a few details of color and size, and a description has been passed on effectively. But what if you are describing something the reader does not already have a general picture of in his or her mind?

For most people, the major problem in describing things accurately comes from not paying much attention to physical details. What do we mean by that? Unlike children who continuously explore physical reality by biting, rubbing, and banging every new object encountered, we adults often forget about physical detail. Most of us live in cities or towns, in houses we didn't build ourselves. We travel enclosed in cars or walking in shoes on concrete pavement. Our water comes from some mysterious source at the other end of our plumbing, and our food comes packaged in plastic from large supermarkets. How often do *you* pay attention to detail in an intimate, physical way?

To describe something effectively, we must do three things:

1. give the reader a general picture
2. fill in the physical details

Fulfilling these three requirements of a good description means that we must force ourselves to observe whatever is to be described in the same ways: First, we must see it as a whole; second, we must focus our attention very carefully on every possible physical detail; third, in gathering details, we must take full advantage of our senses.

Seeing the Whole First

The story of the blind men and the elephant illustrates the problem of not seeing the whole thing first:

> Beyond Ghor there was a city. All its inhabitants were blind. A king with his entourage arrived nearby; he brought his army and camped in the desert. He had a mighty elephant, which he used in attack and to increase the people's awe.
>
> The populace became anxious to learn about the elephant, and some sightless from among this blind community ran like fools to find it. Since they did not know even the form or shape of the elephant, they groped sightlessly, gathering information by touching some part of it. Each thought that he knew something, because he could feel a part.

When they returned to their fellow-citizens, eager groups clustered around them, anxious, misguidedly, to learn the truth from those who were themselves astray. They asked about the form, the shape of the elephant, and they listened to all they were told.

The man whose hand had reached an ear said: "It is a a large, rough thing, wide and broad, like a rug."

One who had felt the trunk said: "I have the real facts about it. It is like a straight and hollow pipe, awful and destructive."

One who had felt its feet and legs said: "It is mighty and firm, like a pillar." (Robert Ornstein, *The Psychology of Consciousness*)

Perhaps this story exaggerates the problems that come from not getting the general picture straight, but talk to a police officer sometime. Ask if witnesses to an accident ever give conflicting reports on what happened. Before we can be sure what a thing looks like we must see it whole, otherwise we risk being like one of the blind men.

Paying Attention to Detail

The second step in observing effectively is also the most important: Much of what we encounter in our world has become so familiar that we no longer pay close attention to what we see. Rows of brick ranch houses, hundreds of beer cans, thousands of people, dozens of campus buildings—we rush past them all paying little attention to detail as we go. It takes a real effort of will to stop and look at something carefully, to look at it not just as a whole but to look instead at all the rich detail. We've said it is important to get the whole picture first, but having done that it is equally important to discover the significant details that make this particular object different from all the similar ones. Stop for a minute and look at a row of tract houses that "all look alike." Do they? Perhaps one has an odd cap on the chimney, another has a forsythia bush planted by the corner of the steps, a third has curtains in the front window that seem to droop in an odd way. How much attention do you actually pay to things around you? Even to things very familiar, things you would think you could describe easily? For example, could you describe in detail the face side of a nickel from memory?

Using All Our Senses

To collect a rich stockpile of details, we have to work hard at observing through all our senses. The blind men, of course, could not give an accurate picture of the elephant because they literally could not see. The description they did give relied entirely on their sense of touch. To turn this story around slightly, relying on any one of our senses completely without the help of the others can result in experiences much like those of the blind men. Our sense of sight is important in getting to know something, but the other senses add vital information to our knowledge. We can help someone else see what we are trying to describe by appealing to as many senses as possible.

As human beings, our dominant sense is sight, and most of us do not make much effort to develop the other four senses. This is why the use of details that appeal to smelling, tasting, touching, and hearing adds so much to a description. In writing we so seldom give or get other than visual information that when our other senses are activated the effect is like a sudden shock. Just think how powerful any of our senses can be—the smell of baking bread, for example, may stir images of teeth crunching through a golden brown crust dripping with melted butter or honey. It may also stimulate feelings of warmth and security, of childhood happiness.

SUMMARY

The point of this chapter is that before you can describe something accurately, you must first *observe* it accurately. Here is a summary of the three steps in careful observation:

1. Get the whole picture straight.
2. Focus on details and unique features.
3. Collect details from every sense possible—not just your eyes.

Writing Description

Good observation is the key to good description, but careful observation alone will not guarantee an effective written description. Now we must move on to the problems involved in putting words on paper in such a way that your reader will see what you saw. The general rule to keep in mind is that *you can never assume your reader knows what you mean.* Thinking about the house you grew up in as a child, you may know exactly what you mean when you write, "It's a big, old house in a kind of run-down neighborhood," but every reader will most likely get a different picture, or no picture at all. The child in the following story encounters this problem in communicating a description:

> I pondered deeply, then, over the adventures of the jungle. And after some work with a colored pencil I succeeded in making my first drawing. My Drawing Number One. It looked like this:
>
> I showed my masterpiece to the grown-ups, and asked them whether the drawing frightened them.
> But they answered: "Frighten? Why should any one be frightened by a hat?"
> My drawing was not a picture of a hat. It was a picture of a boa constrictor digesting an elephant. But since the grown-ups were not able to understand it, I made another drawing: I drew the inside of the boa constrictor, so that the grown-ups could see it clearly. They always need to have things explained. My Drawing Number Two looked like this:
>
> The grown-ups' response, this time, was to advise me to lay aside my drawing of boa constrictors, whether from the inside or the outside, and devote myself instead to geography, history, arithmetic and grammar. That is why, at the age of six, I gave up what might have been a magnificent career as a painter. I had been disheartened by the failure of my Drawing Number One and my Drawing Number Two. Grown-ups never understand anything by themselves, and it is tiresome for children to be always and forever explaining things to them.
> (Saint-Exupéry, *The Little Prince*)

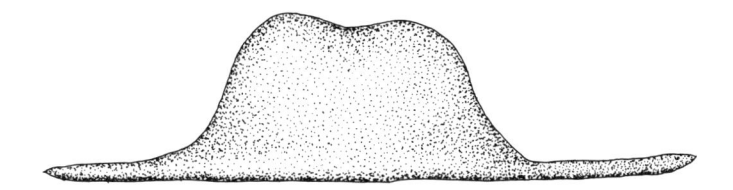

Readers are just like the grownups in the story—it may be tiresome, but it is absolutely essential to be "always and forever explaining things to them." Moreover, drawing a picture with words is a little more difficult than with pencil and paper.

Words

Actually, words do not represent precise *things*, but ideas or concepts of things. In a sense, each word is like a general picture—like Drawing Number One—and needs to be filled in like Drawing Number Two if you want to be sure your reader gets the same meaning from the word that you do. Even when we think the meaning of a word is obvious, there may still be problems. For example, when you hear someone say, "I bought a dog this morning," the first picture of the dog may be of the pet you have at home. The dog purchased by your friend may really have been a Chihuahua, but you picture a Labrador retriever or an Airedale. In a conversation it is possible to ask questions to get a clear picture of what the other person is talking about, to ask for the information necessary to complete your picture ("Why should anyone be frightened by a hat?"). In writing, all the reader has is the words on a page, which sometimes raise more questions than they answer. Take a look at these common, everyday words:

home	train
mother	bus
black	horse
brown	city
pride	beautiful

Every person looking at these words will have a unique set of associations with them. The word "home" might be the immediate place someone lives, or the word can call up a picture of a childhood home. For one of the authors "home" is associated with the thatched roof, stone cottage in the lowlands of Scotland where he spent his childhood. "Mother" means a different thing to a person whose mother is living than it does to someone whose mother died years before. A city can be anything from Brooklyn to Cedar Falls, and judgments made about life in cities with Brooklyn in mind can't be understood by someone who has lived only in Cedar Falls.

The point here is that very often we can't just use a word and expect our reader to know what we mean. Many times we have to fill in details—do a lot of explaining—if we want to be sure our reader shares the same meaning that we have in mind for a particular word. This problem's true in all writing, but focusing on it in writing description makes the difficulty clear.

Mark Twain shows us the associations surrounding the idea of "home":

> I can see the farm yet with perfect clearness. I can see all its belongings, all its details: the family room of the house with a "trundle" bed in one corner and a spinning wheel in another, a wheel whose rising and falling wail, heard

from a distance, was the mournfulest of all sounds to me and made me homesick and low-spirited and filled my atmosphere with the wandering spirits of the dead; the vast fireplace, piled high on winter nights with flaming hickory logs from whose ends a sugary sap bubbled out but did not go to waste, for we scraped it off and ate it: the lazy cat spread out on the rough hearth-stones; the drowsy dogs braced against the jambs and blinking; my aunt in one chimney corner, knitting; my uncle in the other, smoking his corn-cob pipe; the slick and carpetless oak floor faintly mirroring the dancing flame-tongues and freckled with black indentations where fire-coals had popped out and died a leisurely death; half a dozen children romping in the background twilight; split-bottomed chairs here and there, some with rockers; a cradle, out of service but waiting with confidence; in the early cold mornings a snuggle of children in shirts and chemises occupying the hearth-stone and procrastinating—they could not bear to leave that comfortable place and go out on the windswept floor-space between the house and kitchen where the general tin basin stood, and wash. (Mark Twain, *The Autobiography of Mark Twain*)

Twain lets us see the inside of that house, feel the warmth of the fire, and hear the sound of the spinning wheel. We are able to participate in the experience and this participation enriches our own perceptions. Rather than simply tell us "the farm was comfortable" and "I felt good there," Twain shows us the things that made it comfortable and secure. Notice how he uses details from several senses to help us "see" the home he is describing.

EXERCISE

Take a common word such as one of those on the list on p. 56 and write out the details that will make the word come alive with your meaning, details that will show a reader exactly what you mean by the word.

Steps in Writing Description

To describe a person, place, or thing effectively, you must first observe it well. *Careful observation is always the first step in any description.*

1. Observe carefully (See "Understanding Description," p. 51).
2. Make a list of details drawn from all senses.
3. Write a general statement giving the broad outline of the whole thing you are about to describe. For example:

58 STRATEGIES FOR WRITING

"My boss is a stylish forty-year-old black woman." (person)
"There is a pretty cobblestone alley behind our old office building on Franklin Street." (place)
"My stereo is an attractive Pioneer component system." (thing)

4. Decide how the whole subject can be divided into parts. For example:

In writing about your boss, you might divide the description into face, dress, walk. For the purpose of describing the stereo, you could divide into tuner and speakers.

5. Group the specific details from your list (Step #2) under each general part. For example:

TUNER	SPEAKERS
brushed chrome front	dark walnut cabinets
black glass panels	smell of oiled wood
glowing meters	soft, black foam covers
smooth chrome slide controls	brushed chrome trim

6. Organize the groups in a logical *space order* (see Chapter 2, pp. 40–41). For example, describe the tuner as the center of the system before moving out to the speakers.

EXERCISE

Read the following description carefully.

1. Examine it to find the basic pattern for description.
2. Is there a beginning general statement? Could you supply one?
3. Identify as many details drawn from the senses as you can in the description.
4. How are the details grouped under parts of the whole subject?

I remember real clear the way that hand looked: there was carbon under the fingernails where he'd worked once in a garage; there was an anchor tattooed back from the knuckles; there was a dirty Band-Aid on the middle knuckle, peeling up at the edge. All the rest of the knuckles were covered with scars and cuts, old and new. I remember the palm was smooth and hard as bone from hefting the wooden handles of axes and hoes, not the hand you'd think could deal cards. The palm was callused, and the calluses were cracked, and dirt was worked in the cracks. A road map of his travels up and down the West. That palm made a scuffing sound against my hand. I remember the fingers were thick and strong closing over mine, and my hand commenced to feel peculiar and went to swelling up out there on my stick of an arm, like he was transmitting his own blood into it. It rang with blood and power. (Ken Kesey, *One Flew Over the Cuckoo's Nest*)

SUMMARY

1. Good description depends upon careful observation. Train yourself to notice and to note down physical details.
2. "Descriptive" words are often very general and need to be fleshed out with specific details.
3. Organize your description carefully; help your readers form the picture you want them to see.

WRITING ASSIGNMENTS

Now you are ready to write your own description of something. Try the following:

1. Get a potato (or an orange, a cucumber, or some other vegetable). Get a pencil and a sheet of paper. Jot down observations on the size, shape, and color of the potato. You are starting with those features the eye sees first. If you were drawing a picture of your potato, you wouldn't begin with the worm hole on the bottom (does a potato have a bottom?). Look for distinguishing characteristics on the surface of the potato: bumps, bruises, sprouts, warty things, freckles, scars, and so on. These features make this potato unique.
2. Experiment with the potato. What lies under the surface? Scrape off some skin and jot down observations about what you see inside: color, texture, taste. Cut the potato in half and look at it in cross section. Does this potato resemble anything else you have seen (besides other potatoes)?
3. Asking questions such as these should help you to observe the potato carefully and to prepare an extensive list of details. Once you have made this list, begin at Step 3 above and write a description of the potato.

STRATEGIES FOR WRITING

Remember the *pattern* for most written description:

1. General descriptive statement
2. Subject divided into parts and organized by space order
3. Details supplied for each part

Here are some additional writing assignments that will help you sharpen your skills in observation and description.

1. Describe a candle. Write one version from memory. Write another while you are actually looking at a candle, touching it, smelling it, hearing it sputter.

2. Go back to a place you have worked, or go to a place you might work some day. Observe carefully and write a detailed description of the work place itself (not of the work being done) for someone who has never been there. Select details to *show* the readers instead of *telling* them what it's like. Remember, descriptive words often have to be filled in.

3. Describe your favorite food, using all your senses. Write first as if you are describing the food to a friend. Then write a version as if you were an ad man trying to sell the product.

4. You have suddenly been accosted by Martians and taken aboard their space ship. On your release, the local newspaper asks you to write a description of what you saw. Write it.

5. Arrange with some of your classmates to write independent descriptions of the same object, experience, or event. Compare the results.

6. Go into a grocery store, a bus station, or some other place where you might see someone "unusual." Write a description of this person for your classmates.

7. Select a piece of equipment important on your job (a typewriter, a drill press, or some other). Write a description for someone who would not be familiar with it.

4

COMPARING

Understanding Comparison

Comparison and Contrast

In Chapter 3, we emphasized observing physical details about a person, place, or thing to describe it. Description provides basic information about physical appearances. *Comparison* goes beyond descriptive information to note which details are similar and which ones different between two observed things—that is, in what important ways do they compare and contrast?

Actually, comparing one thing with another takes up a large part of our thinking time. We automatically make comparisons and contrasts: We compare products before making a purchase, restaurants before going out to dinner, teachers before signing up for a class, movies before recommending one to a friend. Both simple and complex decisions depend on comparison. The decision to go downtown and hang out rather than stay home and study is based on comparison. More serious decisions are also made by weighing the advantages and disadvantages of two different courses of action. Will the economic benefits of building a new dam outweigh the ecological benefits of not building it? In its simplest definition, comparison means looking at two things and seeing significant ways in which they are similar and significant ways in which they are different.

Significant is an important word here, because there must be a point to any comparison. If two things are so completely alike that they have no significant differences—say, for example, two identical units in an apartment building—there would be no point in comparing them. On the other hand, if two things are so completely different that there are no significant similarities—a new house and a potato—there is no point in comparing them either. Only when there are significant likenesses and significant differences does comparison make sense. For example, there might be some value to comparing an apartment with a house.

Any given comparison will focus on and stress *either* the likenesses *or* the differences between two things. Both likenesses and differences must be present, but the interesting information (the point) will come from emphasizing one or the other. Most often, the focus will be on the significant differences between two similar things (this is often called *contrasting* them). In comparing (or contrasting) renting an apartment and buying a house, not much will be gained by stressing the significant likenesses; both have living rooms, kitchens, and bedrooms. The point to this particular comparison would be to stress the differences: One provides maintenance, repairs, and some utilities; the other requires you to provide your own. With one the monthly payment goes to a landlord; with the other the payment goes toward paying off a mortgage and building equity. Many times our thinking follows this pattern of first noticing the general ways in which things are similar and only later focusing on significant differences that help us learn something important. Very small children, for example, often start out calling all four-footed animals "doggies" or "horsies" because they are all alike in some important ways; but children learn as they grow older that there are significant differences between dogs, horses, cows, and cats. Looking for and understanding significant differences is one of the most basic ways we learn.

Occasionally, a comparison is more informative when we stress the ways in which two things are similar. A book and a television set may at first seem only to have differences, but you may find significant similarities between them: both are sources of information and entertainment; both provide ways to relax and escape everyday concerns.

SUMMARY

In brief, comparison is the everyday process of weighing similarities and differences. To make a comparison (or contrast) between two objects:

1. They must have both significant similarities and significant differences.
2. The comparison must have a point—provide some worthwhile information.
3. The point of the comparison will be found by stressing either the similarities or the differences, depending upon which emphasis provides the more important gain in knowledge.
4. Equivalent factors—engines, comfort, cost, whatever—must be examined for each of the subjects being compared.

EXERCISES

1. Which of the following statements could generate valid comparisons?
   A. Cigarettes are like trees.
   B. Whole grains have more nutritional value than those that have been treated and refined.
   C. Pink roses are prettier than red ones.
   D. Brick houses are superior to wooden ones.
   E. Airplanes have several advantages over doll carriages.

2. In the following groups of items, decide whether stressing the likenesses or differences would provide the more useful information:
   A. German shepherds and dachschunds
   B. Sewing machines and typewriters
   C. Movies and television
   D. Drinking and smoking
   E. Jogging and playing tennis

Types of Comparison

We think comparatively about many things, and the different types of comparison we make are closely related to our purposes. Using comparison as a way of studying a subject usually serves one of several purposes:

> To state preference or make a choice
> To balance advantages against disadvantages, risks against benefits, before against after
> To explain an unknown in terms of a known, an abstract idea in terms of something specific, that is, to use an *analogy*

Preference

One reason for writing a comparison is to make a choice or state a preference. We perform this thought process automatically every day, consciously and unconsciously. One person might prefer to write with a pencil, another prefer a fountain pen, another a ball-point, and another might compose on a typewriter. These choices result from comparing the experience of using each writing instrument, then establishing a preference for one over the others. As consumers, we can refer to many different types of consumer guides to help us choose what product we are going to buy. Supervisors and executives are often asked to compare the qualifications of candidates for a specific job and recommend the best person. The following passage uses comparison to state an important preference:

> The concern in all this is not death, but life. No one is asking for a moratorium on dying, only on the kind of senseless death that is going on all around us.
>
> When a man like Bertrand Russell dies, simply of old age, we feel little need for mourning. Whatever our sense of loss, we know he had lived his life to the full, and there was even a certain correctness to his end.
>
> This is not the feeling we have when we think of those adolescent girls who were killed by cancer of the vagina because their mothers while pregnant were given the drug, Diethylstibestrol during the early part of their pregnancies. Even years later there is still grief in the homes of these girls, still the sense of guilt we all feel for lives unfulfilled. The drug should have been destroyed a decade ago. Yet meat producers still want to add it to the diet of cows, to provide greater weight gain with less feed. The sad fact is that the use of DES as an additive for animal feeds is still under consideration by government regulatory agencies. (Ronald Glasser, *The Greatest Battle*)

The issue here is more serious than choosing between two different brands of cologne. The comparison between two ways of dying—one with dignity after a useful life, the other premature and without dignity—compels us to choose which we prefer for ourselves. The comparison leads to a statement of opinion: "The drug should have been destroyed."

Advantages and Disadvantages

We have all heard or read or participated in discussions weighing the advantages of a course of action against the disadvantages, or risks against benefits. If you remember the controversy surrounding the Alaskan pipeline project, for example, you are familiar with comparison used in this way. Boiled down and oversimplified, the controversy set the risks to Alaska's fragile ecological system (the permafrost, the migration patterns of wildlife) against the benefits of an increased oil supply and a major boost to Alaska's economy. The final judgment as to which side was right in this controversy will probably be made through a before and after comparison (Alaska's ecological system before the pipeline balanced against the circumstances that develop after the pipeline has been in use for a number of years).

The following passage compares advantages and disadvantages of buying a condominium in a Planned Unit Development (PUD):

> There are people who buy into PUDS because they are attracted by the housing designs, by the sort of neighbors they find, or by the fast appreciation and opportunity for easy resale. Then there are some who find that their PUD homes tend to fall apart in their hands and who become involved in running battles with the developers over the necessary repairs.
>
> Don and Elaine Wong, a pharmacist and teacher, respectively, fit all of the above descriptions. They like almost everything about Harbor Bay Isle—the lagoon, the people, the school—but they've found a few score of construction defects in each home they've owned there. (Charles Haas, "The Great Condo Con," *Esquire*)

Weighing advantages and disadvantages provides useful information for deciding on a course of action. The couple mentioned in the above passage bought three different homes in the same development. Each time, the disadvantages of many construction faults were outweighed by the social and financial advantages.

The advantages of a course of action can also be determined by before and after comparisons. Local law enforcement officials might compare accident statistics during a temporary crackdown on drunk drivers with the figures from the same period the year before. If the data indicated a real decline after the crackdown was in force, a police department or city council could use this comparison to justify a permanent program to control drunk driving in the locality.

Analogy

Comparison can explain and clarify new ideas by looking at them in terms of more familiar concepts. This use of comparison is called *analogy*. An idea is explained in terms of something more familiar. For example, we might use the analogy of the *ocean* to explain how the *mind* works: thoughts are like the waves on the surface, while subconscious forces are like powerful currents deep below.

Explaining a difficult idea by using a familiar analogy makes good use of comparison. The analogy must be kept fresh in the reader's mind, however. Notice how the author of the following passage uses the analogy with finding scattered beads to illustrate a method for determining the availability of oil resources.

Suppose it were actually true that the rate of finding new oil in the United States is declining because we are really running out of oil. Then, as new oil fields are found, and the number remaining to be found is thereby reduced, each additional new field would become progressively more difficult to locate. A more familiar analogy might be trying to find all the beads scattered from a broken necklace. The first few beads are easy to find, but the task becomes increasingly difficult as there are progressively fewer beads to be located in widely dispersed places. In the beginning, the ease of finding (as measured, for example, by the number found per minute) will not diminish: but when only a few beads remained to be found, the rate of finding them would begin to decline.

Now, suppose that you were unaware of the number of beads originally on the string, and wished to know, nevertheless, when during the progress of the search you had found all or nearly all of them. This could be done by keeping a record of the number of beads found per interval of time. As long as the rate of finding beads increased or remained constant, you could be sure that a significant number of them were still to be found. After a time, when the rate of discovering new beads began to decline, you could expect that there were only a few remaining ones. When a long time passed and no new bead was found, you could assume that you had run out of findable beads, and probably had the entire necklace in hand.

In the same way, if the number of accessible but as yet undetected oil fields in the United States were now being appreciably reduced by current discoveries, then the effort needed to find each new field should be increasing. If we chose not to increase the exploratory effort, and the amount of oil discovered per unit of exploratory effort remained constant with time it might be concluded that there was still a good deal of oil left to be found. Thus, as in the hunt for scattered beads, the rate of discovery of new oil can be used as an indicator of the phase of the discovery process, a year by year record of the rate at which oil is found and of the inevitable process of exhausting the discoverable fields of oil. (Barry Commoner, *The Poverty of Power*)

EXERCISES

1. Compare two brands of some product you might plan to buy, maybe a stereo receiver, a refrigerator, or a pair of shoes. Note the likenesses and differences. List the differences that seem most significant to you. Mark the ones that are most important in making your choice.

2. You have all seen before-and-after ads for various products from weight-lifting devices to dieting gimmicks. Do a before-and-after comparison between yourself today and the you of five years ago. In addition to physical details, think in terms of finances, health, job security, political opinions, and so forth.

3. We said earlier that there must be some significant similarities to have

a basis for comparison—that you could not compare a house with a potato. But using strange comparisons (analogies) can sometimes lead to interesting ideas when you find *imaginative* similarities between two very different things. Recall our comparison of the human mind to the ocean: thoughts are like waves on the surface; subconscious forces are like deep ocean currents. Think of some other imaginative points of comparison between the ocean and your mind. Try to come up with imaginative points of comparison for some of the following:

A. School and a bowl of mixed vegetables
B. Life and a tree
C. Cars and sports
D. Writing and boxing

Standards of Comparison

A comparison works only if you measure the things being compared with the same yardstick. In other words, things, people, or situations must be looked at in terms of the same set of standards. You know the problems caused by a "double standard." A man, for example, might be admired by peers for his sexual activities, while a woman who has similar activities might be frowned on or condemned. Similarly, women with equal qualifications and experience often earn less money than men performing the same job because a different set of standards is often unfairly applied to women. In fact, if a single, scientifically determined standard is used, our society's clear distinction between men and women would be blurred:

> Everybody's blood chemistry is part male and part female in varying ratios affected among other things by age. Sex identity based on hormones would help abolish silly notions of 100 percent men and women and curtail discrimination against homosexuals and bisexuals. (Lowell Ponte, "Quotas, Taken to Extremes," *Skeptic*)

We cannot make intelligent choices unless we have clearly established standards of comparison. Most of us shop around before making a purchase. This allows us to examine various brands of the same product in terms of our individual circumstances and needs. Most of us do this automatically, but the more conscious our choice of standards becomes, the more our choices become efficient and productive.

For example, a man who wants to purchase a business suit might do some very deliberate comparison shopping. To begin with, he would go to an expensive men's store to look at the merchandise there. Color is one basic consideration in buying a suit, and the shopper would quickly notice that most expensive suits are dark grey or dark blue. Next he would examine the fabrics carefully. What do they look and feel like? How soft are they? What is their texture? After noting the fabric qualities, he will study the details of workmanship. How is the lining done? How many and what type of pockets are there? Do interior pockets have buttons? How many buttons are on the jacket sleeves? What are they made of? How are the lapels cut? Having taken careful notes, the comparison shopper now goes to a more reasonably priced store, one more in line with his budget. He might even go to a discount outlet for the lowest possible price. In both cases he will check out the lower priced suits for qualities found in the most expensive ones. With a little luck and attention to specific details, he may find a suit that appears to be much more expensive than its actual price.

What are the standards suggested here? Having decided to buy a business suit, the comparison shopper uses four definite standards of comparison:

1. The color
2. The look of the material
3. The workmanship
4. The cost

Similarly, when you are writing out a comparison, you should make clear to your reader what standards of comparison you are using.

EXERCISES

1. You are trying to decide which of two houses you will buy. One standard of comparison you are using is the cost of heating and cooling. What factors will you look at in each house to compare them on the basis of this standard? Name one or two additional standards that would be important to use in your comparison. For a house, you may substitute cars, stereo equipment, sewing machines, or other such items. In any case, determine the most important standards you will use to compare these items.

2. A friend asks for your opinion of a movie. You say it is "great." Your friend isn't very trusting and asks why you think it's so good. List the standards of comparison you would use in comparing this movie to others in order to judge it.

Writing Comparisons

The methods for organizing a written comparison follow naturally from our habits of thought. These methods help communicate effectively because our readers use the same patterns of thought to make comparisons themselves. To rely on the consumer example again, there are two major ways we compare products. We can go into a store featuring one brand of, say, stereo equipment and examine the product carefully in terms of our needs and standards. Then we can go across town, visit another store, and examine its brand of stereo. Now that we have looked at two types of the same product, we have a frame of reference within which to make a comparison. On one sheet of paper we might list all the attributes of one brand, then on another sheet, list the attributes of the other. This is the *whole-by-whole* method of organizing a comparison. We examine one thing in its entirety, then we examine the other.

The second method is the *point-by-point* method of comparison. This method puts individual qualities of the objects or situations being compared next to each other. If the same store carries two brands of stereo equipment, we can set them side by side and compare them point by point: the turntables, the cartridges, the amplifiers, the speakers. In effect, we examine and compare the two products piece by piece.

Both methods are effective and both depend for their effectiveness on clearly established standards of comparison. The choice of method depends a great deal on the subject matter. The whole-by-whole method shows one subject at a time and shows how the various parts of that subject relate to the established standards. The point-by-point method has the advantage of showing both subjects simultaneously. Our examples will help you make the decision which method will work best for your purposes. In general, however, your reader will find a lengthy, detailed comparison easier to follow if it is arranged in the point-by-point method.

Whole-by-Whole Method

The organizational pattern for the whole-by-whole method of comparison looks like this:

1. Statement of purpose of the comparison: to suggest that economic class may be more important sometimes than race.

2. Discussion of Subject #1: working-class kids
3. Discussion of Subject #2: affluent kids
4. Summary: White working-class kids are very different from affluent white kids.

The following example uses this structure:

Purpose: The kids of the working class have a lot more in common with the black kids than they do with the children of the middle and upper classes. *The working kid* [italics added] is starting at the same point his father did—he's got to survive in the system, beat the system, just like the black kid does. You know the pattern: "Get your house, raise your family, be a good citizen even though it's not the best system, O.K., but a certain amount of psychological and economic security and you will have it made in America." *The affluent kids,* on the other hand, don't have these needs. Somebody is paying their bills through college; they don't have to work. They have no roots, no goal; they think history is going to end tomorrow. They have spent a lot of time watching television and they believe in the instant answer. They drift. They get bored, they move on. They can worry about the large social problems. They're worried about Vietnam. They're worried about the "noble savages" in the ghettos. But they're terribly unhappy; they are really a mixed-up bunch of kids. What's happened to the Peace Corps? To VISTA? These were the programs of middle-class kids.

Summary: Where has the great generosity of the young people gone in the last five years? At least the working-class kid has a specific goal—security. He's got to do the fieldwork so the liberal affluent kid can worry about the world. (Bill Moyers, *Listening to America*)

Subject #1:

Subject #2:

The following hints will ensure your comparison is clear:

1. Stating the purpose of the comparison before developing the whole-by-whole method helps your reader focus on the main details of the comparison. If the first sentence were left out of the passage above, a reader would have a difficult time figuring out what was going on. The switch to "affluent kids" in the middle of the paragraph would have come as a surprise. The purpose statement is the *topic sentence* of a one-paragraph comparison; it is the *central idea* of a comparison using several paragraphs.
2. The whole-by-whole method requires balance. Each subject must be treated in the same way. The type of information pre-

COMPARING | 71

sented and the standards of comparison used in discussing Subject A should be repeated in discussing Subject B.
3. The facts should also be presented in the same order, as they are in the following example. This careful organization—along with a clear statement of purpose—helps the reader see the points of comparison between two subjects.

Collecting an unemployment check every two weeks beats working for a living. Before I lost my job, I grossed 500 dollars every two weeks. State and federal taxes took their bite. Deductions were made for Social Security and retirement. Union dues were taken out of the check. It cost me 10 dollars a week for gasoline and another 10 dollars or so to eat lunch. Babysitting cost 50 dollars a week. By the time the deductions were taken out and I paid expenses I had about 200 dollars left to live on. My unemployment check, on the other hand, is only 150 dollars every two weeks. But there are no deductions for taxes and I don't have to pay Social Security or retirement. I no longer pay union dues. My car sits in the garage most of the time, except for really necessary trips. Best of all, I have more time with the children instead of relying on babysitters. On unemployment, I seem to have more money to spend than I ever did while I was working.

4. This example illustrates a further characteristic of whole-by-whole comparison. When one thing or circumstance is judged better than the other, the preferred subject is discussed second in the comparison. The subject discussed last has more impact on the reader.
5. The summary statement—the last sentence in this example—draws together the main point of the comparison, and, if appropriate, reasserts the writer's judgment or preference.

SUMMARY

We have made the following points about whole-by-whole organization:

1. Begin with a clear statement of the reason for comparing two things.
2. Present all the relevant details about Subject A, then do the same for Subject B.
3. Present similar facts and information about each subject. Discuss each subject in terms of the same standards.
4. Present the facts in the same order.
5. If one subject is preferred over the other—if the point of the compar-

ison is to make a choice or state a preference—discuss the preferred subject second.

6. Summarize the main point of the comparison at the end.

EXERCISE

1. Read the following example of whole-by-whole comparison:

> Liberals do of course tend to be permissive toward socially disreputable psychoactive drugs, especially when they are used by young and hairy persons. They thus favor decriminalizing marijuana and treating rather than punishing heroin users. However, they are not at all permissive toward nonpsychoactive drugs that are allegedly unsafe or worthless; they thus favor banning certain artificial sweeteners (cyclamates) and the controversial cancer drug, Laetrile. The inconsistency betrays the liberal's fantasy of the state as good parent. Such a state restrains erring citizens by imposing mild, minimal, and medical sanctions, and it protects ignorant citizens by pharmacological censorship.
>
> Conservatives, on the other hand, tend to be punitive about socially disreputable psychoactive drugs, especially when they are used by hirsute youths. They therefore favor criminalizing the sale and use of marijuana and punishing rather than treating those who use heroin. At the same time, they favor a laissez-faire attitude toward nonpsychoactive drugs that are allegedly unsafe or worthless, such as cyclamates and Laetrile. This inconsistency betrays their fantasy of the state as the enforcer of the dominant ethic. In their view, a state should punish citizens who deviate from the moral precepts of the majority but should refrain from meddling in the self-medication of the people. (Thomas Szasz, "A Different Dose for Different Folks," *Skeptic*)

  A. List, in order, the three main points of comparison used for both Subject A (liberals) and Subject B (conservatives).
  B. List some of the similar details used to develop points in each half of the comparison.
  C. Write a clear introductory statement of purpose for the passage.
  D. Write a summary statement at the end. Is it possible to tell if the author has a preference here?

Point-by-Point Method

The point-by-point method of comparison puts the individual qualities of the objects or situations being compared next to each other. Rather than looking at one subject as a whole then looking at the other, particular characteristics of each subject are discussed one at a time. We think this way when we have established quite firmly what characteristics or criteria are most important to us in making the comparison. An outline of a comparison organized by the point-by-point method looks like this:

I. Statement of purpose: One fitness club is a better deal than the other.

II. Characteristic #1: Distance from home

   Subject A: International Spa

   Subject B: Briarwood

III. Characteristic #2: Hours of operation

   Subject A: International Spa

   Subject B: Briarwood

IV. Characteristic #3: Facilities

   Subject A: International Spa

   Subject B: Briarwood

V. Characteristic #4: Cost

   Subject A: International Spa

   Subject B: Briarwood

VI. Summary: Subject B (Briarwood) is a better deal.

Here is an example of the point-by-point method:

> In looking for a fitness club, I find Briarwood to be the best deal. To begin with, of the two clubs in our county the International Spa is nearly ten miles away, while Briarwood is only six miles from my home. Convenience is not just a question of closeness; hours of operation are important also. International Spa is open 7:00 A.M. to 7:00 P.M. six days a week and from noon to 6:00 P.M. on Sunday. Briarwood, however, is open 7:00 A.M. to 10:00 P.M. daily and from 9:00 A.M. to 9:00 P.M. on Sundays. In terms of facilities, Briarwood wins again. International Spa has a Nautilus room, indoor track, and steam room, but Briarwood has all these plus an indoor pool. And when it comes to the cost of membership, International Spa charges $125.00 to join and a $20.00 monthly fee, while Briarwood charges $115.00 initiation fee and only $15.00 a month. Obviously, Briarwood is by far the better choice for me.

In this passage, the most general standard of comparison (best deal) is stated in the topic sentence. The best choice appears second in each category, following the principle that the thing mentioned last takes on the greatest emphasis. Comparisons of both types should have a closing summary that makes a choice or brings out the central point of the comparison.

The question of which method to use has no hard and fast answer. Try to decide which would be easier for your reader to follow in any given case. Experienced writers often set up short and fairly general comparisons in the whole-by-whole pattern, while lengthy, detailed comparisons with many points to look at are easier for readers to follow in the point-by-point form.

EXERCISES

1. Rewrite the passage about liberals and conservatives (p. 72), this time using the point-by-point method.
2. Prepare a brief comparison of two people you know. Use the following points in the comparison: size, style of dress, and attitude toward other people.
3. Make a list of three or four points suitable for a point-by-point comparison of two colleges. What order would you arrange these points in? Why?

Combination of Methods

In the real world, much comparative writing does not model either a pure whole-by-whole method or a pure point-by-point one. Sometimes you will find it most effective to combine the two methods, that is, to follow a paragraph developed by one method with a paragraph developed by the other.

SUMMARY

1. Comparison depends on noting *significant* similarities and differences. Making the point of a comparison usually means stressing the differences between basically similar things.
2. We use comparisons to indicate preferences, to weigh advantages and disadvantages when faced with a choice, and to explain one thing by showing its similarity to something else that is better known or understood. When indicating a preference or making a choice, the item we favor is presented last.
3. Comparisons are arranged by either the whole-by-whole method or the point-by-point method, although a combination of methods may be used. Try to let your reader's needs decide which method is best.

WRITING ASSIGNMENTS

1. Examine these stories about unemployed people. Assume you are writing a report to a political action group that either favors or is opposed to extending unemployment benefits. Write a comparison of two of the men, their attitudes toward finding work, and the problems they face. Write the comparison first using the whole-by-whole method, then rewrite it using the point-by-point method.

   The man made an offer: carry a few panels up a single flight of stairs and make a quick $5.00. Two of the men hanging around carpenter's hall here accepted, but John Martorano declined.
   Not that Mr. Martorano doesn't need the money.... Still he decided against leaving the union hall for $5.00. You never know when a job call might come.
   ... Mostly, he travels to job sites hoping for work. He is in his 26th week of $95.00 a week of unemployment benefits and has 13 weeks left. Like many older workers, he has not taken non-union or odd jobs. "I'd lose my pension benefits," he said. "Besides, the union's always got me jobs." ("Long Island Construction Men Wait in Vain for Jobs," *The New York Times*)

   Jimmy Richardson thinks 11 months is a long time. That's how long the 27-year-old asthmatic black man has been out of a full-time job. "I just want to work," he says. "It don't make no difference what it is. ..."
   He has had a lot of jobs, none for very long. He has chopped cotton; driven farm machinery; worked at a California cannery; run conveyor belts in a lumber mill and glue machines in a furniture factory; put up sheetrock for a contractor; sanded cars in a paint and body shop; greased parts in a bicycle assembly line and sung lead in a local soul band...
   "I didn't like 'em all," he says of his jobs, "but they was jobs. And any job beats nothin' at all." ("The Search for Work," *The Wall Street Journal*)

   Leon J. Green, 33, found shelter at the Salvation Army Emergency Lodge with his wife, Shirley and their three young daughters.
   Weeks ago, the Greens left Coolidge, Arizona, to look for work. Mr. Green lost his job as a janitor in the Coolidge public schools and his wife was laid off at a munitions plant. He said they couldn't qualify for enough aid under Arizona law to subsist there.
   The Greens sold all their belongings that couldn't fit in their car. En route to Chicago, Mr. Green spent almost the last of his money for gasoline and auto repairs.
   "This is the first time in my life I haven't been able to find work. I'll wash dishes if I have to. You got to keep trying and hope for the best, because if you don't, you're done for." ("Okies of the 70's," *U.S. News and World Report*)

2. Go to the library and find information on one of the new technological advances, such as cloning or recombinant DNA, that has significant advantages and disadvantages. Write a comparison of this new technology with the development of atomic power, which also has had advantages and disadvantages. The audience might be people in the community where your college is located, and your purpose could be

to decide whether your school should engage in such research. Think carefully about an appropriate written voice.

3. Choose two job possibilities in your career field, for example, one in private industry, the other in government or military work. Write a comparison of the two jobs, weighing the advantages and disadvantages of each. Act as if you are actually faced with the choice and that writing out the comparison will be the way you think through the problem. Consider such points for comparison as starting salaries, location, general working conditions, fringe benefits, possibilities for promotion or for paid education, necessity of travel and/or periodic relocation, and so on.

4. Consider that you are having a disagreement with someone of the other sex regarding proper male-female roles in marriage and work. Compare two television programs (or books, or movies): one that you think presents a good image of proper male-female roles, and one that you think presents a bad image. Write the comparison to the person you are disagreeing with, as a way to explain your views. What would be an appropriate voice?

5. A common dilemma in the medical field is how to respond to a patient (or a patient's family) who has chosen to reject medical procedures that will temporarily extend life in the face of terminal illness. Choose a specific medical situation and write out a comparison of the two alternatives for a terminal patient (or family) faced with such a choice. Consider carefully whether you want to be objective in your written voice.

6. Write a comparison between your college and one other you considered attending. Your audience is a friend who is now considering both schools and who will probably major in the same field as you did.

7. Select an abstract quality such as love, patriotism, or fear, and decide on a very specific, concrete analogy you may use to explain what you mean by that quality. (Recall the ocean being used as an analogy for the mind.) Write a comparison of the quality chosen and its concrete analogy. Find several specific points of comparison between the two and develop each one.

5

CLASSIFYING

Understanding Classification

Classifying and Dividing

In Chapter 4, we saw that comparison and contrast depend upon noticing significant similarities and differences. When we do notice that a number of items share a major similarity, we often group them together because of this common feature. For example, when we look at a pair of socks, a blouse, a skirt, a pair of slacks and call them "clothes," we have classified these different items. That is, we have grouped them together because they share the one basic characteristic of covering the body. They are all similar in this characteristic, or principle. On the other hand, we also know that these various items are different in important respects so we form subgroups that show these differences. Keeping all these items in the bedroom and calling them "clothes" is *classification*. Putting socks together in one drawer and skirts or slacks in the closet is *division*. A *class* is simply a group of things that are similar in at least one basic or defining characteristic. The *divisions* of a class are smaller subgroups (or subclasses) that are different from each other on the basis of another characteristic. Division is actually another layer of the classification process. First we classify, then we divide. Then we can treat each subdivision as a class and subdivide further if we wish. "Socks" could be divided into "white" and "colored," for example.

Obviously, classification and division are strategies for organized writing that use habits of thinking common to everyone. Classification builds on comparison. Division is based on seeing differences. Human beings seem compelled to classify and divide things in the environment in every conceivable way:

> *Geographically:* The East, the West, the Midwest, the South, Europe, Asia, Africa, North America
> *Ethnically:* Norwegians, Swedes, Germans, Jews, Italians, Native Americans
> *Ideologically:* Left wing, right wing, conservative, reactionary, Republican, Democrat
> *Architecturally:* Gothic, Romanesque, modern, Cape Cod, split-level, ranch, Victorian.

EXERCISE

Name the most specific common characteristic of each list of items:

1. Alabama, Mississippi, Louisiana, Florida, Texas
2. Calculator, typewriter, copy machine, dictaphone
3. Mercury, Venus, Earth, Mars, Jupiter, Saturn
4. Europe, North Africa, Asia, South Africa, Australia
5. Opal, iron, silicone, quartz, copper, silver

Finding a Principle

What you have learned about grouping material and the generalization process (pp. 23–35) prepares you for writing classification and division. In fact, those exercises in Chapter 2 required the basic step you use here. In finding the "common denominator" of items in the data pools, you were discovering what characteristic of each item made it similar to all the others in the group. This is the first step in classification.

Keep this in mind as we examine the following advertisement from a telephone directory, showing how one business classified and divided various forms of printed material:

Mix-a-print
PRINTING IN MINUTES

WHILE YOU WAIT • BIG SAVINGS • VOLUME DISCOUNTS

| COMPLETE PRINTING SERVICE | **XEROX** | OVERNIGHT & WEEKEND SERVICE |

COMPOSER TYPE SETTING • REPRO-TYPING • ART WORK

INSTANT HALF-TONES

SOME POPULAR USES:

ACCOUNTING
STATEMENTS
MINUTES

ADMINISTRATIVE
BUSINESS SURVEYS
CONTRACTS
SYSTEMS

ADVERTISING
PROPOSALS
SURVEYS
TECHNICAL

ARCHITECTS
RENDERINGS
SKETCHES
SPECIFICATIONS

ATTORNEYS
AGREEMENTS
APPEAL BRIEFS
BY-LAWS

BROKERS
CHARTS
MAPS
PICTURES

CONSULTANTS
PROCEDURES
REPORTS
VISUAL AIDS

PROMOTIONAL
CERTIFICATES
CLIPPINGS
PRESS RELEASES

SALES
BROCHURES
CATALOGS
CHARTS

SALES
FLYERS
PRICE LISTS
TRAINING MATERIAL

GENERAL
ANNOUNCEMENTS
APPLICATIONS
BULLETINS
BUSINESS CARDS
DIRECTORIES
ENVELOPES
FORMS
(OFFICE & SHOP)

GENERAL
INSTRUCTIONS
LABELS
LETTERS
MANUALS
NOTICES
POST CARDS
PROGRAMS
PUBLICATIONS
REPORTS
RESUMES
SIGNS
TAGS
TICKETS

MAIL ORDERS FAST • SHIPPED SAME DAY RECEIVED

COMPLETE BINDERY
BUDGET MAILINGS

994-2883   **994-2330**

14624 VICTORY BLVD., VAN NUYS
(SOUTH SIDE OF STREET • 1½ BLOCKS WEST OF VAN NUYS BLVD.)

The class of items is "types of printed material or printing service." Now notice how many different types of material are offered by this company (statements, minutes, business surveys, and so on). Instead of just stringing the names of each of these types across the page, as we started to do, the persons who wrote the ad decided to arrange the material into closely related subgroups. To do this, they had to think of a principle or single point that would divide the class into subgroups and use this same principle for each group. They selected the principle of "some popular uses," as their heading indicates. More specifically, their principle is "some popular uses in different business fields."

Always subdivide the class according to the same principle. Because "uses" is the principle, all the types of printed material here are grouped according to the field in which they are most often *used*. It's possible to subdivide a class according to cost, for instance. That would result in entirely different groups so that "Sketches," which is now under the subgroup of "Architects," and "Signs," which is now under "General," might be in the same group. But because the printing company wanted to make it easier for customers to locate the special type of printing they are interested in, the groups are arranged according to use only.

The telephone company recognizes the importance of using only one principle to classify or divide information. The "yellow pages" section of your telephone book is entirely a *classified* directory. Businesses and agencies are grouped according to the type work they do. When the class is a large one, it is divided into smaller groups on the basis of more specific work. In a big city, the hundreds of contractors in the phone book are divided according to the type of work they do. Thus, the index to the yellow pages may read:

CONTRACTORS

Acoustical   Electric
Air conditioning   Fencing
Awning   Heating
Building   Paving
Concrete

If you want air conditioning service, you needn't walk your fingers through several thousand pages of business listings looking for a name that suggests the type work offered. You don't even have to read through the entire list of contractors in general. You go directly to the few pages listing the precise type of contractor you want—one who repairs air conditioners, not driveways.

But how would you locate air conditioning contractors if the class of contractors were divided not according to one principle, but several, like this:

CONTRACTORS

Years in business
Rates charged
Size of business
Type of insurance carried

Each of these subdivisions is a characteristic worth knowing before hiring someone, but because several principles were used in the division, the contractors are not arranged in a consistent order that helps you find them quickly. Each subdivision would have contractors of all types thrown together.

For another example, notice that the following college courses (the *class* of things) are *divided* according to the type of knowledge studied:

One Division or Subclass: FOREIGN LANGUAGES

German
Spanish
French   } Individual Members of the Subclass
Italian
Latin

Another Division or Subclass: MATHEMATICS

Arithmetic
Algebra
Calculus   } Individual members of the Subclass
Geometry
Trigonometry

Another Division or Subclass: SOCIAL SCIENCES

Economics
Government
History   } Individual Members of the Subclass
Geography
Education

This classification and division organizes the available college courses. Without it, the list could have looked like this:

German
Calculus
Spanish
Geography
Economics

Even a simple alphabetical order would have been better than such a random list:

Algebra
Arithmetic
Calculus
Economics
Education
Geography
Geometry

These lists show that the same class can be divided according to different principles, depending on your purpose. The courses were first arranged according to the type of knowledge studied, then randomly, then divided according to which letter of the alphabet they begin with.

The students in your class could be divided by the number of college credits they have accomulated, say:

1. 0–10 units
2. 11–20 units
3. 21–30 units

Or they could be divided by age groups:

1. Age 17–20
2. Age 21–24
3. Age 25–28
4. Age 28–50
5. Age 50 and above

Grouping in these ways places different students in different groups for each purpose. It is unlikely that all students who would fall into Group 1 of 0 to 10 college credits would also be in Group 1 of age 17 to 20. Different purposes yield different divisions. Notice also that it would be confusing to divide part of the class by one principle and other parts by different principles.

EXERCISES

1. Determine what principle is used to group the following items and check for any item that, according to that principle, doesn't fit. Select the *most specific* principle.

A. Guitar, banjo, harp, mandolin
   B. Drum, flute, saxophone, trumpet
   C. Alabama, Alaska, Florida, Georgia
   D. Lincoln, Mercedes, Chevette, Cadillac
   E. Calculator, typewriter, desk, copy machine

2. Classify the following individuals according to at least three different, clearly stated principles: Joe DiMaggio, Stan Musial, Yogi Berra, Roy Campanella, Mickey Mantle.

3. Classify these items according to two different principles. Be certain that your principle is stated clearly: diamond, emerald, pearl, ruby, sapphire, opal.

4. Visit a large supermarket and examine the system used to help shoppers find various types of food. What principle of classification is used? List the main categories.

5. Think of another principle that might be used to classify grocery items. Using this principle, prepare a diagram of your unique grocery store.

A Caution

Analysis is the process of dividing a single member of a class into its several parts. We can't classify and divide one house into its foundation, framework and interior decoration because these three are *parts of a single house* not *types* of houses. Test whether you are using analysis or classifying and dividing by using the term in question as an adjective to modify the noun that names your class. We can say *chemistry* course, *math* course, *history* course to arrive at three divisions of college courses. We can't say *foundation* house, *framework* house, *interior decoration* house. We can, however, classify houses by their style: Cape Cod, colonial, Georgian, ranch, Victorian, and so on. Or we could classify by their functions the types of rooms in houses: living room, dining room, family room, and the like.

SUMMARY

The basic steps of classification and division are:

1. Determine the essential characteristic that makes each item similar to every other item you are examining. This forms the *class*.

2. Determine what is different about the individual items on the basis of *one* principle. This begins the division.

3. Avoid overly simple divisions, ones that provide no useful information.
4. Don't mistake analysis for classification and division. Remember the adjective/noun test.

EXERCISES

1. Make up lists of items showing subdivisions of these classes:

   College students   Energy savers
   Musical instruments   Health hazards
   Luxury cars   Uncomfortable situations

2. The list below classifies different kinds of jobs available in a particular career field.
   A. Examine the list:

   ... Work with children ... in emergency shelters, in foster and adoptive homes, in protective services for neglected, abused or parentless children, in child guidance clinics, in schools, day care centers, hospitals, convalescent homes, clinics and curative workshops. ... Work in rehabilitation centers and training schools for the mentally retarded.
   ... Work with teenagers and young adults in Y's, community centers, settlement houses, schools, clubs, and on the streets and in storefront meeting places, in juvenile courts and youth councils, in detention homes, in narcotics addiction treatment centers, in reformatories and parole departments. ... Work with the physically handicapped as part of the rehabilitation team in hospitals, rehabilitation centers, sheltered workshops and homes; work with the acutely or chronically ill as part of the medical team.
   ... Work with families troubled by faltering personal relationships and other problems; work with alcoholics, the mentally ill, drug addicts, prisoners and their families. ... Work with the aged in recreational and day care centers, in hospitals and clinics, in their own homes, in residences, housing projects and communities.
   ... Work with community leaders and groups in community planning councils, on urban renewal teams, model cities programs and community projects to meet health or welfare needs. (Patricia W. Soyka, *Unlocking Human Resources: A Career in Social Work*)

   B. Now, do the following:
   (1) Write a sentence that names the class or type of profession involved.
   (2) Assign a descriptive term to each subdivision listed. What title would you give the person who does this work?
   (3) Choose one of the subcategories and write a paragraph that provides details about the kind of work a person with that job would do.

Writing Classification

We all classify and divide the objects, people, and ideas in our environment to help us make sense out of a complex environment. Classifying and dividing the things around you is a valuable strategy for organizing facts and ideas in writing because your readers can easily follow the pattern of your thinking. People working in law enforcement, for example, are alarmed by the rising murder rates in the United States. To understand the problem before trying to correct it, they classified and divided the murders from various points of view. Classifying the kind of weapons used turned up some important facts: In 1974, 54 percent of the murders in America were committed with handguns, 5 percent with rifles, and 9 percent with shotguns; firearms were not used to commit the remaining murders. This classification and division put the facts into a neat order that anyone can understand. On the basis of these facts, what action could be taken to reduce the murder rate?

Classifying and dividing organizes things and ideas into a meaningful pattern. We then use this pattern to store information in memory, to recall it, to uncover new information, and to communicate this information to others.

Getting Started

The first few sentences of a paragraph or essay organized by classification have a very important function. These sentences tell the reader what sort of information is being classified and indicate the principle used to classify the information. The introduction can be brief, or it can be fairly long depending on the complexity of the information. The following examples illustrate various types of introductions to a classification:

    Example: "Hood's Department Store has three major sections."

This sentence tells us that Hood's merchandise has been divided in some way, but the sentence needs additional information to help the reader.

    Example: "Shopping at Hood's is a pleasure when you know how the store is organized. Hood's has three major sections: Women's Wear, Men's Wear, and Sporting Goods."

This version makes the purpose clear: to make shopping easier. Moreover, naming the categories helps the readers find their way through your presentation.

Example: "Several types of television cameras have been developed; each has special characteristics and special uses of its own."

This introduction could help the reader more by naming the different types of cameras. However, the purpose of this introduction, to show the special uses and characteristics of each type, is made clear.

The following examples from published writers illustrate effective introductions to information presented through classification:

Names the class of organs and indicates purpose. Outlines the main categories.

About 25 different kinds of organs and tissues have now been used in human transplantation with varying degrees of success. In general, these fall into three categories: Major organs, such as the kidney, heart, liver, lung, pancreas, spleen, bone marrow and skin; nonvital organs and tissues, such as eye corneas, bone, cartilage, fascia and teeth; hormone and endocrine tissues, such as thymus and pituitary. (Irving Ladimer, "The Challenge of Transplantation," *Public Affairs Pamphlet*)

Names the class of instruments. Tells us how many divisions.

Orchestral instruments [emphasis added] are divided into four principal types, or sections. The first section, of course, is that of the strings; the second, of the woodwinds; the third is the brass; and the fourth is the percussion. Each of these sections is made up of a related group of instruments of similar type. Every composer, when composing, keeps these four divisions very much to the front of his mind. (Aaron Copeland, *What to Listen for in Music*)

EXERCISE

Add one or two sentences to the following statements to show the purpose of the classification and to name the major categories:

1. There are three kinds of teachers at this school.
2. Several types of tires are available for winter driving.
3. Restaurants in our town fall into one of three categories.

CLASSIFYING | 87

Making Transitions

Effective classification and division requires that the reader be aware of each new category introduced. Clear signals showing the change from one category to the next are essential to this method or organization.

The following selection tries to help consumers protect themselves from faulty products and services. We have italicized the key words that signal the beginning of each new category.

> The following defenses are not legally valid, and you should at all costs avoid them. In reading about them, the reasons for avoiding them seem self-evident, but you'd be surprised how many people who should know better, attempt to use them:
>
> 1. A *defective-merchandise defense* when you accepted the defective merchandise knowingly. If you know the merchandise was defective and bought it anyhow, it's your problem, not the seller's. When your defense is based on a defect in the merchandise, never blurt out that you saw the defect before buying. The merchandise looked perfect and it wasn't until you got it home and either examined it, tried it on, or used it, that the defect became apparent.
>
> 2. *Rudeness on the part of the salesman* is not excuse for nonpayment. Of course, if the salesman happened to slander you or push you around a bit, you may have a counter-claim.
>
> 3. *The delivery of the goods or performance* of the service was late. Legally speaking, time is not of the essence (as you may notice from the way the courts operate). The only exceptions to this rule are when a contract specifies a delivery date (and has no escape clause) or when the urgency was made clear to the seller at the time of the purchase and thus became a condition to the verbal sales contract. This legal doctrine works both ways, because time is also not of the essence when you pay for what you bought, as long as you do eventually pay for it.
>
> 4. *The merchandise is defective*, and the seller is making attempts—however feeble, incompetent or misguided—to fix the defect. He's off the hook, and you're legally supposed to pay him. (Bruce Goldman, Robert Franklin, and Kenneth Pepper, Esq., *Your Check Is in the Mail*)

EXERCISE

The first sentence of each main paragraph has been omitted from the following essay. Supply a suitable transition sentence that signals the beginning of a new category.

> ... At a large fund-raising dinner, a man stood before the group and announced that he would like to make a $10,000 gift to the cause anony-

mously. Contradictory as a public announcement of an anonymous gift may seem, the fund raisers understood the man's action and gauged the promotional impact of that announcement. Anyone who organizes and promotes a successful charity drive, civic or religious, understands that different motives prompt people to give money to charity. Experienced fund raisers know that contributors fall into four groups.

... In response to an appeal made on the street corner, they hand over a dollar, but the same appeal made in the presence of friends would cause them to flash a five or ten. At civic drives and church drives, this group is the first to embrace the cause vocally and the first to sign pledges publicly. They are always seen giving.

... Believing that their own sins can be expiated, they dig down deep and give generously, feeling perhaps that some of their unfair profit given to worthy causes, to help the poor they have made poorer, may in the long run, exonerate them. In this group are men who are haunted by feelings of guilt and who trust a sizable donation to absolve them of their guilt. Fund raisers expect many of the $1000 checks to come from this group.

... They protect their own feelings and identify with the human situation. Some remember the bread lines of the thirties, droughts and disasters, illness, and setbacks. Some have been there themselves. This group responds with sincerity to charity because they have a humanitarian outlook and genuinely desire to promote human welfare. They can accept the responsibility of everyman to be his "brother's keeper," and they realize also that improving the world of others improves their own world.

... This group does not hesitate to write checks for $100 or more to different charitable organizations, even though they have not stopped to think whether they are in sympathy with the drives to which they contribute. Often oblivious to the merit of the cause, they are moved less by the spirit of giving than by the argument that the more they give, the less the government will get. Their gifts are a retaliation against the government. It is not that the cause needs it, but that the government needs it less. (Adapted from "The Mantle of Charity," in Sidney T. Stovall, Virginia B. Mathis, Linda A. Craven, G. Mitchell Hagler, and Mary A. Poole, *Composition: Skills and Models*)

The following reading selections are organized by classification and division. Each begins with a precise statement of the class and its division. The *Submariner* selection tells us the principle of classification and division in the first three sentences. The others begin with introductory paragraphs that identify the class and indicate the general characteristics. The body of the essay supports and develops the points mentioned in the introduction.

Petty Officer Keating told the class that as a submarine traveled along through the water, the secret of its being able to dive and then surface again was the principle known as *buoyancy*.

"There are three kinds of buoyancy," he said. "*Positive* buoyancy, *negative* buoyancy and *neutral* buoyancy." He explained the difference among them by using a very simple example—a bottle. "If we jam a cork into the neck of an empty bottle and put in in the water, it floats. That is *positive* buoyancy," he said. "If we take the cork out of the bottle and fill it with water, the bottle sinks. That is *negative* buoyancy. If we put just the right amount of water into the bottle, then cork it, the bottle will stay at whatever level we put it, either on the surface or below the surface. That is neutral buoyancy." Then he added, "If you want a fancy name for this principle of buoyancy, you can call it Archimedes' Law. He's the guy who discovered it, back in ancient Greece." (Henry B. Lent, *Submariner: The Story of Basic Training at the Navy's Famed Submarine School*)

The essential purpose of any switch is to connect or disconnect two metallic conductors. When the conductors touch, electric current can flow from one wire to another—the circuit is *closed*. When the conductors are separated, an air gap remains and electricity can't flow between the wires—the circuit is *open*.

All switches, therefore, open or close the electrical connection between two or more of their terminals. The simplest form is the *knife switch*, so named because of its cutting action as the blade is pulled down between two springy contracts that are wired to one terminal on the switch. The pivoted end of the blade is wired to the second terminal. The conductive parts of this switch must be mounted in plastic or wood or other nonconductive material so that the switch does not *short out*, that is, provide an alternate path for the current to flow around the open switch contacts. In addition, the knife blade itself must have a nonconductive handle so that you can open or close the switch without touching any of the conductive parts.

This design is fine for certain laboratory work on low-current and low-voltage circuits. The trouble is that too many of the conductive parts are unprotected—a careless finger or tool would bring the electric voltages and currents into dangerous contact with the human operator. And so a switch for home use must be completely enclosed—no conductive parts open to prying fingers at all.

A second requirement for the household switch is that the contacts open and close at high speed. The reason for this is that electric current has a form of inertia—once started it hates to stop. If a large electric current were flowing through a knife-blade switch and you slowly lifted the knife blade, current would continue to flow from contact to contact even when they were physically separated. It would flow in the form of a bright spark jumping across the gap between contacts. This is dangerous—the spark is exceedingly hot and it can easily start fires in wire insulation, and in the plaster-and-wood walls of our houses.

The normal household wall switch satisfies these requirements. It is completely enclosed, has fast closing and opening action and it is enclosed in a small metal box embedded in the wall so that even in the unlikely event of a spark, as between exposed broken wires, the flame would be contained by the box.

The snap action of a switch gives it its high speed. In the household switch, the toggle you push is forced by a spring to swing fully down or up—no middle position is possible. As the switch toggle is slowly pulled away from one position, it approaches the point of no return. Once past the center balance point, the spring snaps the toggle over the rest of the way. The contacts are arranged so that one position of the toggle brings them into close contact, the other position separates them.

Another style of switch takes advantage of the buckling characteristics of a saucer-shaped disk of spring metal. When you push down on the convex side of the disk, it resists until you raise the pressure beyond its buckling point. At that point, the disk inverts so that the convex side becomes concave, and vice versa. When inverted, the contacts are brought together; when in normal unstressed condition, the contacts are held apart by the curved shape of the disk. There are dozens of variations of this design.

One last kind of switch should be mentioned here. The *mercury switch* is called a silent switch because it doesn't operate on the snap action of a spring and so it is much quieter. Mercury is a metal that stays liquid (molten) even at room temperatures that are comfortable for people. Actually, it "freezes" at $-38°F$. Since it is a metal, it is a good conductor, and two wires dipped into a jar of mercury will act just the same (electrically) as if a solid bar of copper had been welded between them. Of course, when the conductors have been lifted out of the jar of mercury, the current will cease to flow. (Richard M. Koff, *How Does It Work?*)

As a result of my week-long vigil, this is what I've learned: Daytime TV consists of talk shows (aptly named since everybody talks and nobody listens), game shows (where winning six stainless steel kitchen knives worth $49.95 will bring a woman to the brink of orgasm), and soap operas (which should be called snoop operas). Punctuating the programs are the commercials. If I must have commercials, then let me have them after dark when airplanes fly across friendly skies to desert islands and sensational beauties lather their hair to a froth. They put a touch of glamour in my life. By day, the commercials belong to the detergent drones.

Soap operas offer little action, but if talk could be converted like solar energy, the characters on the soaps would heat and light this nation. The verbose types on "Days of Our Lives" or "The Guiding Light" or "Another World" look like manikins that have slipped out of Bonwit Teller's windows. The men get their hair styled as opposed to cut. The women have manicured nails and use lots of hair spray. I have seen people like these shopping at Saks at two in the afternoon, but they don't look real either. I can't imagine them pushing shopping carts around Grand Union, doing their laundry or standing in lines. They've been homogenized beyond recognition; their bland speech from which every trace of regionalism, every idiosyncrasy has been bleached. Yet here they are on my TV screen, impersonating average middle class Americans. Their houses look like Holiday Inns—beige rugs, beige walls, a few forgettable pictures, a sofa. No clutter, no books, no newspapers, no plants. There are no children's drawings scotch-taped to the refrigerator, no bowling trophies, no souvenirs from Mexico. While the women in the commercials are down on their knees scraping crust out of their ovens, the women in soap operas are sitting in immaculate living rooms writing love notes on scented stationery. We never see them cleaning, and though we meet some of them on their way to and from work, even in their offices on occasion, we never actually catch them doing any discernible tasks. We do see them talking—constantly. (Sylvia Rabiner, "Daytime TV: What You're Missing (or Not Missing)" *Working Woman*)

ANOTHER EXERCISE

Study the preceding examples. In each one:

1. Identify any major classes and the principle used to form them.

2. Identify any dividing principles and state the names of any subdivision.

3. If there are any problems with these selections as accurate examples of classification/division, point them out and explain why they are problems.

4. Based on the kind of information contained and on the writer's "voice" in each selection, identify a probable audience for each piece.

SUMMARY

1. Groups, or classes, are formed by finding a common principle, some important feature that all members of the class share.

2. Classes can be subdivided by finding a different feature that separates members of the class into smaller groups, which in turn can be subdivided, and so on.

3. In writing out a classification, it is important to make clear what principle is being used to classify or divide, and to use a transition statement that identifies each new class or subdivision as you come to it.

WRITING ASSIGNMENTS

1. Nearly everyone has encountered the encyclopedia seller, and some of us have tried to make a living selling encyclopedias. The following passage is taken from an article describing one man's experiences selling encyclopedias:

> It is my theory that three classes of people were hired: "Fishes," "Sneakers" and "Con-men." The fishes actually believe they are advertising representatives and they stay with the company not only for the money, but because they believe in education and in the product. (These people become very defensive of their jobs to outsiders and bristle at the mention of any other encyclopedia). The sneakers figure the sales pitch isn't all on the up-and-up, but for the money they aren't going to bother with details. If they

realized the extent of their deception, the sneakers probably would be forced by their disquieted consciences to quit. They need the rah-rah of product emotionalism to keep their minds from wandering where it might not be economically advisable. The con-men will do anything for the money offered. Even though the con-men don't always know precisely how they are misleading the public, they are fully aware that the public is being misled. Consequently, the fishes and the sneakers are protected from the truth by the con-men who build up fine rationalizations to keep everyone enthusiastic and productive. Strangely enough, management is not composed primarily of con-men. It is easier for these people, too, to believe they are doing something worthwhile for mankind than to try to live with a conscience of conflict; some have become almost fish-like themselves. (Lynn M. Buller, "The Encyclopedia Game," in *Life Styles: Diversity in American Society*)

A. What type of people would be most likely to buy a set of encyclopedias?
B. What kind of people do you think encyclopedia sellers look for as most likely buyers?
C. Write a detailed set of guidelines for a new salesperson, *classifying* at least three types of likely buyers.

2. The following essay classifies women in a unique way:

... We refer to the passive woman as Doris Doormat. When Doris is being non-assertive, she is typically functioning at a low level. She allows other people to make her decisions for her, even though she may later resent them for it. She feels helpless, powerless and inhibited. Nervousness and anxiety are not uncommon to Doris. She rarely expresses her feeling and has little self-confidence. She does best when following others and may be fearful of taking the initiative in any situation. Frequently she feels sorry for herself to the point of martyrdom and wonders why others cannot rescue her from her plight. When a woman has *only* passivity as her style of relating to the world and she has failed in turning to others, she frequently turns to alcoholism, drugs, physical complaints or suicide to escape her misery.

On the other hand, the aggressive woman, Agatha Aggressive, is very expressive—mostly to the extent that she humiliates and depreciates the person with whom she is relating. You could call her obnoxious, vicious or egocentric. No matter what you label her, she has the same destructive effect on you; you feel devastated by an encounter with her. Her message to you is that she's OK and you definitely are not OK. In our society one might say it takes a lot of courage for a woman to be aggressive, especially since this style of behavior has been viewed as totally non-feminine. So, the price the aggressive woman has paid is usually alienation from almost everybody. What a heavy price for anybody to pay just to get what they want!

Because of the reaction accorded to the aggressive woman and the misery experienced by the passive woman, many women develop the ability to get what they want by indirect means. In our chart, Iris Indirect illustrates this style of behavior. Iris has learned her lesson well; in order to achieve her goal, she may use trickery, seduction or manipulation. She sees indirectness as an avenue open to her because society includes this trait in its definition of woman. A woman is expected to use her "womanly wiles" to get what she wants. Therefore, at times Iris is seen as "cute and coy." However, when she is angry, she is likely to use sneaky ways to get revenge. She can be so indirect that the person with whom she is angry may never even know that she was angry or what her anger was about. Iris and many like her enjoy these games that keep her fighting spirit strong enough so that she doesn't succumb to the depressions of Doris.

Many women have been unaware that there is another alternative way of responding to people and situations, i.e., assertively. An assertive action is an alternative to passive or aggressive actions. In our chart, April Assertive, like Agatha, is expressive with her feeling, but not to the point of obnoxiousness. She is able to state her views and desires directly, spontaneously and honestly. She feels good about herself and about others too; she respects the feelings and rights of other people. April can evaluate a situation, decide how to act and then act without reservation. The most important thing to April is that she is true to herself. Winning or losing seem unimportant compared to the value of expressing herself and choosing for herself. She may not always achieve her goals, but to her the end-product isn't always as meaningful as the actual process of asserting herself. Regardless of whether April has something positive or negative to say to you, she says it in such a way that you are left with good feelings about what was said. (Stanlee Phelps and Nancy Austin, *The Assertive Woman*)

  A. In this selection, women are classified on the basis of one principle.
  B. Think of a similar way of classifying men and explain your classification in an essay modeled on the example.
  C. Use the same "self-help" purpose, only now the audience will be men.
  D. Decide on an appropriate voice.

3. Write an essay in which you classify the kinds of social pressures that affect your behavior, or the behavior of people you know. Write as if you have been asked for advice about the social pressures that develop when you leave home for college or work, or those that come with getting married, or moving into a supervisory position, or some other situation that creates classifiable types of social pressures.

4. Select a general subject such as "education," "recreation," "cities"—any subject you're interested in. Make a free association list (Chapter 1, p. 16). Sort through the items on the list and find a principle you can use to classify some of them. For example, if you made a list relating to "cities," among other things on the list might be the names of several cities that could be put into classes according to population size: under 25,000 people; 25,000 to 50,000 people; 50,000 to 100,000 people; and so on. Set up at least three classes drawn from your list according to one principle. See if these classes can be subdivided. Write an essay using these three classes and their subdivisions for its basic structure. You will need to develop each class with specific examples and details. Once you have established the basic classes, consider an appropriate audience and purpose for the essay; who would be interested in this explanation of your subjects? Why?

5. The U.S. Department of Labor uses three broad categories to classify all jobs. List as many jobs as you can think of in ten minutes, all kinds—from working on a factory production line to being a corporate pres-

ident, from being a welder or auto mechanic to being a doctor or a lawyer, and so on. See if you can come up with three broad groups that will take in all these jobs. These jobs categories have little to do with money or prestige; for example, the Labor Department would group trash collectors and airline pilots in one broad class, a counterperson at McDonalds and a social worker in another, a philosophy teacher and a U.S. senator in the third. When you have decided on your classifications, write an essay to your classmates explaining how your system of grouping jobs could be useful in helping people decide what kind of career would be best for them.

6

DEFINING

Understanding Definition

Relationship of Definition to Classification and Division

Definition is actually a special form of classification and division. When you define something, you first place it in a class and then divide it off from other members of that class. For example, look at the dictionary definition of the word "specialist." Most dictionaries have an entry that reads something like, "a physician who limits his or her practice to a specific field." This *simple definition* tells us what class we are concerned with (physicians) and what makes a specialist different from other doctors. Simple definitions are satisfactory for many purposes, but we often need more information to complete the job of defining, that is, of isolating the term in question from other members of its class so that the reader will know exactly what is meant. Read the following definition of "specialist:"

How can you be sure that the specialist you employ is a specialist?

96 STRATEGIES FOR WRITING

You look him up in the *Directory of Medical Specialists,* which you'll find in the public library.... The 1970 edition lists some 108,000 board certified specialists in active practice. This is only about one-third of the total number of practicing physicians in the U.S.A. However, as we noted earlier, 80 percent of the physicians in this country describe themselves as practicing some sort of medical or surgical *specialty* [emphasis added]. This means that some 40 percent of those doctors who claim to be *specialists* are in fact misrepresenting themselves and hoodwinking the consumer of medical care into paying more for their services than they should. *Specialists* charge more than general practitioners for their services.

Consider these figures published in the *Journal of the American Medical Association.* The number of board-certified *specialists* in anesthesia is only half the total number of those physicians who actually practice anesthesiology in the U.S.; among those who call themselves internists only 45 percent are board-certified; of psychiatrists only 48 percent are board-certified; of the surgical sub-specialty colon and rectal surgery only 55 percent are board-certified; finally, only 58 percent of the practicing urologists are board-certified.

The *true specialist* has to undergo a required number of progressively graded years of approved residency training in a major teaching hospital. He has then to take extensive oral and written examinations supervised by these specialty boards. Upon satisfactorily passing these examinations, he receives a certificate that he has been admitted to the specialty in question, and he is then listed in the *Directory of Medical Specialists,* where you can find his name.

Many non-qualified *"specialists"* claim varying years of experience or training in their specialty and indeed they may have some exposure to the field they claim. But the fact remains that they are not board-certified and should not be allowed to practice as *specialists* and charge specialist fees any more than a person who has spent a couple of years at a medical school should be allowed to practice as a doctor. Some physicians who *fail to pass their specialty* examinations nevertheless go on to describe themselves as *specialists,* and this should not be permitted. (Dr. Morris N. Placers and Charles S. Marwick, *How You Can Get Better Medical Care for Less Money*)

This *extended definition* subdivides "specialist" further into "true specialist" and those we might call "self-proclaimed specialists." The longer definition provides the detail necessary for the reader to understand all the significant differences involved.

EXERCISES

1. Without asking anyone else, jot down your own definitions of:

>   young   good pay   fast
>   speed   old   fine
>   machine   gay   sheet
>   investment   good job   rich

Now compare your definitions with the answers of those around you.

2. Find several places displaying signs such as, "Trained Mechanic on Duty," or "Trained Specialists," or "Certified Specialists." Apply the following seven-point consumer's quiz to determine if the meanings are consistent from place to place. Write a paragraph explaining the results of your quiz.

Who?: (Who did the training? Authorizing? Certifying? and so on.)
What?: (What, exactly, was taught? Authorized? Certified?)
Where: (Are standards the same everywhere?)
When?: (Recently or years ago? Does time matter?)
Why?: (What was the real purpose?)
How?: (By lectures? Films? Field practice? Self-instruction?)
To What Degree?: (How was the person's learning measured? Is the person competent? Excellent?)

Simple Definitions

Knowledge of simple definitions will help with the extended definitions that follow. For some things, a single sentence or two of definition is all we want. Can you imagine reading a long essay defining a hairpin? A hat? A blouse? A nail? Though you already know what each of these items is, notice that the dictionary defines them in a particular way. The three parts of a simple definition are the *term* to be defined, the *class* of things to which the term belongs, and the *characteristics that distinguish* the term from all other terms in the same class:

TERM	CLASS	DISTINGUISHING CHARACTERISTICS
hairpin	a piece of wire	U-shaped, used to fasten up the hair
hat	a shaped covering	for the head, usually with a crown and brim
blouse	a garment for women	covering the body from neck or shoulders to the waistline
nail	a rodlike piece of metal	having a pointed tip and a flattened head, usually hammered into wood as a fastener

The class is simply a group of similar things. This is the first step in limiting the meaning of a term. As soon as you identify a blouse as a member of the class of garments, you have limited the meaning. At least we know that a blouse isn't a plant or animal. But because there are other items in the class of garments, it is also necessary to distinguish a blouse from every other garment. You must identify those features that make a blouse a blouse and not a sock or a glove.

EXERCISE

To each of the following classes add two terms to be defined and their distinguishing characteristics.

TERM	CLASS	DISTINGUISHING CHARACTERISTICS
	a machine	
	an instrument	
	the act of	
	practice of	

Problems in Definition

Clear definitions are immensely important to effective communication with readers. But two sources create problems in defining terms. First, in simple definitions you have to be careful about the process of definition:

1. Avoid defining a word with some form of the same word. This chases us in circles. It's no help to say that "courage means to be courageous."
2. Avoid defining with a synonym only: "Courage means bravery." This method is of some value if we know the synonym, but don't rely on it alone; very few words, if any, have the very same meaning.
3. Avoid using the phrases "is where" and "is when," such as in "A tornado is when strong winds can uproot trees and smash brick buildings." The problem here is that definition requires you to say what something *is*. The word "where," however, refers to place. "When" refers to time. Neither one of these is an *essential* aspect of a tornado. Uprooting trees and smashing buildings is what a tornado can do. As you'll soon see, there is value in using this type of information in a

definition, but don't depend on it only. If we insist on knowing what a tornado *is*, we need information about its essential nature as well as what it does. *Essential* characteristics are those that must be part of a thing to make it what it is. The color white is not essential to a house. Walls are essential to a house. And there are dozens of tornadoes every year that do not uproot trees or smash buildings. The following definition tells what a tornado *is*.

> Tornadoes are the smallest but by far the most violent of swirling storms. Their winds sometimes reach velocities as high as 500 mph, five times greater than hurricane winds. About 1,000 feet in diameter, the cone-shaped tornado combines super high winds with extreme low pressure to produce a tremendous vacuum. The suction effect of this storm causes total destruction wherever the tornado touches the surface of the earth.

The second kind of problem can develop when you have a complex term that may have different definitions according to the purpose, or reason, you have for defining it. Look at the following example where a *legal* definition and a *medical* definition operate at cross-purposes:

> Another social *problem* arising from recent improvements in medical technology has to do with *definition* of death. Legally, death is defined as occurring when the heart stops beating. Today, with assisted respiratory devices and heart pacing, it is possible to keep a patient breathing and his heart beating for long, perhaps indefinite, periods of time. This has proved invaluable in tiding patients over potentially fatal periods of respiratory or cardiac arrest. But what happens when these assisting devices are used in a patient who unfortunately has undergone irreparable brain damage? Is the patient still alive because his heart is beating even though the cells in his brain are dead and show no evidence of activity on an electroencephalogram? This is the legal status of such an unfortunate individual. The physician has not the right or permission to shut off the assisting devices and allow the heart to stop beating so the patient may be pronounced dead, even when the possibility of recovery of brain function is nil. The possibility exists that such an action may result in murder charges being pressed against the physician. Clearly a society which is unable to distinguish whether its members are dead or alive may expect difficulties thereby. (Alexander Leaf, "Social Consequences of New Developments in Medicine," in *The New Technology and Human Values*)

The only solution to the problems caused by defining complex terms is to make very clear your *purpose*; let the reader know what end your definition will serve. Informing the reader of your purpose allows you to limit the scope of the complex term before starting the process of definition. A complex term and a specific purpose often point to the need for extended definition.

EXERCISES

1. Redefine the following terms; avoid the problems of the given definitions:
   A. "Sexy" means to be sexually appealing.
   B. "Old" is when you retire and start to have physical problems.
   C. To be "assertive" is to be pushy.
   D. "College" is where you study for your future profession.
   E. "Intelligent" is defined as having great powers of intellect.

2. Study the following complex terms.
   A. Note at least two different ways you could approach a definition of each. For example, "success" could be defined *materially* or *spiritually*.
   B. Jot down some ideas that would go into a definition according to each different purpose:

   Life   Democracy
   Strength   Freedom
   Moral   Guilt

Writing Extended Definitions

The basic difference between a simple definition and an extended definition is the amount of information given to your reader. As we have said, because you can have different purposes for defining a term and because some words have complex meanings, it is frequently necessary to expand the explanation beyond a single sentence so that your reader can share the full meaning intended. The following example makes this point:

THE EYE

(simple definition): "the organ of sight, in vertebrates typically one of a pair of spherical bodies contained in an orbit of the skull." (*The Random House College Dictionary*)

DEFINING

<table>
<tr><td>(extended definition)
Comparison to camera
Places eye in class of organs
Essential parts

Develops comparison to camera shutter
Function of:
lens
optic nerve
brain

Eyelids placed in class—"flaps of skin" and distinguished by function
Function of tears

More essentials and functions

Example of cat's night vision</td>
<td>Whenever you marvel at the performance of a camera, the artistry and detail, remember that its construction was inspired by the human eye!

The eye is a hollow, globular organ, fitting smoothly into a depression of the skull. The white part, the sclera, is transparent where it crosses the front of the eye to form the cornea, permitting light rays to penetrate. Behind the cornea is the colored iris, with the pupil in the center. This acts as a shutter, by dilating or contracting, to control the amount of light which enters. The clear, crystalline lens located just behind the iris focuses an image on the retina, which is the inside coat of the eye, and the optic nerve carries this image to the brain. Because of the criss-crossing of light waves as they pass through the lens, the retina receives an inverted image, and it is the responsibility of the experienced brain to set it upright again.

Nature has also devised excellent protective devices for the eye: the eyelids are simply two flaps of skin, opened and closed by muscles, to guard the eye against injury or too much light; the conjunctiva lines the inside of the eyelid; the eyelashes are coarse hairs which can also protect the eye against foreign particles. Finally, tears from the tear ducts in the upper, outer corner of the eye continuously lubricate and wash away foreign matter from the surface of the eye.

Day and Night Vision. Our eyes possess several mechanisms for controlling the amount of light which enters: the muscular fibers of the iris contract and constrict the pupils; the lids also blink and shut out light. However, eyeshades or sunglasses should be used to control excessive glare, in summer from the sun and in winter from snow. We can see surprisingly well at night in dim light because our pupils become dilated, i.e., fully expanded to permit all available light to enter. You have probably noticed that a cat's eyes seem to be all pupil in the dark because they are fully dilated. (Benjamin F. Miller, Good Health: Personal and Community)</td></tr>
</table>

This example uses four of the five points you'll learn to develop extended definitions. It used points one through four of the following:

1. Place the term in a *class* of similar things.

2. Distinguish it from others in the class by:

    A. Describing the essential *parts* or *characteristics*
    B. Describing essential *functions*

3. Make a *comparison* to a commonly known thing.

4. Use an *example*.

5. Use a negative *example* that might be mistaken for the thing being defined.

After studying each of these points, you can, with some thought, define complex terms in such a way that your reader will share the meaning you have in mind for the term.

Placing the Term in a Class

This first step depends upon classification, which, as you know from Chapter 5, means grouping items according to one or several shared characteristics. Moreover, in the section "Seeing the General and the Specific" (pp. 25–26), we discussed the generalization ladder and used this example:

> Transportation
> Vehicles
> Motor vehicles
> Cars
> Fords
> Mustangs
> Sue's 1965 Ford Mustang

Each term on this ladder is a class except the last. A class is a group of things sharing common attributes. Since all Mustangs share something in common, they form a class. The generalization ladder indicates that the higher a term is on the ladder, the more *inclusive* it will be; that is, the more characteristics it will include.

Defining things by putting them into a class begins to identify them for the audience. Imagine yourself saying to a friend, "I saw a fine mustang last week." A curious child overhears you and asks, "What's a mustang?" You could give two different answers, each would require the act of classification; (1) "It's a type of horse," (2) "It's a type of car." With this information, the child knows at least that a mustang isn't a flower, tool, or whatever. But notice that this knowledge is also quite general. To identify a mustang, the child now knows to look either for horses or cars, but needs more information to know exactly what you are talking about. You always have to go up the generalization ladder to put a term to be defined into a class. Then in *step two* you move back down to provide the specific information that distinguishes the thing from others in the same class.

Our extended definition of the eye first placed the eye in the class of organs, then provided details that distinguished the eye from other body organs.

DEFINING | 103

EXERCISES

1. Complete the first step of definition by placing the following items in a class. That is, for each group, name a class that would include all the items in the group:

A)	B)	C)
The Beatles	marijuana	typewriter
Elvis Presley	vodka	computer
The Eagles	cocaine	lathe

2. Classify six of the following items. But be careful not to make your class too broad or too narrow. Begin with the term to be defined and think your way up and down the generalization ladder. In thought, fill as many rungs of the ladder as possible, as we did with "Transportation." Then place your term in a class one or two rungs above it. If, for example, to define *mustang* we jumped up to the top of the ladder, saying that mustang is a mode of transportation, the class would be so broad it would be of little value to the reader. There are so many subclasses of transportation that it's impossible to know if mustang is a cart, animal, car, or cycle. On the other hand, to define boots as rubber coverings for the feet, worn over shoes, restricts boots too narrowly. Not all boots are rubber; not all boots are worn over shoes.

Darvon	silicon	Underwood
chemotherapy	tax	silo
telephone	stethoscope	weed
pigment	wire	volcano
embryo	taxonomy	species

Distinguishing the Term from Others in the Class

Once you have classified the term for your reader as a tool, horse, car, and so forth, then provide distinguishing *parts, characteristics,* or *functions* to separate it from other items in the same class.

By Essential Parts

The fact that the eye belongs to the class of organs does not in itself define the eye narrowly enough, because there are other organs. So the author of our extended definition describes the essential *parts* of the eye. The eye is made up of the sclera, cornea, iris, pupil, retina, optic nerve, and other parts that distinguish the *eye* from the ear, kidney, and all other organs.

By Essential Characteristics

All horses share the same essential parts—heads, legs, tails, and so forth. Moreover, patches of black and brown on a horse do not make it a mustang; these are nonessential attributes. Essential *characteristics* of size, structure, and line of descent distinguish a mustang from a Clysdale or other horse.

By Essential Functions

The lathe is first classified as a "machine." But there are thousands of machines. We need distinguishing *functions*: "used to shape a piece of wood or metal by rotating it about a horizontal axis while pressing a sharp tool against it." These details set the lathe apart from presses, saws and other types of machines. Defining a person or thing by function is very important in the business world. The following definition uses *function* to define two similar jobs.

> Traditionally, the supervisor's job is considered the management of people and the solving of problems related to their particular jobs. The manager's job is generally more diversified. It is to set objectives, to organize personnel and resources in order to achieve these objectives, and to establish ways of measuring the degree of success or failure. It is also the manager's job to motivate and communicate with people, and to develop their skills. (Muriel James, *The OK Boss*)

EXERCISES

1. In the following definition of the heart, underline the class to which the heart belongs once and the essential parts, characteristics, or functions of the heart twice.

   The heart is a muscle that pumps blood through your body. The heart is divided into left and right halves by a wall called the septum. Each half is divided into an upper and a lower chamber, separated by a valve that allows blood to flow in only one direction. The upper chambers are the left and right atria; the lower chambers are the left and right ventricles. The right half of the heart pumps returning blood into the lungs to be oxygenated. The left half pumps the oxygen-rich blood from the lungs back into the circulatory system.

2. Write out simple definitions for the following words. Underline the class to which the object belongs once and the essential parts, characteristics, or functions that distinguish the object from others in the same class twice:

    thermoscope   oxygen
    microscope   hydrogen
    fluoroscope   nitrogen

3. Check a standard dictionary for simple definitions of the following terms. Determine which words have been defined by function. Write out the function.

    wrench (the tool)   horsepower
    voltage   torque
    welding   springs
    tachometer   rust
    pinion gear   oil

4. Choose two of the following words. Write extended definitions for them. Be certain that the parts, characteristics, or functions you refer to are *essential*. Some people hang deer heads in their den, but most of us would not agree that the essential function of a deer is to be shot and mounted on a wall.

    nurse   lobotomy   tree
    vasectomy   court (of law) contract (document)
    union (trade)   calculator   teacher

Comparing a Term to a Commonly Known Thing

Comparisons (or analogies) also clarify meaning, especially if you make your comparisons to a simpler, more commonly known thing. The idea here is to pick something you are sure your reader is familiar with. More than one scientist has found it helpful and informative to compare electricity and water:

> The idea that electricity flows as water does is a good analogy. Picture the wires as pipes carrying water (electrons). Your wall plug is a high-pressure source which you can tap simply by inserting a plug. The plug has two

prongs—one to take the flow to the lamp, radio, or air conditioner, the second to conduct the flow back to the wall. A valve (switch) is used to start or stop flow. (Richard M. Koff, *How Does It Work?*)

Our extended definition of the eye compares the eye and the camera. The author assumes that most of us are more familiar with the working parts of a camera than we are with those of the eye.

The British philosopher Bertrand Russell talks about man's quest for happiness by comparing two types of people to *sausage machines*:

> Life is too short to be interested in everything, but it is good to be interested in as many things as are necessary to fill our days. We are all prone to the malady of the introvert, who, with the manifold spectacle of the world spread out before him, turns away and gazes only upon the emptiness within. But let us not imagine that there is anything grand about the introvert's unhappiness.
>
> There were once upon a time two sausage machines, exquisitely constructed for the purpose of turning pig into the most delicious sausages. One of these retained his zest for pig and produced sausages innumerable; the other said: "What is pig to me? My own works are far more interesting and wonderful than any pig." He refused pig and set to work to study his inside. When bereft of its natural food, his inside ceased to function, and the more he studied it, the more empty and foolish it seemed to him to be. All the exquisite apparatus by which the delicious transformation had hitherto been made stood still, and he was at a loss to guess what it was capable of doing. This second sausage machine was like the man who has lost his zest, while the first was like the man who has retained it. The mind is a strange machine which can combine the materials offered to it in the most astonishing ways, but without materials from the external world it is powerless, and unlike the sausage machine it must seize its materials for itself, since events only become experiences through the interest that we take in them: if they do not interest us, we are making nothing of them. The man, therefore, whose attention is turned outward can find within, in those rare moments when he examines his soul, the most varied and interesting assortment of ingredients being dissected and recombined into beautiful or instructive patterns. (Bertrand Russell, *The Conquest of Happiness*)

EXERCISE

Develop definitions of one or two of the following words or phrases by comparison to the subjects given:

   heart / pump
   ear / drum
   getting an education / a war
   working / a game

social classes / movies
the body's use of food / an automobile

Using an Example

Naming and explaining examples of your term also takes us down the generalization ladder. By their very nature, definitions are generalizations. Examples are particular instances. Not every term is easy to exemplify. The more abstract the term is, the more difficult it is to find specific examples of it, but when you can provide them, you will help the reader.

Consider how much examples help a beginner in math understand the concept of square root. The definition alone does not clarify the concept: a square root "is a factor of a number that when squared gives the number." Part of the problem here is the use of a word to define itself ("the square root" and "squared"). Avoid these verbal circles. Instead, here is an example:

In 3 x 3 = 9, 3 is the square root;
In 5 x 5 = 25, 5 is the square root.

A dictator is "one holding complete autocratic control, ruling absolutely, often oppressively." This definition from a dictionary contains many abstract terms. It helps your definition to add that Hitler and Stalin are examples of dictators. If your readers don't know much about the meaning of *autocratic* and *oppressive*, but they do know about Hitler and Stalin, they will understand your definition. Wouldn't you like to have an example to support this definition: "ergastoplasm: ribosome-studded endoplasmic reticulum"? (The authors of this text still don't know what it means.)

EXERCISE

In at least one paragraph for each, define two of the following terms using examples. Remember to explain the relevant aspects of your example whenever necessary.

strike (as in labor)	hero	monopoly
picket (as in strike)	coward	socialism
bargain	leader	metamorphosis
work	maturity	responsibility
dedication	ambition	adulthood

Using a Negative Example

Negative examples show what things might be confused with the thing being defined. Negative examples are helpful, for instance, in distinguishing edible from nonedible mushrooms, berries, and herbs, many of which look very much alike. Abstract terms such as "love," "art," "beauty," "freedom," "duty," and others lend themselves all too well to being defined quite differently by different people. For this reason, if you use one of these terms it is wise to state what you do *not* mean by the term. Assume that your readers already have their own definition of the term. You want to clear the air before confusion results.

The author of *Sex and the Single Girl* begins her definition of the essential characteristics "for a single woman to lead the rich, full life," by first giving negative examples:

Here is what it *doesn't* take.

> Great beauty. A man seems not so much attracted to overwhelming beauty as he is just overwhelmed by it—at first. Then he grows accustomed to the face, fabulous as it is, and starts to explore the personality. Now the hidden assets of an *attractive* girl can be as fascinating as the dark side of the moon. Plumbing the depths of a raving beauty may be like plumbing the depths of Saran Wrap.
>
> What it also doesn't take to collect men is money. Have you ever noticed the birds who circle around rich girls? Strictly for the aviary.
>
> You also don't have to be Auntie Mame and electrify everybody with your high-voltage personality. Do *you* like the girl who always grabs the floor to tell what happened to *her* in the elevator? Well neither does anybody else.
>
> And you don't have to be the fireball who organized bowling teams, gets out the chain letters and makes certain *somebody* gives a shower for the latest bride.
>
> What you do have to do is work with the raw material you have, namely you, and never let up. (Helen Gurley Brown, *Sex and the Single Girl*)

The very first page of *The Organization Man* begins with a negative definition, then shifts to the positive:

> This book is about the organization man. If the term is vague, it is because I can think of no other way to describe the people I am talking about. They are not the workers, nor are they the white-collar people in the usual, clerk sense of the word. These people only work for The Organization. The ones I am talking about *belong* to it as well. They are the ones of our middle class who have left home, spiritually as well as physically, to take the vows of organization life, and it is they who are the mind and soul of our great self-perpetuating institutions. Only a few are top managers or ever will be.
>
> In a system that makes such hazy terminology as "junior executive" psychologically necessary, they are of the staff as much as the line, and most are

destined to live poised in a middle area that still awaits a satisfactory euphemism. But they are the dominant members of our society nonetheless. They have not joined together into a recognizable elite—our country does not stand still long enough for that—but it is from their ranks that are coming most of the first and second echelons of our leadership, and it is their values which will set the American temper.

The corporation man is the most conspicuous example, but he is only one, for the collectivization so visible in the corporation has affected almost every field of work. Blood brother to the business trainee off to join DuPont is the seminary student who will end up in the church hierarchy, the doctor headed for the corporate clinic, the physics Ph.D. in a government laboratory, the intellectual on the foundation-sponsored team project, the engineering graduate in the huge drafting room at Lockheed, the young apprentice in a Wall Street law factory.

They are all, as they so often put it, in the same boat. Listen to them talk to each other over the front lawns of their suburbia and you cannot help but be struck by how well they grasp the common denominators which bind them. Whatever the difference in their organization ties, it is the common problems of collective work that dominate their attentions, and when the DuPont man talks to the research chemist or the chemist to the army man, it is these problems that are uppermost. The word *collective* most of them can't bring themselves to use—except to describe foreign countries or organizations they don't work for—but they are keenly aware of how much more deeply beholden they are to organization than were their elders. They are wry about it, to be sure; they talk of the "treadmill," the "rat race," of the inability to control one's direction. But they have no great sense of plight; between themselves and organization they believe they see an ultimate harmony and, more than most elders recognize, they are building an ideology that will vouchsafe this trust. (William H. Whyte, Jr., *The Organization Man*)

EXERCISES

1. Pick two of the following terms and write a brief negative example of each. Do not simply name the negative example, develop it in a brief paragraph.

    | alligator | friend | success |
    | herbs | love | lady |
    | toad | politician | man |

2. In the margin beside the following definition of IGP, write the term that names each specific method of definition used (e.g., classifies, essential parts or characteristics, essential functions, comparison, example, negative example).

110 STRATEGIES FOR WRITING

The International Group Plan Insurance Company in Washington, D.C. is a company selling group insurance plans to organizations ranging from the American Association of University Women to the National Rifle Association. The firm started with 3 employees and a $3,000 investment 12 years ago. It now employs 350 workers with a yearly volume of $60 million.

IGP is a community, a classroom, and a company. On Thursday afternoons at 3:30 the public-address system announces: "Fellow workers, it's time for our weekly bingo game." Several hundred employees stop their normal work assignments, pick up their bingo boards, and play (for money) over the PA system for 45 minutes. Then it's back to work as usual.

IGP is a worker-owned, self-managed company. The file clerks and secretaries have an equal vote (under law) with the president and other officers in making company policies. The employees work in committees and are responsible for appointing management, setting working hours, fixing salaries and incomes, and determining long-range financial policies. Employees are free to join many committees and to attend and take part in meetings of committees they have not joined.

According to IGP President Jim Gibbons, the guiding philosophy of the community is that the company exists to serve the working members. At IGP, "Providing an opportunity for self-fulfillment is the real goal, much more than just having discontented workers making piles of money." (Adapted from Jeremy Fifkin, *Own Your Own Job: Economic Democracy for Working Americans*)

SUMMARY

1. Simple definition is a special form of classification and division: A term is placed in a class, then distinguished from other members of that class.

2. Simple definitions should avoid going in circles, relying solely on a synonym, or taking the "is when" and/or "is where" form.

3. Extended definitions explain in detail the essential parts, characteristics, or functions of the term to to be defined. They frequently use comparisons, examples, and negative examples for clarity.

WRITING ASSIGNMENTS

1. Write an extended definition of one of the following terms, using as many of the five points of definition as you can. Begin by identifying your readers. Note what they probably know about or mean by the term.

DEFINING | 111

Lamarckism	servomechanism	tolerance
sex hygiene	vitamin(s)	stalagmite
horticulture	gyroscope	trap
metabolism	vivisection	materialism
nepotism	opportunism	scapegoat
tycoon	swindle	work

2. Assume you are setting up a business.
   A. What questions would you ask and what answers would you expect to receive before hiring the service of companies that advertised the following? Make notes on your answers.

   Direct impact advertising
   Factory-trained technicians
   Advertising specialties, Exciting sales promotions
   We solve your problems
   Qualified contractor
   Expert sales and service
   Immediate service
   17 years experience
   Large inventory
   Total comfort installations
   Award-winning custom painting
   Discount prices

   B. Now assume that you are running a business that advertises one of the services or characteristics listed above (or one that is similar). You have just received an inquiry from a potential customer asking *you* what you mean by the advertised statement. Write an extended definition in reply. Consider your notes from (A) in working out your definition. To make this situation a little more interesting, let's say this potential customer would mean a huge increase in your business, that a good relationship with this customer could make your financial future secure.

7

ANALYZING: PARTS, FUNCTIONS, and PROCESSES

Understanding Analysis

Analytic Thinking

We began this section with a chapter on description, which informs the reader about the physical appearance of something. Comparison, classification, and definition go beyond informing to explain similarities, differences, relationships, and meanings. *Analysis* is a complex form of explanation that draws in many ways on all of the above skills.

Like description, the method of thinking and writing called analysis grows from observation, but with a difference. Description depends upon observing and recording *surface* details, but doesn't grapple with questions that go beyond or beneath the surface. Description doesn't ask "how" or "why"; analysis does. In other words, when you are observing something in order to analyze it, you are not just trying to *see* it, but to *understand* it—to understand how it is put together, how it functions, why it is the way it is. To achieve this understanding, analysis breaks a thing down into its components. Description is like looking through a camera and taking clear pictures of what you see, for example, pictures of a computer. Analysis is like tearing down that computer in order to identify all its parts and explain how they work together. To use another comparison, we could say that writing description is like observing a nude model and painting a detailed, full-length figure study, while writing analysis is like studying human anatomy by dissecting a cadaver. In short, description is concerned with surface appearance; analysis with basic structure, parts, and the relationship of parts to each other and to the whole.

As with all the strategies discussed in this section, we present analysis as a way of *writing* about things because it is first of all a way of *thinking* about them. We apply analysis all the time as a basic way of thinking about and understanding things we experience. When we encounter something new, our natural curiosity pushes us to understand it, and we start to ask analytical questions. Suppose for a minute that you have never seen a pocket calculator before and you encounter one on display in a store. A series of questions automatically comes to mind as you study this strange device: *What is it made of? What does it do? How do I use it?*

A helpful salesperson might supply the information that it is a calculator made up of a silicon chip and other electronic components, a battery, a keyboard, and a display; that it is used to perform arithmetic and other mathematical operations; that you push the "on" switch, punch the numbers and the key for adding or subtracting, then the "Equals" key to display the answer, and the "Clear" button to go on to the next problem. But we don't always have someone at hand to explain things, and we often have to rely on our own processes of observing, taking apart, and experimenting with things to answer our analytical questions. Once you have grappled with a subject in this analytical way, you are in the position of the salesperson, ready to save someone else the trouble by passing on your understanding.

EXERCISES

1. Pick a common object such as a toaster, typewriter, refrigerator, or desk lamp and ask yourself the three analytical questions. What is it made of? What does it do? How do I use it? Write down your answers in complete sentences.

2. Pretend that you are a supervisor training salespeople who will be offering a new product or appliance to customers unfamiliar with it. Choose any product and explain it by writing an analytical paragraph for your sales staff.

Types of Analysis

When faced with writing tasks involving analysis, you are being asked to apply analytical thinking to understand something, then to relay this understanding to a reader. Most frequently, you are called upon to do one of these four kinds of analysis; that is, to break something down one of these four ways:

1. Into parts or components
2. Into functions
3. Into steps in a process
4. Into causes or effects

The first three kinds of analysis are discussed below. Causal analysis is discussed in Chapter 8.

Analysis of Parts or Components

This kind of analysis explains *what* something is made of by breaking it down into assemblies, or groups of related components, breaking assemblies into subassemblies, and subassemblies into individual parts. The following passage breaks a motorcycle down into its component parts:

> A motorcycle may be divided for purposes of classical rational analysis by means of its component assemblies and by means of its functions.
>
> If divided by means of its component assemblies, its most basic division is into a power assembly and a running assembly.
>
> The power assembly may be divided into the engine and the power delivery system. The engine will be taken up first.
>
> The engine consists of a housing containing a power train, a fuel-air system, an ignition system, a feedback system and a lubrication system.
>
> The power train consists of cylinders, pistons, connecting rods, a crankshaft and a flywheel.
>
> The fuel-air system components, which are part of the engine, consist of a gas tank and filter, an air cleaner, a carburetor, valves and exhaust pipes.
>
> The ignition system consists of an alternator, a rectifier, a battery, a high-voltage coil and spark plugs.
>
> The feedback system consists of a cam chain, a camshaft, tappets and a distributor.
>
> The lubrication system consists of an oil pump and channels throughout the housing for distribution of the oil.
>
> The power-delivery system accompanying the engine consists of a clutch, a transmission and a chain.

The supporting (running) assembly accompanying the power assembly consists of a frame, including foot pegs, seat and fenders; a steering assembly; front and rear shock absorbers; wheels; control levers and cables; lights and horn; and speed and mileage indicators.

That's a motorcycle divided according to its components. (Robert M. Pirsig, *Zen and the Art of Motorcycle Maintenance*)

Analysis of Functions

This kind of analysis explains *how* the identified parts and assemblies work; it tells us what the components are for. Robert Pirsig continues his analysis of the motorcycle by discussing the functions of the parts:

A motorcycle may be divided into normal running functions and special, operator-controlled functions.

Normal running functions may be divided into functions during the intake cycle, functions during the compression cycle, functions during the power cycle and functions during the exhaust cycle.

And so on. I could go on about which functions occur in their proper sequence during each of the four cycles, then go on to the operator-controlled functions. . . . (Robert M. Pirsig, *Zen and the Art of Motorcycle Maintenance*)

Analysis of Steps in a Process

This kind of analysis breaks a complex process down into individual steps; it tells us *how to do* something. For example, the following steps tell someone unfamiliar with doing laundry how to proceed:

1. Sort the dirty laundry according to color and fabric. Light colors should be separated from dark; lighter weight, permanent press fabrics should be separated from heavyweight items such as jeans or towels.
2. Within a load of items similar in color and weight, the largest ones should be placed in the bottom of the tub.
3. Load the tub evenly, but do not wrap items around the agitator. Move from the largest items on the bottom to smaller, lighter ones such as socks or handkerchiefs at the top.
4. Measure the amount of detergent according to the directions on the package and add to the loaded machine.
5. Set the machine on warm wash, cold rinse for most normal laundry. Exceptionally dirty items may require hot wash, warm rinse. One hundred percent cotton items are likely to shrink and should be washed in cold water.
6. When the load is finished, to prevent wrinkling, shake out each item before placing in the dryer.

Analysis of Causes

Causal analysis examines the component forces that worked to bring something about. This kind of analysis will be discussed at length in Chapter 8.

Obviously, many complete analyses will involve more than one type of analytical thinking, but you must be careful to keep the types separate as you are writing them. Each type of analysis is actually a different *reason* for doing analysis. Each type of analysis, or reason for doing it, provides a consistent point of view or principle for controlling the organization of the analysis. An analysis of only one type should stick to that clear principle of organization throughout; an analysis of more than one type should clearly separate the types into different sections. Our very brief example about the calculator (p. 114) contains three types of analysis: the first explains the components of the object; the second type explains its functions; the third explains the process of how to use the mechanism.

EXERCISES

1. Read the following passage. What type of analysis does it represent?

   Do not face your opponent directly. Turn your body to the side so that your left leg is closest to your assailant. Draw your right hand down and allow it to rest on your hip, palm up. Keep both hands closed very loosely. Keeping the feet in place, move your hand toward the opponent's throat. Simultaneously start to shift the hips forward. As the arm goes outward, keep the elbow in place close to the body and under the arm. About 70 percent of the power will be lost if the elbow goes out of place. Your wrist must be a straight extension of your arm. If the wrist bends, there is a danger of breaking it.

2. Read the following analysis of a movie-camera tripod. Identify the two different types of analysis in the passage.

   The tripod itself is a simple mechanism. It consists of three legs that can be spread to create a steady base; each leg can be adjusted to any height so that the camera will be level even when the terrain is not. At the juncture of the legs is a platform. The camera can be screwed to the platform to make the camera absolutely solid. The long handle beneath the platform is held by the cameraman as he films and is used to direct the aim of the lens. A little experimenting will show you how this handle can be loosened to allow the lens angle to swing in an arc or be elevated or lowered. It can also be tightened to keep the camera frozen in one position. . . .
   Sometimes a tripod is absolutely required, for instance, when filming with a telephoto lens on a zoom camera that is set on full zoom. If the camera

in this situation is not absolutely steady, the magnified image will jump about unacceptably on the screen. A tripod is also required when panning through more than a 45 degree angle. The length of the pan requires that the cameraman shift position, a trick difficult to accomplish smoothly with a hand held camera. Filming animation, too, necessitates that the camera be rigidly fixed. In other situations there are advantages and disadvantages to the use of a tripod. (Ann W. Gulliver and William C. Gulliver, *A Guide to Creative Filmmaking*)

3. Read the following passage. This example randomly mixes two types of analysis. Rewrite it, separating the material into two sections, each one organized by a different principle of analysis.

   A common tool for many jobs is a pencil. This simple device can be found all around the world. A pencil usually has five basic components. Artists, draftsmen, grocery clerks, nurses, police officers, and teachers rely on pencils every day. The heart of the pencil is a thin rod of lead, which is actually not lead at all but compressed graphite. Pencils are not only useful for writing and drawing, but have some other surprising possibilities as well. Jammed between a door and its frame, a pencil makes an effective emergency lock. Surrounding the graphite core of the pencil is the wood sheathing. The eraser, a piece of soft rubber attached to the end of the pencil, is used to remove the graphite marks. Have you ever considered a pencil as a lethal weapon? Always handy, a pencil properly employed can kill very efficiently. The final components are metal and paint. A small metal band holds the eraser to the pencil itself, and most pencils are brightly painted. In fact, an important use for pencils is as advertising gimmicks. Many businesses distribute pencils imprinted with their names.

Writing Analysis

Analysis of Parts and Component Assemblies

The basic form of analysis—simply dividing something into its parts—seldom occurs by itself in actual situations calling for written analysis. Certain technical reports, however, may have a section of this simple analysis, often called "technical description," to list and give specifications for all the parts of a machine or components of a system. Such simple analysis may also be used to break down a complex organization, for example, to divide a government agency into its various branches and offices. Most often, however, division into parts is used together with functional analysis to tell us what those parts are for, or how they operate. In any case, the procedure for analysis into parts and component assemblies has four steps:

1. *Identify in a general way* the object, organism, or organization to be analyzed, and *indicate the purpose* of the analysis.
2. *Divide the subject into its major component assemblies,* that is, related groups of parts. These major assemblies should be roughly balanced in their importance to the whole. You would not, for example, divide an airplane into "propeller assembly" and "everything else assembly."
3. *Subdivide the major groups into subassemblies,* if possible. One way to analyze an airliner, for example, might be to divide it into a "flight operations assembly" and a "cargo assembly." The first major assembly could be subdivided into "engine," "control," and other subassemblies. The "cargo assembly" could be divided into "passenger" and "baggage" subassemblies, which in turn could be subdivided; the "passenger subassembly" would consist of flooring, seats, lights, rest rooms, food-service facilities, and the like.
4. Break each assembly or subassembly down into individual *parts*. The food facilities would consist of a refrigerator, a microwave oven or other unit for heating food, serving trays, and silverware, among others. In the case of very simple subjects there may be no assemblies or subassemblies, and the object may be divided into individual parts as step two. A cup, for example, cannot be divided into assemblies, only into a bowl and a handle.

Obviously, complete analysis of anything very complex into all its component assemblies and parts can be an almost endless undertaking; therefore, the extent of any actual analysis will be determined by your audience and purpose. Notice, however, that simple analysis can be an extremely powerful tool for *exploring* a subject and *generating* ideas about it. Notice also that this analysis *organizes* material by moving from general to specific.

EXERCISES

1. Read the following analysis. In two or three complete sentences, point out how the four steps we have just covered are present here:

    The basic kneehole desk is designed for maximum efficiency. This kind of desk provides a flat work surface and utilizes most of the space under that surface for storage. In the center there is an opening, or "kneehole," into which a person's legs extend when he or she is sitting at the desk. On both sides of the kneehole are columns of drawers. The separate drawers that fit into these stacks serve different purposes. Some are deep enough to hold file folders, while others are subdivided to hold envelopes, paper, and other common office supplies. A shallow center drawer for pencils, paper clips, and other small items, along with flat shelves that can be pulled out above each set of drawers, complete a system for keeping all the worker's materials well-organized and close at hand, while providing an expandable work surface suitable for many different tasks.

2. Choose a common object in your home or apartment, perhaps a piece of furniture or an appliance. Analyze this object by breaking it down into parts and component assemblies, following the four steps you have learned. Try to generate as much information as possible by detailed analysis into major assemblies, subassemblies, and parts.

Analysis of Functions

A simple breakdown into parts and assemblies is not done for its own sake very often. More frequently, this breakdown is part of a functional analysis—the examination of how something works. The three basic tasks of functional analysis are:

1. *Identify the general subject and indicate the purpose of the analysis.*
2. *Break the subject down into component assemblies, subassemblies, and/or individual parts.*
3. *Explain how the parts or assemblies work, what they are used for.*

Notice how the following example illustrates these elements:

General description	The big news in coffee makers is still the automatic drip filter (single-pass) units that range in price from $25 to more than $50. These are fairly compact appliances made up of a
Significant parts	water tank or reservoir, a heater, a basket to hold the coffee, and a filter. They have a carafe or pot that rests on a hot plate to keep the brewed coffee at serving temperature. Making
How they work	coffee in these units is very easy. Cold tap water is poured into the tank, where it is heated and then released or pumped over the coffee in the filter basket. The coffee then drips into the carafe. (1976 Consumer Buying Guide)

Recall that on page 117 we said that an analysis of more than one type (e.g., both dividing into parts and explaining functions) should clearly separate the types into different sections. The above example achieves this separation by first listing all the parts, then explaining their functions. Here is a brief outline to show this organization:

I. Parts

    A.

    B.

    C.

II. Functions

    A.

    B.

    C.

Another method of separating the two types of analysis in a single piece of writing is to take each part or assembly and explain its function before moving on to the next. Notice how the following example on solar heating is organized in this manner:

I.

    A. Part 1 (collectors)

    B. Function (trap sun's heat)

II.

    A. Part 2 (fan or pump)

    B. Function (removes heat)

III.

    A. Part 3 (rock or water)

    B. Function (stores heat)

> Solar Heating and Cooling—Of all the possible applications of solar energy, water heating and building space heating are the most advanced and the most nearly economic. Generally, the so-called "active" solar systems use flat trays called collectors which first trap the sun's heat. The front of each tray consists of a transparent material such as glass. Solar radiation passes through this material to a black metal surface at the back where it is absorbed. A fan or pump circulates a fluid—usually water or air—through the hot collectors removing the heat. The heat may be used immediately to warm the building or may be stored in rock, water, or some other substance for later use. (*Solar Energy: Progress and Promise*)

Functional analysis can, of course, be applied to systems and organizations as well as to mechanical subjects, as the following paragraph by a former Central Intelligence Agency (CIA) case officer illustrates:

> The bulk of the Clandestine Services is divided into operating divisions and senior staffs. The operating divisions are in charge of geographical areas and certain specialized services. The senior staffs are in charge of coordination

and review of all operational activities within the functional category of each—which are reflections of basic CIA operational theory. There are three senior staffs: the Foreign Intelligence (FI) staff; the Psychological Warfare and Paramilitary (PP) staff; and the Counter-Intelligence (CI) staff. The FI staff is concerned with intelligence *collection* operations, the PP staff with *action* operations and the CI staff with *protection* of FI and PP operations. The difference between collection and action operations is that collection should leave no sign, whereas action operations always have a visible effect. (Philip Agee, *Inside the Company: CIA Diary*)

EXERCISES

Read the following analyses.

1. Outline each example to identify the three elements of functional analysis and to show how they are arranged.
2. Write a brief paragraph explaining how the author's purpose in each case affected the focus and extent of the analysis.

   While all participants share the same profession and general aim of protecting the national security, the intelligence community has developed into an interlocking, overlapping maze of organizations, each with its own goals. In the words of Admiral Rufus Taylor, former head of Naval Intelligence and former Deputy Director of the CIA, it most closely resembles a "tribal federation."

   The Director of Central Intelligence heads up several inter-agency groups which were created to aid him in the management and operation of the intelligence community. The DCI's two principal tools for managing intelligence are the Intelligence Resources Advisory Committee (IRAC) and the United States Intelligence Board (USIB). The IRAC's members include representatives from the State Department, Defense, the Office of Management and Budget, and the CIA itself. (Since the agency's Director chairs the group in his role as DCI, or head of the intelligence community, the CIA is also given a seat.) IRAC was formed in November 1971, and it is supposed to prepare a consolidated budget for the whole community and generally assure that intelligence resources are used as efficiently as possible. However, it has not been in existence long enough for its performance to be judged, especially since three different DCIs have already headed it.

   The USIB's main tasks are the issuance of National Intelligence Estimates and the setting of collection requirements and priorities. Under it are fifteen permanent inter-agency committees and a variety of ad hoc groups for special problems. Working through these committees and groups, the USIB, among other things, lists the targets for American intelligence and the priority attached to each one, coordinates within the intelligence community the estimates of future events and enemy strengths, controls the classification and security systems for most of the U.S. government, directs research in the various fields of technical intelligence, and decides what classified information will be passed on to foreign friends and allies. (Frank Marchetti and John D. Marks, *The CIA and the Cult of Intelligence*)

While sonic booms, explosions, and gunfire can be felt also, most other noises are only heard. Your ear is a marvelous and sensitive organ. It detects minute changes in pressure—sound waves—and sends information about them to the brain for perception and analysis.

The human ear has three major divisions. The outer ear is the fleshy shell and ear canal at the side of the head. Originally designed to gather sounds, the shell lost that function evolutionary eons ago. Dividing the outer and middle ear is the pearl-gray eardrum which is shaped not like a drum but like the cone of a tiny loudspeaker. Connected to it from behind is a chain of three tiny bones called the ossicles. They do more than transmit sound to the inner ear. When the sound listened to is weak, they can amplify sound thirty times; or, thanks to two tiny muscles connected to them, can lower the efficiency of their transmission of sound when it is too loud. The muscles do this in an important reflex action, on command from the brain, a few hundredths of a second after a loud noise is heard. This Acoustic Reflex automatically protects the inner ear much like the narrowing of the iris protects the retina of the eye from too much light.

Snail-like in shape, and filled with a liquid which closely resembles sea water, the cochlea, or inner ear, is located deep inside the protective temple bones of the skull. Sound waves transmitted by eardrum and middle ear create waves in this liquid; these waves, in turn, cause tiny and sensitive hair cells (cilia) to be thrust against an overhanging ledge. This action triggers the electrical impulses that travel along nerves to the hearing center of the brain.

There are about 23,500 cilia in a cochlea, arranged so that those in front, or the outermost point of the cochlea, sense the highest frequencies, while those at the innermost peak of the spiral sense the lowest frequencies.

Here is where noise can impair. If the noise is loud enough (over 85 dB), your ear can suffer temporary inability to hear because these hair cells are fatigued. If the cells are given a rest, they can recover. But they can't if the noise is too prolonged or repeats itself too soon. What then happens is that they become permanently damaged. The result is that the noise-damaged ear is deaf to certain frequencies of sound. The sensors which go first are those responding to high frequency sounds. Neither hearing aid nor surgical operation can bring back the ability to hear those frequencies. (Theodore Berland, *Noise—The Third Pollution*)

Analysis of Steps in a Process

Most commonly, process analysis means explaining to someone else how to do something. The millions of "how-to-do-it" books on everything from sex to moneymaking are all examples of process analysis at work. Written instructions on how to operate a piece of equipment or how to perform a technical task are a very common form of job-related writing. We will discuss writing instructions more fully in the last section of this book, but the basic principles are useful for other types of writing also. Here are the elements necessary in writing that explains a process:

1. *State the objective.*
2. *Describe any equipment or tools* necessary to complete the task.
3. *Divide the operation into steps. Use transitional signals* such as *first, second, third* or—if there are many steps—use numbers.
4. *Tell why each step is necessary* and what it should accomplish.

Stating the Objective

The reader who is going to perform the operation needs some idea why you are giving the explanation of the process in a particular way. A note left for a friend who will mow your lawn while you are on vacation might begin like this: "My old lawn mower can be a little stubborn, but if you follow steps exactly you will have no trouble getting it started." The following passage introduces an analysis of the process used to develop an additive for gasolines. The writer begins by telling us why this research was undertaken and what its purpose was. In effect the writer is saying: "Here is how we went about developing a new idea and you can learn something from the process we followed."

> In searching for an opportunity to develop new marketing approaches for a certain product, we had difficulty originating new ideas. The only way to proceed seemed to be to do basic research that would provide information about potential consumers. We thought that with luck such basic knowledge would lead to new marketing strategies. We therefore decided to enter the area of motivational research, using "depth psychology" to understand what motivates buyers. A research project was started that has been active ever since.

Describing Necessary Equipment or Tools

If you tell readers what they need to do the job, the tools can be in hand before they begin. Often you may know of a particular tool that can save time, effort, and money.

> Six-nine-fine tool. This one you have to make or have made. Go to a good tool shop and get a 9mm, deep socket for a ¼ inch drive ratchet. Use just those words to get just that one socket—don't get the ratchet to go with it. Instead, get a 6mm Allen key. The Allen key should just fit into the square ¼ inch hole in the socket. While you are at the tool shop, ask if they know anyone who will braze the socket onto the Allen key. Have the thing brazed. It doesn't have to be perfectly straight—just strong. Seem like a lot of trouble? It is. But it's worth it, especially if your bike has a French changer or brakes. There are

ANALYZING: PARTS, FUNCTIONS, AND PROCESSES | 125

ready-made socket tools, but few are as cheap or as handy as the six-nine-five. If you have a six-nine-fine and a Campognolo T, you don't need to buy a regular socket set, which could contain lots of tools you can't use on your bike. (Tom Cuthbertson, *Anybody's Bike Book*)

Dividing the Operation into Steps

A process takes place in time. The reader must know which step to perform first, which second, and so on. The reader will have difficulty understanding the process if the steps are out of order or are not clearly indicated. Make sure *all the steps* are included. Leaving out an important procedure has serious consequences. Following the steps in a process exactly is important in many professions. Many court cases, for example, are decided on the basis of an error in procedure by a police officer:

> Under cross-examination, Magee said that he did not find the marijuana cigarette, only a rolled-up, red, white and blue matchbook cover, which he left on the floor. Noting that Magee is taking courses in police science, Rittenberry asked, "Do you think your instructor would be proud of you for leaving that evidence there?" Magee gulped, "No." (Ray Kennedy, "Pittsburg Fats Dodges a Silver Bullet," *Sports Illustrated*)

Remember to indicate each new step clearly by a transition signal or number.

Explaining the Function of Each Step

People are not computers or automatons. Readers want to know why an action is necessary, and knowing what is supposed to happen helps someone recognize when something is going wrong. The following instruction could save a motorist much unnecessary trouble:

> If nothing happens when you turn the ignition key, *check the battery terminals* before you call a towing service. Sometimes enough corrosion builds up on the terminals to cut off the flow of electricity. Removing the cables and scraping off the corrosion may be all you need to get started.

Detailed instructions are necessary when you want your reader to duplicate a procedure (as in writing out a recipe), but the analysis of a process often explains how something is done without expecting the reader to perform the operation. The following paragraph explains the procedures for face lifts performed by plastic surgeons. The reader is not expected to duplicate the operation, so detailed directions give way to a more general explanation:

Upper lifts vary, depending on the problem. One lift is a "temple lift" that is done in this country but is particularly popular in Europe. The operation corrects a sagging brow, underbrow, and droop in the outer-eye area. This section of the face is lifted up from behind the temple hairline. The surgeon makes an incision within the hairline; he then loosens a sufficiently wide swath of skin from the underlying tissues, almost down to the eyebrow. Finally he pulls the loosened skin up taut, cuts off the excess skin, and sews up the incision, which of course doesn't show, since it is within the hairline. This temple operation lifts *up* rather than *back*. It gives a good life to the area. "It was *exactly* what I wanted," says one woman who had planned to wait another five years, until she was 58, before having a total face lift. (Harriet La Barre, *Plastic Surgery: Beauty You Can Buy*)

EXERCISES

1. Write out the instructions for a simple process you know well (e.g., how to boil an egg, how to make burritos, how to change a tire). Include all four elements of process analysis.

2. Devise a method for explaining to a preschool child how to tell time. Write this method out in the words you would use talking to a small child.

3. Choose a relatively complicated process that might interest your classmates and explain it to them. Write a general explanation of the process, not a set of instructions on how to complete the process. Choose a process you are familiar with.

SUMMARY

1. In its most basic form, analysis means to break something down into its parts. Simple objects can be divided directly into their parts.

2. More complex subjects are usually broken into major groups, or assemblies, of parts first, then subdivided repeatedly until they have been divided into individual parts.

3. Most analyses include an explanation of how the parts and assemblies work together. Process analysis explains how to do something by breaking the whole process into its component steps.

4. Analysis in any form is a powerful tool for exploring subjects and organizing material.

ANALYZING: PARTS, FUNCTIONS, AND PROCESSES

WRITING ASSIGNMENTS

1. List significant features of a particular make of compact automobile (or some other product). Write a brief explanation to a potential buyer of how these features make this car a good buy. Then do the opposite—select features that contribute to a negative judgment about the car and write an evaluation warning the customer about them.

2. Choose a situation and an audience for a speech you might have to make—a service club luncheon or a college speech class, among others. Write out a ten-minute speech explaining how to do something, such as:

    save money
    stay healthy
    heat a home
    win at golf (cards, or other games)
    throw a party
    raise a child
    survive winter
    get a job

3. Examine the organizational structure of the company you work for, the college you attend, or some other institution or agency. Write a two- or three-page analysis that would be appropriate for a company brochure (college catalog, or the like) explaining the institution to the general public.

4. Write a detailed functional analysis of a fairly complex piece of equipment, for example, a computer of some sort, a sophisticated electric typewriter, a copying machine, a piece of production or medical equipment with which you are familiar. You may substitute an anatomical analysis of an organism or complex organ (other than the ear).

5. Write an instant, 500-word best seller: explain how to make an outrageous profit from something available for free—rain, leaves, used cat litter, or any other item you come up with.

8
ANALYZING CAUSES and EFFECTS

Understanding Cause-Effect Analysis

In Chapter 7, we explained that analysis means breaking something down into its components one of four ways—that is, into (1) parts and assemblies, (2) functions, (3) steps, or (4) causes. In this chapter we will examine the last process—*causal analysis*—at some length.

Anything can be considered an *effect* brought about by one or more causes. If we look to the background of any effect and break that background into the component causes, we are practicing causal analysis. The process can function in the opposite way: we can treat our subject as a *cause* and break down what follows into the different effects created by that cause. Our natural curiosity about why something happened or what will result from our actions keeps us always conscious of causal relationships—in other words, those relationships in which one event or situation depends upon another in a certain logical way.

Sequence Versus Causality

Cause-effect relationships always involve time; causes must come before effects. But because something happened just before something else takes place does not always mean that the first caused the second. There may be a one, two, three *sequence* of events, but that does not necessarily mean that one caused two, or that two caused three. For example, if an airplane lands at National Airport in Washington, D.C., at 8:15 A.M. and another touches down at 8:23 A.M., the first airliner's arrival did not cause the second one, even though one came after the other. But if one event depends upon the other, we have a causal relationship. Returning to our example, say the first airplane has trouble landing, suffers damage to the landing gear and cannot be moved immediately from the runway. The second landing is delayed an hour until the runway can be cleared. The problem with the first plane is a cause; the delayed landing of the second is an effect. For a more complicated example, imagine that you are working in a hospital emergency room when a heart-attack victim is brought in. While you are filling out admission forms, the victim's wife mentions that her husband had just gotten a telephone call informing him that his sister had died suddenly. The patient's wife says this news caused his heart attack. Did it? Was the news of his sister's death the cause of his heart attack? Was his sister's death itself the cause? Perhaps we need to look beyond the surface here. What causes heart attacks?

Medical science doesn't have a complete answer to that question, but we do know that certain factors are usually involved. High blood pressure, excess cholesterol in the blood, lack of regular cardiovascular exercise, smoking, and a few other things are causally related to heart attacks. The victim at hand probably suffered from some or all of these problems. Moreover, he ran across the yard, up the steps, and through the house when he heard the phone ring. The call might have brought good news, and he still could have collapsed.

EXERCISE

Determine in what ways the following situations involve *sequence* and/or *cause and effect*. Write a paragraph explaining your answer in each case.

1. Someone knocks at the door. You open it.
2. You get up in the morning, shower, dress, eat, and go out.
3. A newspaper reports that a member of city council has resigned under investigation of involvement in a contract kickback scheme. A lawyer for the former council member accuses the paper of humiliating her client.

Immediate and Remote Causes

Take a moment to study your motives for being in college before reading this next illustration of someone examining a cause-effect relationship.

I've been reading application folders for the College recently, and I've been struck, as I think you would be, by the poverty of vocabulary and idea shown in the students' statements of why they want to go to college. "I want to be a doctor and I have heard that the University of Chicago has a good pre-medical program." "I want to be a social worker and I have been told that these days a college degree is almost a must for such work." Honest statements perhaps, but otherwise no less depressing than the many attempts to butter us up with clichés about "wanting a liberal education in order to live a fuller life" or wanting to "round out my education before entering on my professional career." One young man talked about the age of leisure that is upon us, and he wanted a liberal education in order to have, in later life, something to do in his spare time.

What disturbs me about these statements is not that any of them are flatly illiterate or wrong-headed but that they are all so mean-spirited. Each of the applications I read showed quite clearly that its author was thinking strictly in terms of the future *uses* of a liberal education. Or at least he thought *we* would be stuck in such grooves. "I want to get a liberal education so that I will be able to do this, that, or the other *with* it." Nobody said anything like "I want to get a liberal education because that seems to me the best possible way to spend my time during the next four years, no matter what happens to me after that." Nobody said, "What a strange question. Is there anything else that a human being my age *ought* to want?" Nobody said, "I want to go to Chicago because I've heard that people have more fun with ideas there than anywhere else in the world." No, it was all "I want to go to Chicago because I've heard that you have a good pre-med program."

Pre-med, pre-law, pre-physics, pre-English, pre-life. I sometimes think, as I look at what has been called the post-Sputnik era in American education, that there is no one left who learns anything because he wants to know it; it is all pre-learning. "Education is Our First Line of Defense—Make it Strong"—so reads the title of a chapter in Admiral Rickover's book pleading with us to educate for Freedom. Any day now I expect to see some educational measure advocated because it is good training for survival in a nuclear attack: get your liberal education packet here, good for filling your leisure hours in the bomb shelter.

Where do the applicants get such stuff? Quite obviously they get it from their mentors, from college catalogues, from articles in national magazines, from books about education. When educators publish statistics proving that college graduates earn more than non-college graduates, it is not difficult for students to infer the reasons for going to college. High school counselors, who have been counseled by college counselors, who have been counseled by graduate school counselors, counsel high school students to get such-and-such courses "out of the way" *so that* when they get to college they can be placed in certain other preparatory courses *in order* to get as quickly as possible into graduate courses *which will prepare them for* a degree *which will be necessary* for good placement in a job *which will lead quickly on up* the ladder toward an indefinite but no doubt finally glorious future. (Wayne C. Booth, *Now Don't Try to Reason with Me*)

It might be interesting to compare your motives to those Booth describes.

Now let's take a closer look at this selection to learn something about different types of causes. Study the piece carefully to determine any differences in the kind of causes behind the students' behavior. What is the difference between magazine articles or college catalogues and what the author describes as "the post-Sputnik era in American education" or Admiral Rickover's idea that we must "educate for Freedom"? The students have immediate contact with the first two, just as they do with high school counselors. These are all *immediate* causes. A student listens to a counselor or reads an article and his or her decision is directly affected. But what about the "post-Sputnik era," or graduate school counselors who counsel college counselors who counsel high school counselors? These are all causes affecting the student's decision, but not immediately. Causes that are removed in time or space from the effects they create are called *remote* causes. Whenever we are looking for causes, we need to consider both the immediate causes and the remote causes behind them. Often the remote causes, although we might not think of them at first, are more important than the immediately recognizable ones. For example, in the preceding section on "Sequence Versus Causality," we could say that running across the yard and up the steps was the *immediate* cause of the victim's heart attack, but obviously the remote causes, such as smoking, excess weight, high cholesterol level, and so forth, were the more important ones. If those remote causes hadn't been present, it is unlikely that the immediate cause would have been sufficient to produce the unhappy effect.

EXERCISES

1. Consider your present job or one you have had in the past. List the reasons why you took this job. Divide the causes you listed into *immediate* and *remote* ones. Can you separate them clearly? Were there more of one kind than the other?

2. Make a list of three immediate and three remote causes for choosing to attend college. Which *one* cause is the most important overall? Is it immediate or remote?

3. Think of something good that happened to you recently (a raise, a good date, an "A" in some course). List the immediate and remote causes associated with this event.

Uses for Cause-Effect Analysis

Looking for cause-effect relationships is a method of generating much factual information and many new thoughts about any subject. Of course, some subjects more than others naturally lend themselves to fruitful study by this method. An understanding of cause and effect is particularly helpful in preparing technical or business reports. Any problem that needs solving will need a study of the possible causes, an estimate of the probable effects, or both. For example, an auto mechanic or a doctor examines a given symptom (the car won't start or the patient's hands tremble) and works back logically from the simplest and most immediate possible cause (there's no gas in the tank or the patient drinks twenty cups of coffee a day) to more complex and remote possibilities. In the same way, a manager or a committee facing a decision needs a carefully prepared analysis of the causes behind the present situation. Only with such knowledge at hand can they make an appropriate decision about the action to be taken. Another very common kind of report analyzes the probable effects of each alternative. For example, a city council meets for two or three hour sessions and must make four to eight policy decisions during each meeting. The members of the council must have information on which to make decisions in a wide range of areas such as insurance, education, public safety, engineering, communication systems, and so forth. Not being experts in all these matters, they rely on reports prepared by the city manager's staff. These two- to three-page reports must provide concise information and indicate the results of the alternatives facing the council member. If he or she votes one way, these will be the probable effects, if the other way, then these results will follow. The same pattern of reports prepared in advance, suggesting alternatives and their effects, is followed in industry, education, social service, and health services. For example, a physical therapist would prepare an analysis of the causes for a patient's present condition and examine alternative plans with their probable effects before drawing up a final therapy program.

In a broader sense, looking for causes and/or effects can help you think your way through situations. Depending on the subject you are examining, you may be able to make a fresh estimate of causes and thus gain insight that will help you understand something in a new way. In the following example, a new insight gained by thinking about causes may prove to have far-reaching effects:

Sheila Tobias, associate provost of Wesleyan University, is a feminist with an interesting theory about why women fail to get certain kinds of jobs. Says she: "I had been deeply concerned with occupational segregation, the tracking of women into 'soft' fields that were considered appropriate for them. When I listened to adult women discussing going back to work, they kept talking about 'working with people.' What they were all avoiding, I realized, was anything based on mathematics. It just went click." A number of studies by educators have substantiated what Tobias has named "math anxiety." Among the findings:

Sociologist Lucy Sells, in a 1973 survey at Berkeley, discovered that 57 percent of male first-year students had taken four years of high school math, while only 8 percent of females had done so. As a result, 92 percent of freshmen women could major in only five out of twenty available fields, since calculus was a requirement for the other fifteen. Sells' charge: "Nobody told girls that they couldn't get jobs in the real world unless they knew math." ("Math Mystique: Fear of Figuring," *Time*)

The next article illustrates in detail how a careful analysis can reveal the causes leading to a problem situation, in this case the lack of suitable sites for low-income housing:

Land for the construction of housing for low-income families is hard to find for several reasons—fiscal considerations, social status, racial discrimination, and price. With central cities largely built up, it is in suburban communities where one must look for vacant land for housing development. Such localities rely heavily upon property taxes for their revenues. The taxes collected from inexpensive houses tend to fall below the costs of public services to the occupants, especially if they are families with school children.

For example, a $15,000 house may be assessed at $10,000 with a tax rate of $40 per thousand. This yields the locality $400 a year in property taxes. A family with two children occupying such a house may require public expenditures of $1,200 or more per year—$500 for each school child plus $200 for other services such as police protection, refuse collection, and street maintenance. The rational thing for the town to do is to exclude housing for such families. And local zoning boards and town councils have shown great resourcefulness in doing just that. Large-lot zoning is widely practiced as a means of permitting only higher-priced houses and higher-income residents into the locality.

The desire to maintain the character of the community is another factor in this reluctance to see land used for lower income housing. In part it is an aesthetic resistance to construction of identical houses on treeless lots or to the loss of parkland; in part, it is opposition to having lower class families as neighbors. Whatever the blend of attitudes, builders are often stymied by the established residents when they seek sites for lower income housing.

The resistance hardens impenetrably when it becomes known that Negro families may occupy some of the new houses. Some towns have even chosen to acquire proposed housing sites for parks—as in Deerfield, Illinois—when faced with the prospect of black residents. Deerfield became a cause célèbre and brought shame on the community, but only because the local officials failed to anticipate the possibility of mixed racial occupancy and permitted the developers to take steps to acquire the land. Most localities have—and most builders accept—unwritten rules against integrated housing developments.

Some housing programs have been stifled by the congress itself when they appeared to foster open occupancy housing. The 1965 refusal to appropriate funds for the rent supplement program is partly attributable to the fear that localities, northern suburbs as well as southern towns, would be unable to deny access to black families. The House Appropriations Committee re-inserted the requirement of site approval by the local governing body or the existence of a workable program (localities could veto all such projects by simply not having a workable program) as the price of subsequent small annual appropriations.

These fiscal, status, and racial factors result in suburban practices that severely limit the supply of land for lower-priced housing. Pressing against this limited supply has been a strong demand among the well-to-do for larger and better homes. The net effect has been a steady rise in land prices at an average rate of 10 to 15 per cent per year during the past decade. Increasing ground cost has a multiplier effect upon the price of new houses: not only is it a larger item itself in the development cost but builders tend to put more expensive houses on more expensive sites. Suppose a builder uses a rule of thumb that the house price should be at least five times the site cost. If improved lots rise from $4,000 to $5,000 he will be inclined to construct homes intended for sale at $25,000, rather than $20,000. When many builders do the same, incremental increases in land cost mean large increases in the prices of new homes, putting them further from the reach of low and moderate income families. (Morton J. Schusshein, "Why We Have Not Built More Houses," *The Public Interest*)

EXERCISES

1. Examine a *decision* you must make.
   A. Determine the important effects that will result from each of the two or more possible choices; for example, a two-alternative decision might be whether or not to move out from your parents' home; a three-alternative decision would be whether to keep your present job and attend school part-time, quit work and go to school full-time, or quit your present job, but take another one and continue in school part-time.
   B. Write a paragraph discussing the potential effects of each alternative decision.
2. Examine a *problem* situation.
   A. Determine the causes behind the situation, which might be a prob-

lem at work, a problem with a personal relationship, a problem at school, or a community problem you care about.
B. Write a paragraph explaining each cause you discover.
C. Study the causes to see if your understanding of them helps to suggest a solution to the problem. Write down any possible solutions and list the effects that might result from each.

Evaluating Cause-Effect Analysis

As we suggested earlier, people seem to have a natural curiosity about causes and an equal interest in speculating about effects. This human tendency often leads to statements and explanations that appear to involve causal analysis, but upon examination reveal little or no actual basis for the cause-effect relationships asserted. When it is simply a problem of mistaking *sequence* for causality, it is not difficult to spot, but sometimes more problems arise. We are constantly bombarded by apparent cause-effect statements that need careful examination: "If you elect me, I will . . ." or, "Nuclear power plants will . . ." or, "The communists are behind the decline of morality today."

Let's take a look at this third example for just a minute. In determining the value of a cause-effect statement (your own or someone else's), you need to examine both halves of the relationship. On the cause side, who are "the communists"? Are they Americans? Russians? Cubans? Yugoslavians? Does the author of the statement give any *specific* causes (specific communist actions or beliefs, for example) that have led to the decline of morality? If specific causes are given, are they accurately presented? See if a little research can provide facts by which to judge the statement of causes. On the *effect* side, make sure first of all that the effect being talked about is real. Is there a "decline of morality today"? Have moral values *declined* or just *changed*? Could it be that the changes are an improvement in morality rather than a decline? Questions such as these can be used to probe the accuracy of the effects as stated.

We will discuss logic and evidence in Chapter 9 on persuasion, but it seems appropriate here to note the particular tendency of cause-effect statements to appear more logical than they may actually be. We can evaluate suspicious causal analyses by investigating both the *cause* side and the *effect* side through *research* and careful *definition*. These techniques can also be applied to our own breakdown of events and situations involving causality to avoid the problems superficial analysis may cause. An exaggerated example can be found in the true case of a freshman who cheated on his first college assignment. When caught, he defended his action as necessary—he had to cheat, because he had to get a "A" on every paper, so that he would get an "A" in every course, so that he would be sure to get into law school. He had to get into law school because his father insisted on it as a guarantee of success. Putting aside his moral values, or lack of them, his causal analysis was pretty faulty as well. The apparent logic of good grades leading to law school leading to success doesn't hold up under even minor investigation. Getting into law school depends as much or more on Law School Admission Test (LSAT) scores as it does on grades, and the idea that a law degree insures success is no longer very accurate either:

> The exact number of young lawyers now driving cabs to survive is anybody's guess, but one thing is clear: the circumstances awaiting the average law-school graduate are, on the whole, wretched.
>
> About 35,000 law-school graduates were confronted by a shrinking job market in 1975. Today, the Department of Labor puts the number of available jobs at 26,400. Most of those out of work in 1975 seem to have remained out of work, at least in the profession for which they were trained, thus compounding the imbalance of supply and demand as more and more lawyers graduate.
>
> The situation is not likely to improve in the near future, since the American Bar Association believes it has no right to intervene with the proliferation of new law schools or with the tendency of established schools to expand their facilities to accommodate a flood of students for whom there are not enough jobs. (Myra Friedman, "Is This Any Way To Make a Living?" *Esquire*)

In short, we should try to be as clear-thinking as possible in our analysis of cause and effect, because our guessing and fuzzy thinking can lead to trouble.

EXERCISE

In 1977, Judge Archie Simonson of Madison, Wisconsin, refused to punish a convicted fifteen-year-old rapist. Judge Simonson stated that the boy reacted "normally" to society's sexual permissiveness and to women's provocative clothing when he raped a girl in a high school stairwell.

1. Is this a legitimate cause-effect analysis?
2. Is rape a natural effect of a sexually permissive society?
3. Write out your evaluation of Judge Simonson's analysis. Be sure to consider the definitions of key terms such as "normal," "sexually permissive society," and "provocative clothing."

SUMMARY

1. We have a strong need to understand why things happen and what may result from our actions. This natural desire leads us into constant analysis of causes and effects. Such analysis is an excellent way to explore a subject, especially to gain insight into a problem situation or to help us weigh the consequences when faced with a decision.

2. We need to distinguish between simple *sequence* and a true causal relationship. We also need to distinguish between *immediate* and *remote* causes.

3. Cause-effect statements tend to sound very logical. We need to evaluate them very closely—to practice careful analysis of causes and effects.

Writing About Cause and Effect

From Cause to Effect

The first way to analyze a cause-effect relationship begins with the subject as a *cause* and examines what the effects have been, or what the probable effects will be. Your decision to enter college, for example, has already had certain effects on your life—perhaps on your income, place of residence, interests, friends, and so forth. This decision will have additional effects in the future as well—you could make a list of what those effects probably will be. This pattern—moving from a cause(s) to the effect(s)—occurs in decision making when the probable effects of different actions are considered before deciding to take a specific action. "Supply-side" economists, for example, argue for large tax cuts, which they forecast will increase spending and investment, which in turn will increase production while reducing unemployment and inflation. Exploring probable effects before taking action also appears commonly when people are trying to figure out the possible effects of some new situation or recent event. For example, the 1980 U.S. census indicated that for the first time in about a century more people are moving into

ANALYZING CAUSES AND EFFECTS

rural areas than are leaving them. Everyone from sociologists to real-estate agents are busy now trying to decide what the long-range effects of this change may be. Whatever the reason for examining real or potential effects, the pattern remains essentially the same:

1. Identify the subject and the general effect(s).
2. Develop each of the effects in detail.
3. Move from the most immediate effects to more remote ones.

Examine the following example for this pattern; the subject (cause) is bad writing in business:

Cause
Forget about inflation for a minute. Put aside those tax problems, union troubles and snotty letters from EPA, OSHA and EEOC. Instead, start worrying about all those people in our outfit who write "at this point in time" instead of "now." They may be costing you more.

So say consultants who have made a mini-industry out of teaching corporate executives, managers and technical people what they never learned in school—how to write clearly. The word doctors say many patients arrive in critical shape, unable to pen a simple thought without Herculean effort or lapses into gibberish.

Effect #1
Development
"We get *people who are swamped by their work* [emphasis added] because they need a whole hour to compose a simple, one-page letter," says Charlene Andolina, executive director of the Pittsburgh Reading and Writing Center, which offers seminars tailored to specific needs at prices ranging from about $200 to several thousand. Another therapist adds: "Some writing at fairly high corporate levels leaves you astonished that the company is still functioning. It's atrocious."

CHOPPING DOWN FORESTS

Effect #2
And expensive. Whole forests go under to chainsaw so managers can finalize the termination of something rather than just end it, and the time consumed in encoding and decoding corporate gobbledygook is the costliest waste of all. *Inevitably much isn't or can't be read, including vital data submerged in the chaff.*

Development
A few years ago an oil company chemicals unit spent a bundle reinventing from scratch a selective pesticide one of its own researchers had found five years before; he'd buried the news 25 pages deep in a hopeless gumbo of report prose that no one apparently could get through. Another, luckier, company accidentally stumbled on a similar in-house report about a new production process just before it began building

Effect #3 Development a plant using the older, costlier way. "We damn near put up the wrong thing," an official says.

Misinterpretation can be just as expensive. Miss Andolina says she's worked with construction project supervisors whose fuzzy building instructions have added hundreds of thousands of dollars to building costs. And a single hyphen omitted by a supervisor at a government-run nuclear installation may hold the cost record for punctuation goofs. He ordered rods of radioactive material cut into "ten foot long lengths"; he got ten pieces each a foot long, instead of the ten-foot lengths required. The loss was so great it was classified, says Douglas Mueller, president of the Gunning-Mueller Clear Writing Institute in Santa Barbara, Calif., which offers six-hour seminars for up to fifty people at $1,500 a session. (William E. Blundell, "Confused, Overstuffed Corporate Writing Often Costs Firms Much Time—And Money," *The Wall Street Journal*)

EXERCISES

1. Look over the lists of causes that follow.
   A. Write a general statement naming one probable effect for each group of causes.
   B. Now select one of these general statements naming an effect. List specific details that could be used to develop a paragraph having this statement as a topic sentence.
      (1) (a) Within a thirty-mile radius of most cities, the cost of land has increased geometrically in recent years.
          (b) Lumber exports have risen dramatically.
          (c) Skilled construction workers are now among the highest-paid personnel nationally.
      (2) (a) Parking has become almost impossible in congested downtown areas.
          (b) Population has shifted to outlying suburbs.
          (c) Massive shopping malls ring the cities.
      (3) (a) Multiple primaries have replaced conventions as the actual way of choosing political candidates.
          (b) Many prominent politicians have switched parties or chosen to run as independents.
2. List across a page the titles of the courses you are enrolled in. Under each course write down first what the immediate goal of that course is—what skills you will have when you finish it. Then write down the possible ways that course will influence your future career.

From Effect to Cause

In the same way that any subject can be viewed as a cause allowing us to write about its effects, a subject may also be seen as an effect for which we can trace the cause or causes. For example, the course you are taking right now is a cause of future effects in your life, but it is simultaneously the effect of past causes. What brought you to this college, this program, this particular section of this particular English course? Were you in control of all the causes involved, or were some outside your power to influence? A computer may have scheduled the course for you as part of a series of required courses. Perhaps the only control you exerted was to enroll in a particular area such as liberal arts, engineering, or med-lab technology. In any event, a given set of circumstances naturally leads us to speculate on what brought them about. Moreover, many circumstances present problems for us and to solve them we must understand the causes. Just as in treating a disease, a proposed solution to any problem is best when it treats the cause and not just the symptoms.

The steps involved are very similar to those used in writing about effects:

1. State the subject (effect).
2. List and develop each major cause.
3. Move from immediate causes to more remote ones.

Examine the following model:

Statement Of Effect

Women are trained to be rape victims [emphasis added]. To simply learn the word "rape" is to take instruction in the power relationship between males and females. *To talk about rape, even with nervous laughter, is to acknowledge*

Cause #1
Development

a woman's special victim status. We hear the whispers when we are children: girls get raped. Not boys. The message comes clear. Rape has something to do with our sex. Rape is something awful that happens to females: it is the dark at the top of the stairs, the undefinable abyss that is just around the corner, and unless we watch our step it might become our destiny.

Cause #2

Rape seeps into our childhood consciousness by imperceptible degrees. Even before we learn to read we have become indoctrinated into a victim mentality. Fairy tales are full of

Development

a vague dread, a catastrophe that seems to befall only little girls. Sweet, feminine Little Red Riding Hood is off to visit her dear old grandmother in the woods. The wolf lurks in the shadows, contemplating a tender morsel. Red Riding Hood and her grandmother, we learn, are equally defenseless before the male wolf's strength and cunning. His big eyes, his big hands, his big teeth—"The better to see you, to catch you, to eat you, my dear." The wolf swallows both females with no sign of a struggle. (Susan Brownmiller, *Against Our Will*)

EXERCISES

1. Read the following passage.
   A. What is the subject (the *effect*)?
   B. List the causes given.
   C. Decide whether the causes have been presented in the order of immediate to remote. Would changing the order improve the explanation of causes?

   The Udall committee's concern about nuclear power was based at least in part on a tour by some of the members of the crippled Pennsylvania plant last week. Three more human errors contributing to the accident were disclosed: 1) The operators not only shut off the auxiliary feed-water system two days before the accident but mistakenly indicated on their check sheets that the water had been promptly restored. (Explained one supervisor later: "I thought I completed that.") 2) A light that warned of the water shutoff was not seen for eight minutes because it was blocked by a tag hanging from a switch above it. 3) The first indication of real trouble, a hydrogen explosion during the first few hours of the accident, went unnoticed by federal inspectors even though a recording gauge registered it. The staff of the Nuclear Regulatory Commission later confirmed that such human errors turned what might have been a minor malfunction into a major breakdown. (" 'Hell No, We Won't Glow,' " *Time*)

2. Consider the following statements. Each one names a general effect.
   A. Write down two or three probable causes for each effect.
   B. Select one of the causes you came up with and write a paragraph that develops the cause in some detail.
      (1) American families will be limited to one, or at most, two children.
      (2) Nuclear power is no longer politically acceptable as the basic solution to the energy problem.
      (3) Most people will not only change jobs, but will change career fields two or three times during their working years.

Combination: Effect-Cause-Effect

A third way of using cause-effect analysis to write about a subject is to look at both. In addition to examining some of the causes of a victim mentality in women, Susan Brownmiller, for example, could (and does) go on to look at the effects of this state of mind on women's lives. Exploring the combination and interrelation of causes and effects often begins with an observed *effect*, because most of the time we experience the effect of circumstances or actions before we understand the cause or causes. The writer of the following example set out to buy a used truck. He found many old trucks abandoned in farmyards, left to rot. He wonders why these "derelicts" or dead vehicles are not traded in for newer machines. He discovers one dominant cause: "The dead vehicles are not traded in on newer models because of the rust."

But this observation does not really tell us anything. What causes the rust?

> The dead vehicles are not traded in on newer models because of the rust. The rust is because of the salt, dumped on the roads all winter to melt the snow. Salt accelerates the oxidation rate of metal. The road salt makes a mushy, corrosive paste that is flung universally about the under- and over-sides of every vehicle. It fouls all the metal parts, pits windshields, scours paint, reduces the useful life of north-country motor vehicles by several years.

One set of circumstances or one action or event can set off a chain of effects. Often in searching for the cause of one observed effect you will discover that that cause also has many other effects. The writer who discovered the damage salt caused to trucks also observes that this was only one of many effects of spreading salt on the highways: "It also kills roadside trees, pollutes streams and wells, and destroys gardens."

And this is not all. Another effect of the highway department's addiction to salt is economic loss to the citizen:

> Salt is an invisible tax. We pay for the salt, pay for the machinery to spread it, pay for the labor to get it onto the roads. And then we pay with our vehicles, in reduced resale value, in hulled-out, rotten, disintegrating cars, untimely mechanical failures, a huge additional tax. Salt damage reduces resale value by about $350 a year. Nobody bitches except the environmentalists. (John Jerome, *Truck*)

The following outline summarizes Jerome's discoveries regarding the effects of salt and shows the pattern of his thinking and writing:

Effect:	Rusted, useless vehicles.
Cause:	Salt on highways.
Further effects:	A) Environmental pollution
	B) Cost to citizens

EXERCISE

Do a little research in the library and write a paragraph that describes the effect, specifies a major cause, then shows the relationship between this cause and several other effects. Use one of the topics below:

EFFECT

1. Highway fatalities
2. Energy crisis
3. Rising divorce rate
4. Need for skilled technicians
5. Two-income families
6. Retirement age delayed to age 70

Organizing a Cause-Effect Analysis

We have not described all the relationships possible between causes and effects nor have we shown every possible organizational pattern for presenting them. The decision whether to discuss causes first, then describe effects, or to describe effects, then specify causes, depends a great deal on the nature of the situation and the writer's purpose. The following outline shows you an organizational pattern for writing an essay examining the multiple causes of one effect. The procedure could easily be reversed to show multiple effects of a single cause, but the pattern of organization would remain the same.

Introduction

    I. Identify the effect and give a general overview of the causes

        Suicides among Americans between the ages of fifteen through twenty-four more than doubled in ten years, from 1,876 in 1965 to 4,747 in 1976. Suicide accounts for one of every ten deaths in that age group. Among the major causes for this phenomenon are the special anxieties of adolescence, a sense of isolation, and pressure to succeed.

   II. Development

      A. First Cause

         Adolescence is full of anxiety growing from self-doubt and the need for acceptance. When these immediate anxieties become too great, a significant number of young people choose suicide as an escape. (This cause would be further developed by evidence and example.)

B. Second Cause

   The changing patterns of American family life create a sense of isolation for many young people. Many parents are so busy pursuing careers and solving their own problems that children feel isolated and alienated from their parents—this feeling can trigger thoughts of suicide. (Further development is provided by evidence and example.)

C. Third Cause

   Successful parents prod their children to succeed, without offering the emotional support the children need. The adolescent who cannot fulfill parental expectations can experience stress leading directly to suicide. (Further development is provided by evidence and example.)

III. Conclusion

   The rising rate of adolescent suicides seems linked directly to the relationship between child and parents. Young people need the support and love of their parents, but also need to form identities of their own. The security and love that grows from a strong family unit provides the environment necessary for well-adjusted, emotionally secure young people.

A chain of cause-effect relationships could be set up by doubling the length of this essay and using the second half to explore three effects of the increased adolescent suicide rate.

In reading the following essay on worker dissatisfaction, pay attention to the organization and to the complex interrelationship of causes and effects. Notice in particular that the author not only reports, that is, *informs*, us of the survey results about causes for job-related unhappiness, but also *explains* these causes.

A major source of disagreement, among union and government officials, employers, and academics when they get together to discuss the problem of worker discontent is the question: "What's bugging them anyhow?" In general, union and government people seem to believe that it's a matter of money, while employers and academics feel that workers are angry because they expect—but do not get—fulfillment from their work.

Of course, when we talk of the "worker" we are talking about a nonexistent person. Some workers are no doubt motivated solely by money and look at the world of work as a marketplace where they can exchange their time for money. Just as certainly, there are other workers who wish to be active in their jobs and express themselves through the medium of work.

We can also speculate that young people might be dissatisfied for different reasons than those in their middle years or older people, that blacks might have different causes of dissatisfaction than whites, and that women might have different grievances than men. Keeping in mind these individual and group differences among workers, the responses to questions asked in the survey point toward some tentative conclusions about what is bugging workers.

Workers were asked how important they considered some twenty-five aspects of work, including pay, working conditions, and relations with coworkers. The results may be surprising to those who believe workers are interested mainly in pay.

Of the five work features rated most important, only one had to do with tangible or economic benefits. And that one (good pay) ranked number five. Ranked above pay were interesting work, enough help and equipment to get the job done, enough information to get the job done, and enough authority to do the job.

Work aspects rated sixth, seventh, and eighth in importance were:
—Opportunity to develop special abilities.
—Job security.
—Seeing the results of one's work.
Of the eight top-ranked work aspects, six had to do with the content of the worker's job.

Some observers contend that workers might overstate their concern with the noneconomic aspects of their jobs in order to put themselves in a more favorable light. I would suggest, however, that we take the worker at his word and seriously question our traditional notions regarding his needs and priorities.

In addition to being asked how important they considered the twenty-five job aspects listed, workers also were asked to what extent each one was present in their jobs. This provided a rough indication of the aspects of work which the most workers felt to be in need of improvement. Where more workers felt an aspect of work to be very important than believed it to be very true of their jobs, a "satisfaction gap" existed. Of the twelve job aspects in which such a gap was found, four were mainly economic, seven had to do with job content, and one involved personal relationships.

The largest satisfaction gap for the work force as a whole concerned feelings about promotional opportunity. Relatively few workers—55 percent of those interviewed—said that chances for promotion were very important to them. The facts of work life, however, created a large satisfaction gap, since only 25 percent considered good chances for promotion characteristic of their jobs. Opportunities for promotion have both economic and noneconomic implications. Money certainly is involved, but so is the possibility for personal growth and achievement.

The aspect with the second largest satisfaction gap was "good pay," with 64 percent ranking it very important and only 40 percent stating that it was very true of their jobs. Third was the "opportunity to develop one's special abilities," and fourth was the "adequacy of fringe benefits." "Interesting work" was fifth, and "enough help and equipment to get the job done" was sixth.

While these figures indicated that more workers feel their jobs fall short with regard to promotions and pay than on other aspects of work, it should be stressed that the satisfaction gap is only a very rough indication of the number who feel a discrepancy exists between their desire for a given work feature and the fulfillment of this desire. It does not measure the relative importance of this discrepancy to the worker.

The overall survey shows that the chance to do meaningful work and to achieve and grow on the job is of great importance to the average American worker—perhaps even overshadowing financial considerations. It also appears that this chance is sadly lacking in the average job.

This need for job satisfaction can best be met through the humanization of work: through restructuring the work situation so that jobs provide autonomy, interesting work, and the opportunity to be active, to grow, and to achieve. Widely varying rates of dissatisfaction in various industries suggest a targeting of efforts to improve the quality of work. Just as society gives particular attention to industries with exceptionally high accident rates perhaps special assistance might be tendered by the Government—and special concern shown by employers and unions—in industries with particularly high dissatisfaction rates. Similarly, special efforts might be made to alleviate the causes of unusually high job discontent among particular groups of workers, such as women, blacks, and younger people.

Work or life dissatisfaction were seldom reported by the self-employed. This supports the theory that independence of action is an important ingredient in satisfaction. It also points out the possibility of improving the structure of work by stimulation—through tax or other incentives and aids-economic opportunities for the very small businessman. A detailed examination of the occupations of the 205 self-employed workers in the University of Michigan sample would be a logical first step.

Major programs to employ the aged are needed. When only 10 percent of the sample of employed persons age fifty-five and older are dissatisfied with their lives, and when previous studies have shown that between 27 and 30 percent of retired persons express negative attitudes toward life, it is time to develop programs allowing older people an alternative to "dropping out" of life. As Erich Fromm points out, the human being is by nature active and, when inactive, begins to die. (Herrick Neal, "Who's Unhappy at Work and Why," *Manpower*)

SUMMARY

1. In writing cause-effect analysis in its simplest form, we treat a subject as if it were a cause, break down the individual effects, and discuss them one by one. Or, we look at the subject as an effect, break down its causes, and treat them one by one.

2. Many cause-effect analyses are complex, involving chains of causes and effects. How far you pursue a chain of causal relationships depends, of course, on your subject, audience, and purpose.

3. The ordinary arrangement of causes (or effects) in a written analysis is to move from the less important *immediate* ones to more important *remote* ones.

WRITING ASSIGNMENTS

1. You are working in the community. Develop and write up some preliminary plans for projects that would aid elder citizens in achieving greater "life satisfaction."

2. You have been hired as a youth consultant by a local business that has been experiencing problems with its younger workers. Prepare a report explaining the causes of job dissatisfaction among young people.

3. Pick a social or political issue you consider important. It may be a national issue such as the debate over abortion rights or a local matter such as a controversy about the "youth takeover" of a city park every weekend. You are going to testify on the issue before an appropriate group such as a city council or a visiting legislative delegation. Take a stand on the issue and prepare a report on the negative effects that will occur if your view is not accepted and acted upon.

4. You are working for a small business firm. Prepare a report for your boss on the probable effects on worker morale if the business is sold and merged into a giant corporation. Think carefully about the difference between working in a close, personal, group atmosphere and working for a large, impersonal organization. Consider both positive and negative effects.

5. You have been majoring in a technical area that offers many secure job opportunities. In your second year of college, you decide that your liberal arts courses are more interesting and you contemplate changing majors. Prepare a written analysis of all the consequences in remaining with your major or in changing to a liberal arts program.

9

PERSUADING

Understanding Persuasion

All acts of communication involve persuasion. If nothing else, we are trying to persuade someone to read and consider our ideas. Persuasive writing calls on all the techniques of thinking and writing we have looked at so far—the analytical skills used in defining, in classifying, in comparing, and in analysis. All these are natural ways our minds organize and make sense of the things and ideas we encounter in the world. When we translate these natural ways of thinking into writing or speech, we are trying to get someone else to see the world in the same way we do.

The root of *persuasion* is *swad-*, a basic form that goes back through many related languages to their dim origins in a single language now thousands of years lost. The basic meaning of the root word *swad-* is "sweet, pleasant, delightful." Words don't always keep their meanings over the years. Most change a great deal as time passes, and we can't always tell what a word means today by what it used to mean. But in this case, the origin of the word *persuasion* can help us understand something essential about the process involved—it's the old saying, "You can catch more flies with honey than you can with vinegar." In other words, *persuasion* is making your ideas appealing to an audience in order to have them respond the way you want them to. You may be able to affect an audience—get them to do what you want—by being aggressive, but this is not persuasion. An employer brusquely ordering an employee, or a teacher rudely demanding something of a student, is achieving an effect, but not by persuasion. Ordering, bullying, heatedly arguing may push an audience into doing what you want, but these behaviors create a negative relationship and will, in the long run, produce undesirable side effects. A positive, persuasive relationship with your audience creates only the effects you want, avoiding reactions such as hostility and resentment. Let's look at a brief example that tries to avoid these problems.

Much has been written and said about the energy crisis, but how much attention do people really pay to the statistics and arguments aimed at them? How many people are persuaded that a real problem exists and that their future may be very different because of it? In the excerpt that follows, Isaac Asimov doesn't try to *argue* with people to convince them that the energy problem may have serious effects, but he does try to *persuade* his readers.

> So it's 1997, and it's raining, and you'll have to walk to work again. The subways are crowded, and any given train breaks down one morning out of five. The buses are gone, and on a day like today the bicycles slosh and slide. Besides, you have only a mile and a half to go, and you have boots, raincoat and rain hat. And it's not a very cold rain, so why not?
>
> Lucky you have a job in demolition too. It's steady work. Slow and dirty, but steady. The fading structures of a decaying city are the great mineral mines and hardware shops of the nation. Break them down and re-use the parts. Coal is too difficult to dig up and transport to give us energy in the amounts we need, nuclear fission is judged to be too dangerous, the technical breakthrough toward nuclear fusion that we hoped for never took place, and solar batteries are too expensive to maintain on the earth's surface in sufficient quantity.
>
> Anyone older than ten can remember automobiles. They dwindled. At first the price of gasoline climbed—way up. Finally only the well-to-do drove, and that was too clear an indication that they were filthy rich, so any automobile that dared show itself on a city street was overturned and burned. Rationing was introduced to "equalize sacrifice," but every three months the ration was reduced. The cars just vanished and became part of the metal resource. (Isaac Asimov, "The Nightmare Life Without Fuel," *Time*)

We said earlier that persuasion depends on making your ideas appealing. At first, the above passage does not seem very appealing, but we do find it persuasive. Although the subject matter is unpleasant, the *relationship* the author establishes with his reader is not, and this good relationship has an appeal for us as readers. Look at the opening lines. The author addresses the reader directly, involving us in the situation. He uses contractions such as "it's," "you'll," informal words like "slosh" and expressions like "so why not?" to give his voice a friendly, casual tone. Remember our discussion of *voice* in Chapter 1. Here the author's voice is pleasant, speaking to us in a way that doesn't make us feel talked down to or ordered about. We don't feel any need to defend ourselves against this voice, and thus we can be open to what the voice is saying. Even if we don't agree completely, we are at least willing to consider what is being said. Creating an open channel is effective persuasion. The job of persuasion is to open a reader's mind, to let new or different ideas flow in and slowly do their work.

Subjects for Persuasion

People argue about everything from baseball, politics, and religion to the color of Aunt Gertrude's eyes, and most often these arguments fail to persuade anybody of anything, except perhaps that the other person involved is a fool. The problem commonly exists because, in fact, many subjects cannot be effectively argued about. There are three kinds, or classes, of arguments and only the third class is suitable for persuasion:

1. Questions of investigation
2. Questions of taste
3. Questions of judgment

On many subjects, our opinion may be one that can be tested by simple *investigation*, without involving anything else. For example, if I am trying to convince you that Army beat Navy in their annual football game in 1975, there is really no room for persuasion in this discussion. Either Army won or it didn't, and the matter can be settled by simply checking the facts. The other kind of opinion that exists outside of any logical process is *a question of taste*. If I want to make you believe that chocolate ice cream is better than vanilla, or that blue is prettier than red, no logic in the world will convince you if you hate chocolate and blue. Only *questions of judgment* lend themselves to persuasion.

A *judgment* involves a choice between two possibilities. The choice cannot be made through simple investigation or on the basis of personal taste. Judgment takes over when there is a good case to be made for both sides of an issue, and we must choose one side or the other. For example, deciding between a liberal arts education and a technical one involves a judgment. Which one prepares us better for the future? The liberal arts education broadens our perspectives, making us more flexible and thus more capable of adapting to unforeseen changes that will come in the future. On the other hand, a technical education gives us marketable skills we will need to survive in an economically competitive society. The decision to choose between the two kinds of education requires a judgment.

EXERCISE

Review the following statements. Identify which ones indicate opinions on matters of *investigation, taste,* and *judgment.* Write a brief explanation of your decision.

1. I hate communists, liberals, and Eastern intellectuals.
2. Chesterfield county is normally Republican, but half of the precincts went against Reagan in the last election.
3. The 1957 T-Bird was the best-looking car Ford ever built.
4. Jackie Robinson was a better role model for black kids than Muhammed Ali is.
5. Muhammed Ali is the greatest athlete who ever lived.
6. There are too many nursing programs around now.
7. She's not a very good person to have as a friend.

Evidence

A judgment differs from a question of taste because it is not "just an opinion." Judgments are *informed opinions,* decisions made on the basis of evidence and careful thought. In writing to persuade, you must: (1) be sure you're dealing with a subject open to persuasion; (2) gather the evidence to support your position. Evidence exists in two basic forms: *facts* and *expert* opinions.

Facts

Generally speaking, facts are those events, things, details, and pieces of information that have some kind of actual reality. We can check on them and demonstrate that they actually exist or did exist. We can classify facts into four basic types:

> Physical facts
> Scientific facts
> Historical facts
> Statistical facts

Physical facts. These facts are the simplest. A statement of a physical fact is nothing more than a statement of what is. At this moment you are physically located in one place and not another. You are home on your sofa, or you are in a specific chair in a certain classroom of one building on your campus—that's a physical fact. If there is a maple tree growing next to the entrance of the building, that's a physical fact. If a car heading west on Grace Street crashes into one heading north on Lombardy at 2:47 A.M., that's a physical fact. Physical facts are established by simple observation of physical reality.

Scientific facts. Scientific facts are special kinds of physical facts established by research and experimentation, which can be demonstrated over and over by repeating the same procedures. We have established scientifically, for example, that water freezes at 0° Centigrade and that nuclear fission produces immense heat. We know from scientific experiment that a car having a certain mass and traveling at a certain velocity, will have a predictable impact if it crashes into something.

Historical facts. Those things or events we "know" to be true about the past are called historical facts. Columbus came to America in 1492; Henry VIII beheaded his wives; Lee surrendered to Grant in the McLean home at the village of Appomattox Court House. Historical facts are established through the records kept at the time of past events, through the writings shortly after the events, through journals, diaries, ledger and account books, through oral tradition, songs, old maps, buildings, roads, and other artifacts.

Statistical facts. Statistical facts are used heavily to make decisions and to persuade people in our society. Computers have given us the ability to collect, analyze, and communicate vast amounts of information expressed numerically. In one sense, statistical facts are physical or historical facts that have been turned into numbers. It is a physical fact, for example, that black families and white families live in a given city. When they are counted, or estimated, and expressed in numerical terms, we get the statistical fact that "11 percent of the families in Anytown are black;" another example would be the statistical fact that "the average American family has 2.2 children." Obviously, statistical facts often exist only as numbers on paper. No real family out there has 2.2 children. Because statistical facts are both "real" and "unreal" at the same time, they may easily be misunderstood or misused.

Expert Opinion

Judges and juries rely heavily on the testimony of experts in reaching decisions. Ballistics experts testify that the bullet recovered from the victim's body was fired by the gun found in the accused's car. Psychological experts testify about the mental state of the accused at the time of the crime. Business and economic experts testify in corporate disputes, and doctors testify in medical cases. There are experts on every subject whose opinions must be considered carefully because of their knowledge and experience. The weakness with expert opinion, however, is that experts will often disagree, and expert opinions contradicting each other are not uncommon.

Sources of Evidence

Facts and expert opinions make up the two main kinds of evidence. The two main sources of evidence are your own knowledge and/or experience and *research*. Depending on the subject, you may have a storehouse of facts available from your own experience. You may well be an expert on a number of things, from what it's like being a student, to what it was like being in a combat unit in Vietnam. Always consider the facts that you know and the expertise that you have to be among the most important resources for your writing. For those subjects you need to know more about, research is the answer. Research may consist of looking in the library for historical facts, statistical information, or the opinion of experts on your subject. It may also consist of going out and doing some first-hand observation yourself. If you are writing about justice, for example, don't just read what's in the library—go sit in a municipal court for half a day and observe how cases are handled and people are treated. Another good form of research is to interview people. Make appointments with a police officer, a prosecuting attorney, a defense lawyer, and a judge. Talk with them and ask for help in finding other sources of information.

In brief, one of the best ways to be persuasive is to do your homework. Find out what physical or scientific facts can be or need to be established, gather any pertinent statistical or historical information that is available, and check into what the experts on the subject have to say about it.

EXERCISES

Consider the career field you plan to enter. To gather evidence about it, do the following:

1. Make a list of everything you already know about jobs in this field—probable starting salaries, availability of jobs, career potentials, and the like.

2. Make an appointment with someone who does the kind of work you think you'd like to do. Ask him or her for specific information on the topics that you have listed and to recommend one book or magazine you should check in the library.
3. Look up the recommended source in the library. In it, see if you can find the names of three other books or magazines related to the subject. Look them up.
4. List the names of three people referred to in the sources you have found. Check the library for books or articles by or about these people.
5. Keep a record of all statistical information you encounter in your search. Be sure to write down the source for any statistical facts you record.

Use of Examples

Very often persuasion relies not on hard evidence but on selected examples that support the point being made. Examples make an idea come alive and this quality makes them particularly effective in written persuasion. In a general statement we tell the reader our opinion or judgment, then provide a specific example to show him or her what we mean. Examples used to support opinions may be very specific and detailed, using extensive description, or they may be general, indicating types or classes of things that illustrate the point. For example, if we wanted to persuade you that smoking is bad for your health, we could illustrate this point with a detailed example of someone who died of cancer or emphysema, describing the yellowed, drawn skin on his face, the hacking cough that wracked his body, the wheezing battles for breath, and so on. Or we could simply say something like, "For example, all of us have known a heavy smoker who died prematurely from a smoking-related lung disorder." In most cases, the more detailed example will be more persuasive. Carefully chosen, carefully developed examples let the reader experience the same kind of observations that led the writer to reach a conclusion.

In the following selection, we have italicized the general points the writer is making. Pay careful attention to the way he uses examples to illustrate them:

> Preachers of the late 20th Century will have to insist that enjoyment of total luxury is a sacred and solemn duty. Penitents will be required to confess such sins as failing to give adequate satisfaction to one's third concubine or lack of attention to some fine detail in serving a banquet to friends—such as forgetting to put enough marijuana in the turkey stuffing. Sure, I am talking with about one half of my tongue in my cheek, but I am trying to make the deadly

serious point that, as of today, an economic utopia is not wishful thinking but, in some substantial degree, the necessary alternative to self-destruction.

The moral challenge and the grim problem that we face are that the life of affluence and pleasure requires exact discipline and high imagination. Somewhat as metals deteriorate from "fatigue," every constant stimulation of consciousness, however pleasant, tends to become boring and thus to be ignored. When physical comfort is permanent, it ceases to be noticed. If you have worried for years about lack of money and then become rich, the new sense of ease and security is short-lived, for you soon begin to worry as much as ever—about cancer or heart disease. Nature abhors a vacuum. For this reason, the life of pleasure cannot be maintained without a certain asceticism, as in the time and effort required for a woman to keep her hair and face in fine condition, for the weaving of exquisite textiles or for the preparation of superior food. Thus, the French distinguish between a gourmand and a gourmet, the former being a mere glutton, a trencherman who throws anything and everything down the hatch; and the latter, a fussy, subtle and sophisticated devotee of the culinary arts.

Affluent people in the United States have seldom shown much imagination in cultivating the arts of pleasure. The business-suited executive looks more like a minister or an undertaker than a man of wealth and is, furthermore, wearing one of the most uncomfortable forms of clothing ever invented for the male, as compared, say, with the kimono or the caftan. Did you ever try the food in a private restaurant for top brass in the offices of a big corporation? Strictly institutional. Even the most expensive night clubs and country clubs pass off indifferent fare; and at $100-a-plate charity dinners, one gets the ubiquitous synthetic chicken, machine raised in misery and tasting of just that.

If the behavior of increasing numbers of young people is any real portent of what may happen by A.D. 2000, much of this will change. Quite aside from cavalierish styles of long hair, men are beginning to wear jewelry and vivid colors, imitating the styles of medieval and Oriental affluence that began to disappear when power shifted from the landed gentry to miserly merchants of the cities—the burghers or *bourgeoisie*. Beneath such outward appearances, there is a clear change of values: Rich experiences are more to be desired than property and bank accounts, and plans for the future are of use only to those who can live fully in the present. (Alan Watts, *Does It Matter*)

EXERCISES

1. Read the passage by Alan Watts again. State in one sentence the main point he is making.

2. Write out a detailed example of your own that would illustrate Watts' main point.

3. Assume that someone you love is a heavy smoker. Write that person a letter using examples to persuade him or her to stop smoking.

4. You are a state government official. The state is losing millions of dollars a year to Medicare fraud because certain people who supply medical, dental, or nursing-home services are cutting corners. Write a presentation using examples that will persuade citizens of the state to report people who are taking advantage of Medicare patients.

Writing to Persuade

We can write persuasively by appealing to our readers in three basic ways: *logically, emotionally, personally*. These types of persuasion may be used singly, but more commonly are used in combination. Let's take a look at them one by one.

Logical Persuasion

Logic is one way to affect our reader's thinking, and logic grows from the habits of thought we have been developing. Most simply stated, logic is an orderly way of thinking through a question. If we are logical in our thinking, then someone else can follow the pattern of our thought easily and see the reasons why we came to our conclusion. When we are consciously trying to persuade, we do want our reader to accept our conclusion as a good one, or at least to find it worth considering. Strictly logical persuasion depends more on evidence than on example.

After we have gathered facts and expert opinions, logic shows how the evidence relates to and supports our opinion. For example, the scientific fact that controlled chain reactions can produce power does not, by itself, support a conclusion that technical training is the best preparation for life. But showing the logical cause-effect relationship between the benefits of nuclear power and the need for technical training to gain those benefits will support our conclusion.

To be a little more specific, there are two common forms of logic: *induction* and *deduction*.

Induction

We have to show the reader the connections between our evidence and the judgments we make. One way of showing these relationships is through *induction*. Induction allows us to make valid general statements after studying individual cases. Let's suppose that at some time in the past, a scientist stuck a thermometer in a jar of water and froze the water. This observer noted that the water froze at 0° Centigrade. After freezing a number of jars of water and noting that in each individual case the temperature at freezing was the same, the scientist reached the general conclusion that all water freezes at 0° Centigrade. We cannot prove that inductive conclusions are absolutely true, but, most of the time, we rely on induction to reach conclusions about the world around us.

To check the validity of our inductive process we should look for three things:

1. A fair number of individual cases on which to base our conclusion
2. Individual cases that are typical
3. Explanation of negative cases (e.g., a jar of water that froze at $-1°$ Centigrade)

A typical case of induction at work might go like this: The manager of a high-volume, discount stereo and television outlet with a large service department hires a graduate from the two-year electronics technology program at a local college. From the first day on the job, this employee excels. Is the manager justified in reaching the general conclusion that the college offers a high-quality electronics program?

Individual cases. We need a fair number of individual cases on which to base our conclusion. The application of this rule, as with the other two, must be decided on the basis of common sense. In this situation, the manager would probably need to hire three or four graduates who all worked out well before being justified in reaching a general conclusion about the program.

Typicalness. The manager does hire a new graduate each year for three years and each one turns out equally well. But, each year, the manager selected the student graduating with the highest grade point average. Is the general conclusion about the program's high quality logical?

The individual cases must be typical. The best student from each graduating class would not be a typical student. It would be difficult to judge the overall quality of the program by hiring only the outstanding students. To be logical, the manager would have to hire several average graduates and see they all performed equally well before concluding that the college has a good electronics program.

Evaluation of negative cases. But what if the manager did so, only to find, after concluding that the program was an excellent source of employees, that the next graduate hired turned out to be late frequently, absent many days, inattentive, and made many mistakes on the job? Must the logical conclusion about the program's quality be thrown out?

Explanation of negative cases. All negative cases must be explained. Perhaps the last individual turns out to have family problems, or a problem with drugs or alcohol, factors unrelated to the quality of his or her training. The problems at work are more easily explained by learning about these personal difficulties than by finding fault with the program in question.

Overall, if the three rules are observed the manager is using inductive logic and reaching a valid general conclusion on the basis of several individual examples. Having proceeded this way, the store manager might then write a report to the district manager of the discount chain to recommend that the company consider that particular college program for special attention in recruiting new service employees throughout the district. The written report would present the individual examples and the inductive reasoning that led the store manager to his or her conclusion.

Organizing an Inductive Paper

1. Gather the facts, examples, and expert opinions you will use to support a general conclusion.
2. State the conclusion early in the paper so the reader will know what the individual items are leading to.
3. Work from your least important piece of support to your most important.
4. Restate the general conclusion after presenting the individual instances that support it.
5. Examine the following model:

Statement of Conclusion Every American-made luxury car weighing 3,000 or more pounds and having an engine displacement of 300 cubic inches or more causes an unjustifiable drain on severely limited energy resources. EPA estimates indicate that such

Individual Details of Support cars average less than 14 miles per gallon as opposed to the 26 miles per gallon average of four cylinder models in the 2,000-pound weight range. Moreover, the cost of energy required to produce each vehicle is nearly double for the larger cars. Finally, the energy cost for ultimate disposal is proportionately greater for the larger car and is not offset by greater recyclable salvage, because the energy costs involved in either disposing of or recycling the greater bulk of materials are also greater. The American who purchases a large car equipped with energy-intensive "luxury" accessories must accept the moral responsibility for unnecessary waste of energy resources.

Restatement of General Conclusion

EXERCISES

1. Check the following example of inductive reasoning by using the three criteria set forth on p. 158:

    DETECTING HEART ATTACKS IN ADVANCE

    Dr. Reams, through individual laboratory test analysis, states that he is able to detect heart attacks in advance.

    In 1975 he warned a man that he was in imminent danger of a fatal heart attack. Dr. Reams told this man how to ward off this heart attack. The man did not believe him!

    Instead, he went to his doctor. The doctor pronounced him in perfect health.

    But at 5 o'clock that afternoon, this man's wife called Dr. Reams to tell him that her husband had just died on the way to the hospital!

    Why was Dr. Reams' advice ignored?

    This individual told Dr. Reams that he was in perfect health. He said:

    I am in excellent health. There is nothing wrong with me.

    But he dies!

    Dr. Reams stresses this one fact:

    You can feel well and yet be in imminent danger of either a major or fatal heart attack.

    In the spring of 1975, a bishop of a church came to Dr. Reams' retreat for tests. The urine test indicated that he would have a fatal heart attack in 6 months.

    He said in disbelief at this report:

    I'm in perfect health!

    He ignored the warning and the preventive procedures.

    In just six days short of six months . . . he was dead . . . of a heart attack!
    (Salem Kirban, *Health Guide for Survival*)

2. State a general conclusion about the quality of your working conditions, or the quality of the educational program in which you are currently enrolled. Exaggerate if necessary, but make your conclusion strongly favorable or strongly unfavorable. List what you believe would be a sufficient number of typical facts to support your conclusion. Identify at least one negative fact and explain why it does not affect the conclusion.

Deduction

The other common form of logical reasoning proceeds in just the opposite manner from induction. With induction, you examine several individual cases and conclude by making a general statement. Using *deduction* you begin with a general statement about a whole class of things and conclude that if what is said in general is true, then it will be true about an individual case belonging to that class. The formal statement of the deductive process is called a *syllogism*. Here is a classic example:

General statement about a class—all men	All men are mortal.
Placing an individual case into the class	Socrates is a man.
Concluding that what is true about the class in general is true about the particular case	Therefore, Socrates is mortal.

One problem with formal deductive reasoning, however, is that we may have difficulty establishing the truth of the general statement (or *premise*) that we start from. An ordinary case of deductive logic might go like this:

"All graduates of engineering programs at M.I.T. are excellent, and Sharon just got her degree in electrical engineering there. She must be good, so I'll hire her."

The premise that all M.I.T. graduates are excellent is open to question, however; for example, some people may just scrape by. We do use deductive reasoning every day, but seldom in the form of strict syllogism with proven premises and a conclusion that is absolutely certain. The common way to use deduction is to *qualify* the premise and conclusion:

"M.I.T. has an excellent reputation as an engineering school, and most graduates are probably well prepared. I'll take a reasonable chance, then, and hire Sharon, who just completed her degree there."

In such a qualified form, a deductive line of reasoning can be very persuasive.

Organizing a Deductive Paper

A deductive paper will be organized very similarly to an inductive one. In fact, the major part of most deductive essays is spent using *induction* to establish the general premise. For example, the inductive model above (p. 159) could be used to establish the premise that Americans must accept responsibility for the wasteful effect of their luxury cars. A deductive paper would proceed beyond this stage to present the argument that the president of your college, as the owner of a new luxury car, must accept some responsibility for the wastefulness of this self-indulgence. To organize a deductive paper:

1. State the final judgment you are aiming at. ("The president of this college is acting in a wasteful manner by driving a new luxury car.")
2. State the general premise you will be working from. ("Americans who drive luxury cars must accept the responsibility for wasting energy resources.")
3. Present *inductive* support for this general statement. (See model paper on p. 159.)
4. Place the particular case within the class identified in the general premise. ("The president of our college has just purchased a large luxury car.")
5. Restate your conclusion about the particular case involved. ("Therefore the president must bear the moral responsibility of wasting limited resources.")

EXERCISES

1. Try to build formal syllogisms from each of the following general premises:
   A. No life can exist without oxygen.
   B. All teachers are dedicated to their students.
   C. All college graduates have a better chance for employment than college dropouts.
   D. Every prolonged period of high unemployment has brought a decrease in the rate of inflation.

2. Now rewrite each syllogism in a less formal, more *qualified* manner. Make each one a reasonable statement generally following the deductive process.

Emotional Persuasion

Appealing to the reader's sense of logic is one way to persuade, and appealing to the reader's emotions is another. These two appeals do not have to oppose each other; often they are used together. The following passage begins a lengthy news article written to persuade readers that there are serious problems with the cost of medical services today. The remainder of the article depends heavily on logic, but note that the readers are being set up by an emotional approach. Although the opening passage does not even mention cost, it does put the readers in a sympathetic mood for the arguments that will follow.

> TEXARKANA, Ark.—Jason White, age 6, handsome, husky and blue-eyed with brown cornsilk hair, looks out his bedroom window, thinking, probably, how nice it would be to play outside in the sunshine again.
> But for now he must wait. He sits in his chair in front of his little desk, his hands folded, patient and resigned. His eyes, made bluer and more luminous by recent tears, are calm now.
> His cheeks, so round, are tinged with pink, flushed from outdoor play in the fort they built for him in the front yard, from riding his bike and from throwing and catching the ball that swings from a rope tied to a limb on his old maple tree.
> Above him in his room, on a metal stand partially obscured by the headboard on his bed, the clear plastic bag of golden parental hyperalimentation fluid has been reattached once more. Soon he must leave the unrestrained world of play and hook up to his life-supporting tube. (Robert Carey, UPI, "The Life And Death Struggle of a Miracle Child," *The Boston Globe*)

Notice the author's choice of words. The words are chosen to affect the reader's emotions. The boy has "cornsilk" hair, thinks about being "outside in the sunshine," sits at "his little desk," has "cheeks so round" that are "tinged with pink" but his eyes are glowing from "recent tears." In this case, emotional appeal introduces an argument; and emotional appeal can often influence people. However, relying on nothing but raw emotion, especially anger or outrage, can turn people off.

Emotional appeal lies at the heart of propaganda and most advertising. Propaganda tries to move people to act without thinking and raising questions. Most advertising aims at the same goal. A number of specific emotional persuasive techniques are commonly found in propaganda and advertising. Among the most common techniques are the use of *sentimentality, glittering generalities, name-calling, testimonial, transfer,* and *bandwagon.*

Sentimentality

The lead-in to the newspaper article above is a good example of the use of sentimentality. Sometimes the emotion of pity is appealed to by using examples of helplessness. Other times a rush of good feeling is triggered by illustrations, in words or pictures, of something humorously cute—puppies, kittens, very young children.

Glittering generalities

In this device, *god-words* are used to persuade us to approve of something, whether it is a commercial product, a political candidate, a government policy, or something else. *God-words* are general terms to which most people respond favorably, without bothering to think. To call a product the *best,* or *improved,* is not to tell us very much about it, but we respond automatically with favorable reactions to those words. See if you can pick out the *god-words* in the following political endorsement:

> Governor Jackson is the man that we need. He has been a fighter from the beginning, courageously upholding the rights of the people against those who would deny them. He is a man of long experience in government, and the record of his years of service is spotless. For your sake, and for the sake of all decent citizens of this great state, keep Governor Jackson.

Name-calling

Name-calling, the opposite of glittering generalities, associates *devil-words* with a subject when we want our audience to disapprove. Again, these words are general and actually tell us little about the subject, but these words are cues to our emotions. We respond automatically with dislike, even fear. Pick out the *devil-words* employed here:

> Governor Jackson has been bought and paid for by the big corporations from his first day as a political hack. His cronies in the board rooms wheel and deal while Jackson tries to fool the people into believing he is on their side. But the people are not being fooled. Jackson's record in office is an open disgrace. It is time for the good people of this state to rise up and to clean Jackson and his fat-cat friends out of the governor's mansion.

Testimonial

In this familiar device, some famous or well-respected person lends his or her prestige to some unrelated product or cause. The football player advertising toothpaste, the politician endorsing a fund drive, the film star speaking out for a political candidate are all engaged in *testimonials*. There is no logical reason why some well-known person's support should influence our opinion, but if we find that person emotionally appealing, we transfer our favorable emotional attitude to whatever he or she endorses.

Transfer

This device is very similar to that of using testimonials. Instead of having a famous person speak on behalf of something, *transfer* tries to have some place or thing lend its positive image to something else. Ads that show a beautifully dressed couple walking on the beach at sunset seek to transfer the glamour of the setting to the product. A classic example of transfer occurred during the Watergate era when President Nixon appeared on television to defend himself against various charges. He spoke from the Oval Office with a picture of his family clearly visible over one shoulder, and a bust of Abraham Lincoln showing over the other.

Bandwagon

Our desire not to be left out makes us susceptible to this technique. We are convinced that "everybody's doing it" or "buying it." Ads frequently present large groups of people happily rushing about in order to stir our desire to be "with it," to be on the bandwagon.

We list these devices of emotional persuasion for two reasons: First, so that you can familiarize yourself with them as they are used everyday by advertisers and others to appeal to your emotions, and, second, so that you can learn to use the emotional appeal judiciously in persuading your own readers. There is nothing wrong with appealing to the emotions; some evidence of sentimentality, glittering generalities, name-calling, or another of the devices presented here will be found in almost all good persuasive writing.

A heavily emotional appeal usually works poorly, however, when you are trying to change someone's mind, and works best with an audience that already agrees with you. The politician who rants on about his opponent's being a liar, a communist, and probably a homosexual is not going to win over any of his opponent's supporters, but he is going to stir up a crowd of his own followers to a fever pitch. Generally, the most effective use of the emotional appeal is to move a sympathetic audience to action.

EXERCISES

1. Make a list of at least ten *god-words* commonly found in advertising.
2. List at least ten political *devil-words*. ("Communist" is the most obvious one in our society. What would be the worst political *devil-word* in the Soviet Union?)

3. Write an example of a television ad based on one you have seen that uses either *transfer* or *testimonial*.
4. Cut out magazine ads that illustrate three of the devices listed and write out your explanation of how each device is used in the ad.
5. Write a sentimental opening for a news story about the effects of inflation on the elderly.

Personal Persuasion

We appeal to both logic and emotion in trying to persuade, but a third manner of winning over an audience is no less important. *Personal persuasion* refers to the effect of the persuader's personality on the audience. In other words, how you come across to your readers will affect their response to your arguments. If you appear to be a reasonable, open-minded person sincerely concerned about the issue, your readers will be receptive to what you say. On the other hand, if you appear narrow-minded, too angry, or as if you are trying to be smart or cute, the personality projected to the readers may turn them off. Look at the two sample pieces dealing with the energy crisis, the one by Asimov on p. 150 and the one on large American cars on p. 159. Read each one carefully to determine your response to the personality, or voice, each one projects. Which is more agreeable, that is, less self-righteous sounding? For most people, the Asimov piece will be more persuasive because the voice is less self-righteous. We have already noted that the voice in it is created by careful selection of casual words and phrases that help the reader feel at ease.

Two methods used to project a reasonable personality to the reader are common: *choice of lanauage* and *identification with the audience*.

Language Choice

Try, as much as possible, to avoid *judgmental* words, such as "right," "wrong," "good," "bad," "guilty," and "responsibility," among others. Obviously, sometimes it will be necessary to use such words, but piling them up on the reader can make you seem hostile or self-righteous.

Remember our discussion of voice in Chapter 1. In some formal situations it may not be possible, but, when you can, give your writing a friendly, personal tone by using *personal pronouns* ("I," "you," "we," and the like); some contractions ("don't," "can't," "I've," "we'll," and so on); and some casual, conversational words or phrases ("O.K.," "you can bet on it," among others).

A WARNING: Don't overdo this stuff a whole bunch, gang, or it'll get real silly mighty quicklike, O.K.?

Identifying with Your Audience

Most importantly, you must understand how your audience thinks and feels about the issue at hand. The traditional model for persuasion has been the courtroom. This is a poor model, however, because the audience here, either judge or jury, is supposed to be disinterested, but in the world outside very few other audiences are without preconceived notions or prejudices. Moreover, in the courtroom the emphasis is not so much on truth as it is on winning. The relationship between the prosecuting attorney and the defense attorney is defined as an *adversary* one. They are opponents—one must win and the other lose. The aim is simply to overpower the other side and impress the objective audience. When the audience is a judge, the contending lawyers try to win by the logic of their cases; when the audience is a jury, the lawyers rely heavily on emotional appeals. But most people will never test their persuasive skills in a courtroom or in any situation where such a beat-the-other-guy approach to persuasion is appropriate. More commonly, our audience is involved in the issue, so an aggressive, competitive form of persuasion may seem an attack on them and their position.

A more common occasion for persuasion might be writing your boss a memo that suggests a new office procedure or that points out some problems caused by an existing one. You might, for example, work in a community mental health clinic and want to suggest to the director some ideas for an advertising campaign to make the community aware of the clinic's services and not to be threatened by the idea of seeking help for emotional problems. On the other hand, you might see potential problems in a newly proposed outreach program and want to convince the director that these should be solved before implementation. Sometimes you might want to work for change in a community organization such as church or school. Or you might be faced with problems as a consumer or citizen—you have a complaint about a product or about your treatment by a government agency.

In cases such as these, the audience you are addressing is directly involved. You are trying to persuade them to favor your position, so an approach that emphasizes your desire to beat or crush them is generally not the best. To understand the audience, you must thoughtfully and sympathetically put yourself in their position. How would you feel if you were, for example, directing the lab in a hospital and one of the technicians wrote you a memo attacking all the current procedures and demanding that things be done his or her way? The answer is obvious, and it is also obvious that if you were the technician seeking a change in procedures you had better think first about the director's attitudes and feelings. He or she is probably proud of the methods employed, but anxious to improve them if approached in the right way.

The best way to make sure that you understand the other person's point of view is to write it out as clearly and as fairly as you can. If you write out the other person's point of view honestly, you can probably spot points of shared interest from which to work. Moreover, a considerate statement of your reader's case is the best possible opening for a piece of persuasive writing. The key is not to *judge* the reader's position, but simply to state it fairly. Any judgment can seem like an attack, but an opening summary of what the reader probably thinks has the opposite psychological effect. Instead of feeling attacked, the reader feels that he or she is understood. We all like to be understood and respond well to those people who obviously understand us, because we don't feel threatened by them. In the above example, the technician should realize that the director wants the lab to run well, if only because it looks good that way for him or her. This is a good point to start from. Rather than beginning with an attack on what is done poorly, the memo could begin by noting all the well-run procedures and commenting on the director's obvious concern for operating an effective lab. From this mutual ground, the technician could suggest his or her ideas about changing procedures and how these changes would benefit everyone involved. Having opened up the reader by presenting a sympathetic, understanding voice, he or she will be more willing to listen to logical and emotional appeals.

EXERCISES

1. Rewrite the passage on American automobiles on p. 159. Use the same information, but change the language so that it seems more personal and less self-righteous.

2. Put yourself in the following situations. In each case, write one paragraph that sums up how your *audience* probably views the situation. In other words, try to see the problem the way your audience would and write out a brief, objective statement of its feelings.
   A. You need to write a memo reminding your boss of the raise promised you at the end of your first six months on the job. The time has come and gone, but she hasn't mentioned your raise. You know the business has had some financial problems lately.
   B. You are an assistant to the city manager and must write a memo to the members of the police department announcing that the city budget will not allow pay increases for the upcoming year. Yesterday, a city police officer was killed in the line of duty.
   C. You have been assigned a new sales territory and discover that the

largest potential customer has bought from the same firm, your main competition, for the last twenty years. You are going to write a letter introducing yourself to the purchasing agent before visiting his office to make your sales pitch.

SUMMARY

What then are the steps to effective persuasion? Let's review them in outline form:

1. Make sure that the conclusion you are trying to persuade someone to accept is a *judgment,* not just a matter of taste or one that can be settled by investigation.
2. Use *evidence* to build a logical base for your judgment.
3. Select appropriate *examples* to support your judgment.
4. Consider your audience carefully to decide whether a strongly emotional appeal is appropriate. Remember: the more they already agree with you, the better they will respond to emotional persuasion; the more hostile they are to your position, the quicker an emotional appeal will turn them off.
5. Honestly try to *identify* with your audience.
6. Open by stating a reasonable summary of what your reader's views probably are. Don't make any judging statements about these views.
7. Try to establish some mutual ground. Zero in on a point where you both agree.
8. Follow up on this point of agreement by suggesting that the ideas you are proposing will be mutually beneficial if accepted.
9. Rewrite carefully for tone of voice. Choose words that will get the kind of emotional response you want. Avoid words and expressions that seem judgmental or hostile to your reader's views. Try to be polite, friendly, perhaps a little bit casual. Establish your image as a reasonable, open-minded person, and your reader will probably respond by treating your views reasonably.

WRITING ASSIGNMENTS

1. Among other forms of citizen action called for by Ralph Nader is pressure on the federal government to pass tough laws requiring many safety features in new cars. Assume you are on the staff of a legislative

committee drawing up a new auto safety bill. There are many safety devices available, from lap and shoulder belts that must be buckled before the car can be started to crash helmets such as those required for motorcyclists. How far can you go in ordering people to use safety devices? Write a report to the committee members persuading them either that the government's obligation to protect its citizens is most important or that the citizen's right to be free of government interference comes first.

2. As a college student, do you feel that teachers' unions are a good idea? Talk with one or two of your professors about why they think unions are a good or bad idea for college teachers. Take a stand on this issue and write a persuasive piece for the college newspaper in which you argue for or against professors' unionizing. Remember that your audience includes faculty and administrators as well as students.

3. Assume that you have purchased a rather expensive item, such as an appliance, a television, or a stereo, that is unsatisfactory in quality and/or performance. The discount chain store where you made the purchase is willing to exchange it for another one, but has a policy of no cash refunds. You have decided that the particular product is simply not what you want and the store does not carry a suitable substitute. Write a letter to the district manager of the chain persuading her that you should be given a cash refund.

4. Decide what would be the ideal job for you at the ideal company. Don't let problems interfere with this choice—just pick your dream job. Write a letter to the president of this company persuading him or her to hire you.

part three

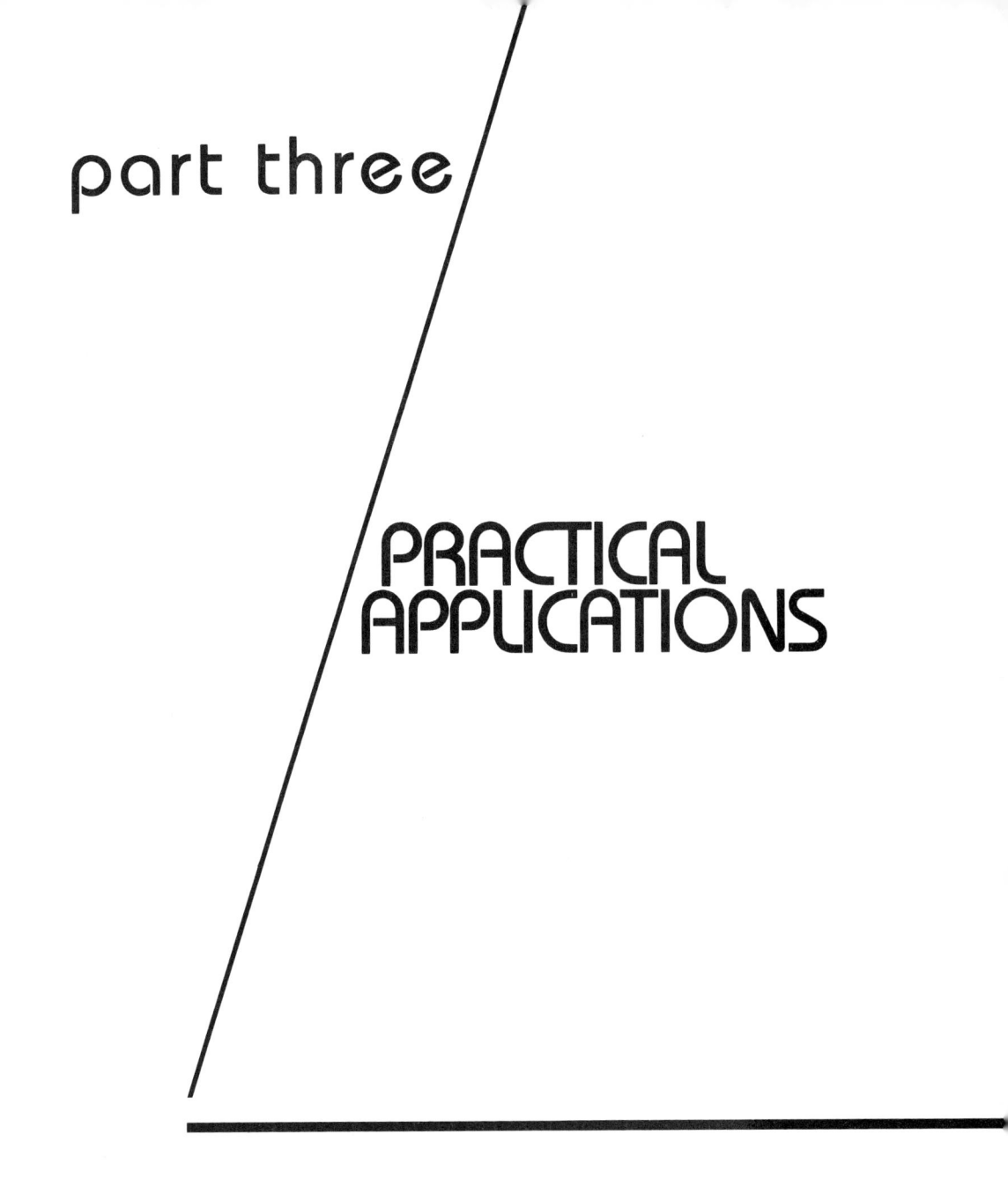

PRACTICAL APPLICATIONS

10

WRITING in COLLEGE

Writing About What You Know

Throughout the section on strategies, we have suggested that thinking and writing go hand in hand. Written work takes the form of comparison, or classification, or analysis because these patterns are basic ways we think about our world. We understand the reality around us by using these basic mental processes to study and to organize what's out there. Often we employ processes such as cause-effect thinking without conscious effort. When we write to communicate, however, it's important to make conscious these thinking strategies and to turn them into deliberate ways to gather and organize material about our subject. In the section on strategies, we isolated each basic thinking and/or writing process and examined how it works. Now we are concerned with the practical application of these strategies in ordinary writing situations, not in isolated exercises. We'll begin by looking at common college writing assignments: essay exams, general essays, summaries, and reviews. Research papers vary widely in approach and format. The handbook or research paper guide specified by your instructor will provide a full discussion. We have already given you the *process* for doing research in the chapter on persuasion, where we discussed gathering *evidence* and *examples* (pp. 152–155).

Essay Exams

In most situations that require writing, we must draw on several of the strategies simultaneously. A typical college writing task, for example, is an essay exam. On an essay exam in history there might be a question such as: "Discuss the three major causes of the Civil War." Writing a superior response could require application of many of the strategies we've been working with:

1. Causal analysis
2. Classification (grouping various causes into three classes: economic, political, social)
3. Division (breaking these classes down into subgroups)
4. Comparison (weighing one set of causes against another to suggest the relative importance of, say, political versus economic causes)
5. Definition (of certain key terms involved)
6. Persuasion (trying to convince the instructor that of the three, economic causes were the most important)

The key to successful answers on essay exams in any field is knowing the basic strategies called for. Pay attention to what you are asked, because most essay questions specify the use of one or more of the basic strategies you have been studying:

1. *Compare* and *contrast* the characters of Othello and Macbeth.
2. *Analyze* Douglas McGregor's approach to management known as "Theory Y"; point out significant *contrasts* with management "Theory X."
3. *Define* at length the term "ergastoplasm."

In each case, you would draw upon your understanding of the strategy named and upon your skill in writing in this mode. In answering a comparison question, for example, you would be careful to establish standards of comparison, to select only significant points, to emphasize either likeness or difference, and to organize either in a whole-by-whole or point-by-point structure. To define fully, you would place the term in a class, note essential characteristics or functions that separate it from other members of the class, use positive and negative examples, and find something to compare it with. In short, conscious application of the elements learned about each strategy in Part II gives you a structured way of responding to essay questions.

EXERCISE

Review the last set of exams you took and list all the essay questions.

1. For each essay question, identify the basic thinking and/or writing strategy called for; note also those strategies not named but that might have been useful in responding.
2. Under each strategy on your list, note the elements you recall from the Part II discussion of that strategy. Check back to Part II and add what you may have overlooked.

General Essays

General essays, those short papers assigned in many humanities, social science, and business classes, frequently use one main strategy as the basic approach to understanding and explaining the subject. Five-hundred word "themes," no matter how long they seem when assigned, actually leave little room for in-depth treatment of a subject. Selecting one basic strategy such as comparison, functional analysis, or the like, can help you focus your attention, sort through material generated by the exploring techniques presented in Chapter 2, and organize the final essay. As in essay exams, however, you will probably be drawing upon and integrating several of the strategies even though you may be concentrating on one. In most cases, it's best to explore the subject first and then let the material you've gathered indicate which strategy or strategies would be most appropriate for developing and organizing your ideas. If you're writing about education, for example, and your free association list contains the names of many different schools, you might begin by trying to group or *classify* them. Having set up two or three categories, you might notice some strong points of comparison or contrast between or among them, and begin to develop your approach along those lines. Free writing about your job, however, you might mention many of the different things you do while at work and then analyze the job's components. Or you might start by describing a piece of complex equipment and wind up doing a functional analysis of it or comparing it to the machine it replaced. Let the material you generate suggest an appropriate strategy, then work at further development and organization by using all that you have learned about the application of that strategy.

Many general essay assignments are "thesis" papers; that is, you are asked to state your opinion (or thesis) and defend it in some detail. In writing a thesis paper, go back to Chapter 9 on persuasion. Apply what you learned about using evidence and example to support a judgment (a well-grounded opinion). Think about the teacher as your audience and what you learned about logical, emotional, and personal appeals. Every teacher has heard the complaint that goes like this: "The teacher says you can write your own opinion, but if you do and you disagree with what was said in class then you get a bad grade." Often, however, not what the student wrote but how it was presented caused the problem.

Say the English teacher has spent two class periods going over William Faulkner's story "The Bear," explaining why she thinks it is the greatest piece of twentieth-century American fiction. You are now supposed to write an essay on this story and have been told to write what you really think about it. You don't like Faulkner's story, and you begin your essay by attacking it, using heavily judgmental words such as "dumb," "stupid," and "confusing." You're relying on an emotional attack rather than a logical appeal and the image you're creating, your "voice," is certainly not taking the audience into account. If you want to persuade the teacher to consider your negative opinion, then you need to draw on what you learned about writing persuasively to an *involved* audience. Using the logical and personal appeals, you could make a case that while critics may find the story excellent, the language, setting, and events of this hunting story are foreign to a contemporary urban reader such as yourself and make it very difficult for you to identify with or care about it. A well-written essay could make your honest opinion known without antagonizing the teacher. It might even persuade the teacher to rethink her approach to teaching this story—not to abandon her opinion, but to find ways of overcoming the problems the story presents for students like yourself.

EXERCISE

Dig out any old papers you may still have from past classes. Reread them and make notes on how conscious application of the thinking and/or writing strategies covered in Part II could be used to improve each paper.

Writing About What You Read

Summaries

Along with essay questions and general essays, summaries are one of the most common writing assignments in college. A summary is often called by other names, such as "abstract," "precis," or "synopsis." Each teacher may mean something slightly different by any one of these terms, so be sure to ask the teacher to explain precisely what he or she wants.

Day in and day out you summarize easily and naturally—you tell a friend about a television show, report a conversation to him, or explain what happened in class on the day he was absent. In most of your courses, you use this same ability to summarize when you take notes on a lecture or on material you read. Summaries often form part of longer compositions, such as essay answers to test questions, book reviews, and research papers. The summarizing section of a paper states, fairly and objectively, the ideas of the original authors.

Whenever you write a good summary, you do three things:

1. Write a shortened version.
2. Write a version that states the thesis, the major supporting ideas, and the conclusions of the author.
3. Write an objective version, omitting your own ideas and evaluations.

A summary is a condensed report of the original material—speech, essay, short story, poem, book, or article. Summaries range in length from a single sentence to several paragraphs. But whatever their length, summaries give the main ideas of the original, omitting details, examples, dialogue, and long quotations. Longer summaries include enough information to indicate how the main points are supported but should never include so many details that the essential argument becomes obscured. Summaries are usually much shorter than the original—25% or 10% of the length of the original if it's an article, or considerably less if the original is a book. As a general rule, the summary of even the longest book should not be more than 400 to 500 words. It may be as short as 25 to 50 words.

A summary may also be called a "precis," a "synopsis," or an "informative abstract." However, a summary is *not* a *response*, a *paraphrase*, or a *descriptive abstract*.

A *response* may include the reader's personal, subjective reaction to the original. ("I agree with X because . . ." or "X fails to say that. . . .")

A *paraphrase* substitutes the writer's own words for those of the original author but does not necessarily reduce the length of the original. A paraphrase is often written to clarify or simplify.

> *Example:* Take an aggressively penetrating approach to the communicative dimensions of the interface between institutions of medicine.
>
> *Paraphrase:* The author says that we should investigate very thoroughly the ways in which medical institutions communicate with each other."

A *descriptive abstract* (or topical abstract) describes what information is contained in the original without stating the conclusions or the supporting evidence. It tells what the subject is but not what's said about it. A descriptive abstract may be useful to you if you are forming an annotated bibliography for a research paper; however, since it states only what information is available, it cannot substitute for a summary.

> *Example:* This article explores selected economic factors in the South during the period 1830–1860 as possible causes for the Civil War.

A *summary* would tell what those factors are and what the author says about them in the original article.

Steps in Writing a Summary

The following steps should help you write a clear summary:

1. Assume that your audience has *not* read the original; your job is to inform them what's in it.
2. Read the entire article or book you are to summarize.
3. Go back over it and decide where it breaks into sections. (Many times this is done for you by chapter titles and headings.)
4. Pick out the main point in each section.
5. Note those main points in order and any *essential* details or examples needed to make them clear.
6. Note the beginning and any conclusions stated or implied at the end. You now have an *outline* of the book or article.

7. Write your summary from these notes, following the original organization you have captured in your outline.

Write briefly, accurately, and objectively. Also consider the following suggestions:

1. Use transitions
   A. Use appropriate transitional expressions to indicate progression of major ideas ("first," "second," also, "finally"). Avoid "firstly," "secondly," "first of all," or "last of all."
   B. Do not overuse "And then . . ." or "Next."
2. Use brief quotations
   A. Use several brief quotations (preferably less than a sentence) to convey the style or flavor of the original, to repeat particularly effective words, and to define the author's terms.
   B. Do *not* quote excessively. Remember that most of the wording should be your own.
   C. Try to blend quotations smoothly into your own sentences, avoiding awkward constructions.
3. Explain all terms, abbreviations, and proper names, so that the reader can understand your summary without referring to the original piece of writing.
4. Reflect the tone of the original to avoid slanting your summary.
   A. Use slang or humor only if it appears in the original.
   B. Be serious if you summarize a serious piece of writing.
5. Carefully proportion your summary to convey the author's idea of the relative importance of each section.
   A. Whenever possible, you should devote the same percentage of your summary to a particular idea that the original author devotes to the development of that idea.
   B. Where lengthy anecdotes, examples, or case histories appear in the original, this proportioning becomes impossible.

To edit and revise your summary, do the following:

   1. Omit all needless prefaces, such as "The author says that. . . ."

2. Be sure that you have followed the organization of the original.
3. Be sure that you have included any recommendations or conclusions that the author presents at the beginning or at the end of an article.
4. Be sure that you have not carelessly included any statement of your own opinion or reaction to the item you are summarizing.
5. Be sure that you have properly identified the original (by author and title) either in the first sentence or in a heading—or in both places.

Often you may be required to write a summary far shorter than 10 percent of the original. A one-paragraph summary of a full book, for example, is a common beginning for a book review. No matter how short the summary, the process is essentially the same. Your summary statements simply become broader and more general. A very brief summary of the industrial robot article that follows might read: "Labor unions are not yet complaining about industrial robots, but experts predict problems when the computerized machines begin to replace assembly-line workers."

Sample Summaries

Here, followed by summaries, are two news articles:

INDUSTRIAL ROBOTS SEEM READY TO ROLL

Industry, on the whole, says never fear. No jobs will be lost. Robots will be good for you.

Labor, the organized kind, so far has taken the first robot beachheads in industrial plants calmly.

About the only ripple in that calm came earlier this year when some workers were reported to have speculated that the closing of Ford Motor Co.'s big Rahway, N.J. plant was actually a scheme to automate it more fully before reopening it at a time when the auto market had improved.

But the union most affected, the United Auto Workers, has pretty much accepted the use of robots in automotive plants. Other unions affected, and there are few so far, have followed suit. But in all cases, with provisos. Any workers replaced must be retrained or reassigned.

"What Charlie McCarthys (as autoworkers have dubbed robots) do in the skilled trades," said Dick Martin, co-director of the UAW's skilled trades department, "is they increase our work force—electrical work, installation, computer operation, that's your skilled trades worker."

"We really end up putting more people into skilled trades to maintain these robots."

"Normally," Martin went on, "people think it's just a piece of equipment that sits there and does the work. But it creates lots of work for the maintenance trades. As automation increases, the skilled trades work force increases."

In fact, robots have so far had little or no effect on the size of the work force. There are only 3,000 of these mechanical arms in use in U.S. production plants. And such robots have been around for 20 years.

But now their numbers appear destined to grow more rapidly. The advent of microprocessors—and, as a result, brainier computer systems tied to newly developed robots that can see and feel—is moving them from limited and specialized production work to true assembly line status.

"Assembly 'robotics' is just emerging," said Dr. Jules Mirabel, who heads what amounts to an in-house automation consulting firm set up by General Electric Co.

"It is a much larger opportunity for industry than the present applications of industrial robots. Assembly is the second largest activity we have and the second largest cost behind the finished product."

"The biggest use of robots, ultimately," observed Dennis Wysnoski, who heads the Air Force-aerospace industry's ICAM project, aimed at eventual development of the automated factory, "will be in assembly, where we have far too labor-intensive operations which limit our ability to change, to respond to surge."

Rather than replacing a relatively few workers from work they didn't want to do in the first place—welding, painting, feeding curing furnaces—robots are expected soon to have a larger role on the production line. But the pace at which the change takes place is likely to be slow, since total U.S. production of robots is now only about 100 a month.

"So long as the replacement (of workers) hasn't exceeded natural attrition," said Gordon Richardson, author of a report evaluating the advent of robots for the financial consulting firm of Arthur D. Little Inc., "robots haven't been resisted by labor. When that is going to change, I don't know."

Other authorities interviewed are equally uncertain. But most feel that the change, in view of organized labor's strength and other factors, will be more evolution than revolution.

In the long run, George Sutton of the Machine Tool Task Force, Lawrence Livermore Laboratories in California, predicted, "On balance, there will be a fewer number of heads, but they will be more professional." (UPI, *Richmond Times-Dispatch*)

SUMMARY A (25 percent of the length of the original article)

The UPI article, "Industrial Robots Seem Ready to Roll," (*Richmond Times-Dispatch*), states that at present both industry and labor accept the advent of industrial robots. The United Auto Workers, for example, agrees to their use as long as replaced workers are "retrained or reassigned." Dick Martin, UAW spokesman, says that "Charlie McCarthys" (the auto workers' name for robots) actually create "lots of work for the maintenance trades." Relatively few robots are in use, but computerization has now made it possible for robots to do actual assembly-line work. Dr. Jules Mirabel, from G.E., and Dennis Wysnoski, an Air Force expert, both point to the growth potential for industrial robots once they take over labor-intensive assembly work. But if the pace of replacing workers begins to exceed natural attrition, labor may begin to resist. Several authorities agree that labor's strength means the changeover "will be more evolution than revolution." In the long run, however, one expert sees the result as fewer, but more professional, workers.

SUMMARY B (10 percent of the length of the original article)

According to the UPI article, "Industrial Robots Seem Ready to Roll," (*Richmond Times-Dispatch*, November 9, 1980), labor unions are not currently objecting to industry's use of robots as long as replaced workers are taken care of. But several experts agree that the use of robots in labor-intensive assembly work may increase rapidly thanks to recent developments in computerization. If too many workers get replaced, organized labor may start to resist and slow the pace of automation. A long-term result may be fewer but more professional workers.

FOREIGNERS RAP U.S. CAMPAIGNS

WASHINGTON (UPI)—Three Europeans studying the U.S. way of life sound like Americans when they criticize the presidential campaign. They say it lasts too long, emphasizes personalities and costs too much.

They say money largely determines who will run and succeed, television advertisements simplify issues and nominating conventions are virtually meaningless, although everybody has a good time.

Ulrich Andersch of West Germany, Marion Creely of Ireland and Niksa Gligo of Yugoslavia are among 2,400 foreigners who come to the United States each year to study its institutions and way of life.

They are taking part in a competitive selection program, sponsored by the International Communication Agency, a federal bureau that attracts prominent foreigners in such fields as government, science and education.

In studying the United States, they found its presidential campaign flawed.

Andersch, a professor of political science at the University of Goettingen, said the long primary season eliminates the need for a convention.

"The conventions look like a carnival in Germany," he said. "It is a media thing. It is a circus, it is redundant."

Miss Creely, music director of the Arts Council in Dublin, said television dominates the campaigns at the expense of the issues.

"People getting information from television rather than from papers don't get much detail." she said. "It is so dominant. Perhaps for this reason, issues have not developed into greater consideration because the television medium fosters quick answers, short answers, rather than more in-depth analysis from written media."

Gligo, director of the music program at the Student Center in Zagreb, Yugoslavia, said the primaries and the candidates' access to television have fundamentally changed the nature of U.S. political parties.

"Media Campaign"

"It is a media campaign," he said. "It is their judgements you hear. The parties are not politically efficient."

All found the voter turnout low.

"In Germany, in our last election, 88 percent voted," Andersch said, "Reagan has been elected by barely a quarter of the total eligible population. That is not a very convincing election."

The length of the campaign "is very inefficient," he said. "I don't think it selects the best candidates, but the candidates that can survive that process, who have enough money to go for it and have enough time."

"You market a personality," Miss Creely said. "Television is not made to mediate any issues."

"There's a very nasty joke going around," she added. "It says: 'If God had intended for the Americans to have presidents, he would have given them candidates.' " (UPI, *Richmond Times-Dispatch*)

SUMMARY A (25 percent of the length of the original article)

A UPI story in the *Richmond Times-Dispatch* reports that the American presidential campaign has been criticized by three prominent Europeans studying in the U.S. as part of a program sponsored by the International Communication Agency. Ulrich Andersch, a German professor, criticized the nominating conventions, while Marion Creely, director of the Arts Council in Dublin, Ireland, attacked television's superficial coverage of the issues. Niksa Gligo, a music program director from Yugoslavia, complained of television's effect on U.S. political parties. All three criticized the low voter turnout in this country. Andersch added that the candidates who have the most money and time, not the best candidates, survive our lengthy campaign. Creely concluded that the American presidential campaign has become the subject of nasty jokes among Europeans.

SUMMARY B (10 percent of the length of the original article)

A UPI story in the *Richmond Times-Dispatch* reports that three prominent Europeans studying in the U.S. attacked the American presidential campaign for its length, superficiality, and cost. All three criticized the role of TV and low voter turnout. One suggested that Europeans view the campaign as a joke.

EXERCISE

Here is an editorial on the glut of physicians projected for the end of the century.

1. Write a summary approximately 25 percent of it in length.
2. Write a second summary approximately 10 percent of the original article in length. Work from your first summary in writing the second one—it's much easier than trying to work from the original.
3. Write a one-sentence summary.

A person who has to wait a long time for a doctor's appointment may find it hard to believe that the nation is on the verge of having a surplus of doctors. But the Graduate Medical Education National Advisory Committee says there are about enough physicians now in many medical fields and there will be an overall surplus of 70,000 by 1990.

The impending surplus is resulting largely from the federal government's program of providing financial aid to medical schools to help them maintain or increase enrollments. The program was launched at a time when there were, indeed, too few doctors, and it has served a useful purpose in helping to alleviate the shortage.

The forthcoming surplus will be in 15 fields such as cardiology, neurosurgery, general surgery, obstetrics-gynecology and opthalmology, according to the study report. But a continuing shortage is forecast in several fields, including child psychiatry, general psychiatry, preventive medicine and emergency medicine. It is a sad omen that the committee predicts a particularly acute need for psychiatrists for children, with only 4,100 estimated as being in practice in 1990 as against a need of 9,000.

The committee said the 375,000 physicians in the nation in 1978 were 44,000 fewer than were needed. Even today, according to the report, there is a slight shortage overall, but the large numbers of medical students now being trained will soon produce a surplus. By 1990, the nation will need an estimated 466,000 doctors, while there will actually be 536,000 in practice.

At first thought, the public might welcome a situation in which there not only were enough doctors but even too many; it would be good, one might conclude, to have medical care easily and quickly available. But the committee that studied the problem warns that an excess of physicians will be reflected in an increase in the nation's total health care cost bill. A committee spokesman explained that more doctors will be doing more things to more people, and this excessive medical service may not make any contribution toward improved health. It's somewhat the same principle as that involved in excessive hospital beds: There is a tendency to fill up available beds with patients who could be treated at home and to keep patients in those beds longer than is medically necessary.

One heartening aspect of the predicted surplus is that it means the federal government can reduce its grants for the education of medical students. Already, Congress has cut "capitation" grants, as they are called, from a high of $2,000 per student in 1972 to the current $639.

Unfortunately, the fact that the doctor shortage is being alleviated, statistically, still leaves one problem: the distribution of doctors. Today, they tend, understandably, to settle in urban areas where practice is easier and income higher, thus leaving some rural areas without adequate medical care. Presumably, when the field becomes more crowded, more doctors will be inclined to put up their shingles in the hinterlands that they now avoid. *(Richmond Times-Dispatch)*

Critical Reviews

By whatever name—"critical review," "critical analysis," "book review"—many college courses require that you read something and write an evaluation of what you have read. Students are often assigned this task by instructors in many disciplines and are often frustrated in their efforts to understand exactly what it is their instructors expect. The greatest problem comes from confusing a *summary* with an *evaluation*. When assigned a critical review, students tend to summarize the book or article, reserving evaluation for a final line that asserts an unsupported, general opinion; for example: "Overall I agree with the author and find this an interesting book that is well written and informative." A critical review does include both summary and evaluation, but most students get the proportion all wrong; instead of one-tenth summary and nine-tenths evaluation, they write just the opposite. How many times have you written a review that provided a detailed summary but an unsupported, generalized evaluation? By consciously drawing on what you have learned about writing in the section on strategies, you can learn to examine the same elements in someone else's written work. You will know what to look for to build a detailed, well-supported evaluation.

Make clear the distinction between summary and evaluation by separating them. Begin with a one-paragraph summary of the book or article, no matter how long it is. From then on, you are not allowed simply to repeat what's *in* the book; you must make judgments *about* the book. When you do tell something that's in the book, it should be as specific support for some general statement you have made *about* the work.

Evaluation means judgment—that is, an opinion that is well-supported. In writing a critical review, you will evaluate (form a judgment about) the following:

1. The author's *thesis* (What is the central opinion presented?)
2. The author's *purpose* (Why was the book or article written? What is its intended effect?)
3. The author's *effectiveness* (How well is the thesis presented? How well is the purpose carried out?)
4. The *usefulness for what audience* of the work (Who would benefit from reading this? In what way?)

5. A *comparison* with other works on the subject (How well does it measure up?)

Thesis

To judge anything else about a book or article, you must first know *what* it says—what is the main idea, the central opinion that the author develops? You may have to read the whole piece once or twice before you can decide what the central point is. You can get help in many books by reading the preface or introduction in which the author may openly state his or her thesis. If you read a work twice and still do not know for sure what its thesis is, this is a point well worth making in your critical review—either the work is much too difficult for a reader at your level in this subject, or the author is much too obscure and fails to make the controlling idea of the whole work clear. Write out your judgment of the author's thesis in a single sentence, then list your reasons for judging this statement to be the author's thesis.

Purpose

In Chapter 1 (pp. 10–11), we discussed the purposes found in most writing: *to express, to inform, to explain, to persuade.* Most of the writing you will be asked to review will not have as its primary purpose the intent to express the author's feelings and little else. Usually, books and articles selected for review in different subject areas will combine the purpose of informing, explaining, and persuading. It's helpful to figure out what the *primary* purpose seems to be, so that you can evaluate how well or ill the author achieves it. News stories, for example, intend primarily to inform. Textbooks, instructions, and the like intend to inform and explain. Editorials and other such writing intend mainly to persuade. Most writing combines all three purposes and by far the majority of works intend to persuade their readers to accept the author's opinion. Even very "objective" scientific papers are examples of the logical appeal, intended to persuade using evidence. Write out your judgment of the author's primary purpose; note also any clear secondary purpose. List your reasons for this judgment.

Effectiveness

You must decide what the *thesis* and *purpose* are for a book or article before you can judge how effectively the author has carried them out. Now to judge effectiveness, consider the following elements:

the quality of ideas
the support for ideas
clarity of organization
appropriate voice
general strengths and weaknesses

Quality of ideas. What are the main ideas used to support the thesis? When you did your summary, what main idea did you find for each section? Now take a close, thoughtful look at this list of ideas. Do you know enough about the subject to judge the quality of the ideas here? You may not be an expert on the subject and still be able to make some judgments. Are the ideas exciting to you? Do they open up new ways of thinking about the subject? Or are the ideas here very common, ones you've run into before? Jot down your honest reaction to be main ideas and note any reasons you have for these reactions.

Support for ideas. Remember our discussion of support for your opinion in persuading an audience. Look at the book or article you are reviewing to judge how well the author uses the two forms of support: *evidence* (pp. 152–154) and *example* (pp. 155–156). Use the following checklists to judge each kind of support:

1. Evidence

    A. Kind (Facts or expert opinion? Type of facts? Review pp. 152–154)

    B. Amount (How many facts? How many expert opinions? Is there enough evidence for each main idea to be convincing? Are some ideas better supported than others? Which ones? What's the ratio of facts to expert opinions?)

    C. Quality (How solid are the facts? What is the source? If statistics are used, where did they come from? Might their source be biased in any way? Who are the experts? What are their credentials?)

2. Examples

    A. Kind (Are they general examples or detailed, specific ones?)

    B. Number (How many examples are used in support of an idea? Are they used in addition to forms of evidence or used alone? Are there enough examples to be persuasive? Are some points better developed by examples than others? Which ones?)

C. Quality (Do the examples seem to be reasonable? To be fairly typical? Are the examples heavily emotional ones?)

If you make notes on anything you find in a book or article related to the support for the main ideas, you should have plenty of material to make up the center of your evaluation; that is, you should have plenty of specific material to cite in support of your own general ideas, the main points you are making in your review. Your notes will allow you to refer to details and parts of the work as *examples* of what you mean in the general comments you are making.

Clarity of organization. Look at the outline you made in doing your summary of the book or article. What is the basic organizational pattern? Does it follow one of the strategies from Part II such as comparison or classification? Or is it a basic pattern of development from Chapter 2 such as general question/specific response, general assertion/specific support, or topic/illustration (pp. 31–34)? What about the internal order for details: are they organized by time, space, least to most important (pp. 35–44)? How effectively does the author use the organization to support the purpose? For example, if the purpose is to persuade and two items are being compared, does the author put the preferred one last? In short, apply what you have learned about organization to judge the organization of the piece being reviewed.

Appropriate voice. How do you judge the author's "voice"? Is it distant and formal, or involved and informal (pp. 11–13)? What details of the style—sentence structure, word choice, use of personal pronouns, and the like—can you cite to support your judgment? Considering the subject, purpose, and probable audience, is the voice appropriate? Why or why not? Does the voice create a pleasing image of the author, one that will have a strong personal appeal for the reader?

General strengths and weaknesses. After considering all the above elements, try to assess the overall impact of the piece. How thorough is the coverage? Is anything significant overlooked? Is there considerable new information here? Are there inaccuracies, facts the author got wrong? What appeals are used—logical, emotional, personal—and how effectively? Is there a good blend? Try to sum up your evaluation at this point.

Usefulness to a Specific Audience

Given your evaluation of everything so far, who would most benefit from reading this book or article? Remember that a work may not be useful to you—either because it is too elementary or too advanced for your level—but it may be very useful to a different audience. Don't judge something negatively just because it doesn't fit your needs—it may be an excellent piece for some other audience.

Comparative Evaluation with Other Works

How does this book or article stand up when compared with others in the field? If you have not yet read anything else on the subject, you cannot of course make a comparative judgment. But if you have knowledge of other works, it is important to your reader that you place the work being reviewed in relation to those others. Is this one the work someone should read first? Or last? Is it good on one aspect of the subject, better than other works available on that point? Is it weaker than other available works on certain points? How would you rank it among the works you have read on this subject? Why?

Obviously, going through and making notes on each of the elements above will provide you with much material, much more than you probably can use in a limited review. But you should no longer be faced with the problem of too much summary and not enough supported evaluation! Actually, many articles or books will not be open to analysis on each of the above points, but consider each one as you go through a review piece and see what you can come up with. Having generated a lot of evaluation material, you may very well find yourself focusing the final review on one or two of your points, and ignoring much of the rest. But doing this will still mean you are writing a well-supported analysis, not a lengthy summary with a general evaluation statement tacked on at the end.

Here is a sample student critical review written by following the guidelines presented above. Notice that the summary is completed in the first paragraph.

YOUR FUTURE IN ACCOUNTING CAREERS

by Lawrence Rosenthal
Reviewed by Kristina Kendall

Rosenthal begins his discussion of accounting careers by observing that all businesses revolve around accounting, which is an analytical history of a business's growth and decline. He briefly discusses some types of accounting jobs by separating them into three major groups: public, private, and government. In giving the reader a concise introduction to the accounting field, the author lists some advantages of being an accountant, gives his view of what an accountant's life is like, and discusses how technology has influenced accounting jobs. He also mentions separately the job of the Certified Public Accountant, the highest of accounting occupations. He suggests some ways that the interested student can begin to prepare for an accounting career, and directs the reader by including lists of terms and definitions, accounting schools, and accounting associations. The book ends with the Code of Professional Ethics as composed by the American Institute of Certified Public Accountants.

Rosenthal's main objective seems to be to introduce the reader to some general facts about accounting. These facts and descriptions compose the major part of the book.

The writer presents ideas which are so simple and standard that they could only have been aimed at an audience of very young people. Rosenthal frequently repeats the same elementary subject matter at several different points throughout the text. The author does, however, make occasional use of examples and fictional characters to demonstrate his ideas. For instance, Rosenthal tells of a small boy who, "while playing in his room at home, was trying to explain to a young friend what his father, an accountant, did at work. He headed for the dresser drawer and, upon opening it, pulled out a bunch of socks all folded neatly together—except for a stray fuzzy yellow sock. 'See?' he exclaimed. 'A deficit. My Dad makes sure that all his company's socks match!'" These little stories tend to be on the corny side, but they do get the general point across.

Though the ideas presented aren't new or unusual, they do seem credible. The book doesn't contain lots of specific details, but it does give a pretty thorough general coverage of the main points. The bulk of the material in the book is organized into chapters which each pertain to a small sub-heading under the general topic of accounting careers. These chapters, though, do not seem to be arranged with any set format in mind.

Rosenthal's style is one of informal chat. To achieve this style, he makes deliberate use of small, simple words and sentence fragments, which he overdoes until he comes across with a very "parent to child," patronizing kind of tone. Occasionally, though, he gets away from his condescending style in some of his explanations of titles and definitions of terms.

For a very young student who is just beginning to explore career possibilities, *Your Future in Accounting Careers* may contain somewhat valuable information. This audience would probably require some general facts and definitions of the accounting profession which read quickly and easily, rather than an elaborate discussion of occupations in the accounting field. For my purposes, however, this book was not very useful, since I already had a basic knowledge of the things discussed. For me, *Your Future in Accounting Careers* would not be as helpful or valuable as an indepth study of each type of job available in the accounting field and what each job entails.

EXERCISE

Reread the preceding sample.

1. Check it against the summary outline that follows, and identify as many of the points evaluated in the sample review as you can.

2. Note where the writer has stated the thesis and purpose, evaluated the support, judged the voice, and so on, of the original.

SUMMARY

1. Essay questions are best answered by focusing on the specific thinking/writing strategy named or implied in the question.

2. Short general essays often lend themselves to development by one dominant thinking/writing strategy. Explore the subject first and then let your material guide your choice of an appropriate strategy.

3. The key to a good summary is to *outline* the main points in the work. Stick to that outline in summarizing; add as much or as little detail as you need to satisfy your purpose.

4. In outline form, here is a summary of what you should focus on in preparing a *critical review*:

   I. Brief Summary
   II. Evaluation
      A. Author's Thesis
      B. Author's Purpose
      C. Author's Effectiveness
         1. Quality of Ideas
         2. Support of Ideas
            a. Evidence
            b. Example
         3. Clear Organization
         4. Appropriate Voice
         5. General Strengths and Weaknesses
      D. Usefulness to What Audience
      E. Comparative Evaluation

WRITING ASSIGNMENTS

1. Select a topic related to your job or to your major field of study. Explore it with the techniques from Chapter 2. Examine the material generated to discover what basic thinking and/or writing strategy from Part II would help you develop and organize your ideas. Use this strategy to develop more material about the subject and to provide a basic structure for a short essay (300 to 500 words) intended to explain it to your teacher.

2. Rework the essay you wrote for #1 above. This time make a judgment on the subject and try to persuade the same teacher to accept your thesis. Pay careful attention to the kinds of changes you make when shifting from explaining to persuading.

3. Ask an instructor in your major field to recommend an important book or article. Write two summaries of this work, one about twice as long as the other. Then write a one-line summary of the work.

4. Beginning with a one-paragraph summary, write a 500-word critical review of the article or book used in #3. Explore all possible points for evaluation first, then focus your review to fit the 500-word limit.

11

FINDING a JOB

Understanding the Job Search

Finding a job will be one practical application of the skills you have been developing. The strategies for looking at the world and organizing your thoughts discussed so far are basic to success in the game of job hunting. A good way to keep your sanity during the process is, in fact, to think of it as a game—one with high stakes but still a challenge to be enjoyed.

Needing a job and not having one presents a problem. How do you go about solving it? You could eliminate the need. Explore this possibility for a while, but if you can't come up with a way to survive without a job, then it's time to focus on the other possibility—filling the need. Remember, however, that you are not the only one with a need. An employer out there needs someone to fill a job opening, and when you accept a position you are answering an employer's need as surely as he or she is answering yours. Finding a job is not, then, a one-sided effort in which you go looking for someone to do you a favor; rather, it is an arrangement for satisfying mutual needs.

The existence of needs on both sides suggests the broad strategies used to meet them. First, employers can advertise their needs and wait for applications; second, you could advertise your need and wait for an employer to respond; or, finally, a third party can bring the two of you together. A comprehensive job search includes all three approaches, and each will challenge your writing and reasoning skills. But before examining each approach in greater detail, let's start with a general look at the job market.

The Job Market

Excluding self-employment, which we will not be discussing here, the remaining sources of employment fall into two huge classes—the government and the private sector. Government employment provides service for society, from military protection of the nation on the federal level to police protection of citizens on the local level, or, for another example, from planning a national health insurance program to working in a community health center. The private sector focuses on the production and sale of goods or commercial services and ranges from international corporations such as AT&T or Exxon to the neighborhood grocery store in your hometown. Private enterprise has been gradually expanding into the traditionally governmental area of social services—especially in child care, health care, education, even police protection, and trash collection. Generally speaking, if your program of study develops production or sales skills, your probable target will be the private sector; but if you are training to provide some service, you may be aiming at either private or government employment. In either case, the process of hunting for a job will be about the same.

For those of you who have not yet selected a specific program leading to a clearly defined type of work, finding a job offers the most difficult challenge, but that makes the hunt all the more exciting. A definite career choice eliminates all the other possibilities, at least for the present; but if you have not yet chosen a career, the world is wide open. Your first step will be to narrow down the possibilities. How do you do that? Well, what do you most enjoy doing? Ask your family and friends what it is that you seem to do best. You may discover an ability so basic to you that you ordinarily never think about it—tinkering with stereo equipment, caring for animals, keeping the family books, making other people laugh. Whatever natural talent you have, there is probably some employment opportunity in line with it. Perhaps you've just never considered making a living that way—it just seemed too *easy*. With a little investigation, however, you may find that what seems easy to you may seem difficult enough to someone else that they are willing to pay to have it done for them. We may find it easy to do our own typing, but pay someone else to fix our car; we may take care of our own car, but pay to have our house painted; we may enjoy painting, but pay a veterinarian to care for our sick dog. Don't minimize and dismiss the abilities you have; learn to profit from them instead.

But many of you will have already made some choices—will have enrolled in a liberal arts curriculum, or in a tehnical one, in the fine arts or the applied sciences. To find a job in whatever broad field you have chosen, your first step will be to learn all you can about the opportunities in it. What branches or specialties are there? Which ones interest you most? Where are the current job openings? Can you match your interests to the special areas that seem to hold the most promise for future employment? The time to think about these questions is now, at the beginning of your college career, not a few weeks or months before you start looking for that first job.

Journals

Get in the habit of reading the professional or trade journals in your field. Every type of work has magazines devoted to it, many published by a membership organization such as those for nurses, engineers, and farmers. The names of these trade, technical, and professional journals fill 138 pages in the most recent edition of *Writer's Digest*. They range from the *Journal of the American Medical Association* to *The American Painting Contractor, Fence Industry,* and *Dairy Herd Management.* Find those journals oriented to your field and read them. Faithfully. If your college library does not carry the journals you want, go to instructors in your department and ask if they subscribe to these periodicals. As long as you return the copies promptly, most instructors will be pleased to lend their journals to an interested student.

These journals often carry lists of job openings in the field. Two other benefits result from studying the basic periodicals in your field. First, you will gather a great store of information, as well as a "feel" for what's going on. This will help you when you arrive at the interviewing stage of a job search. Second, you can spot trends and developments that may help you decide what special area to pursue. Within a year or so you may see that jobs cluster in one or two specialties. If there is an ongoing demand for geriatric nurses, or intensive-care nurses, for example, you might consider one of these specialties instead of pediatric nursing, where you notice that job openings seem few and far between. Moreover, by the time you are ready to start applying for jobs in earnest, you will have studied hundreds of ads and developed your ability to analyze them.

EXERCISES

1. Talk with a counselor at your school's placement service, or with an instructor in your major field. Make up a list of possible job opportun-

ities for someone with your experience, training, and interests. Try to divide the list into private- and public-sector jobs.

2. Do some research. If at all possible, talk with someone actually working at the jobs of most interest to you. Carefully read the job ads in the trade or professional journals in these areas. Make notes on the ads that are of most interest to you.

Steps In the Job Search

This discussion of ads in trade journals brings us back to the first way in which jobs are filled—employers advertising their needs. Much of this advertising is done by word of mouth, so keeping in contact with working friends, instructors, and others who may hear about current job openings is important. But much advertising for jobs is done in local newspapers under "Employment Opportunities" in the classified ads, and for most professional or paraprofessional jobs, ads are placed in the trade journals. These ads usually specify the skills sought and list what the employer is willing to offer. Here is a typical ad that might appear in *Advertising Age* (the trade journal in advertising):

> Experienced copywriter. Some background in layout or accounts desirable. Looking for an innovative, nontraditional person who can meet the challenges of a rapidly growing agency. Full benefits, paid vacation after one year. Salary negotiable. Write Jason Billings. Billings, Drexel, and Smith, Inc. 341 Indiana Ave., N.W., Washington, D.C. 20202.

Having previously examined many ads, you can judge the appropriateness of qualifications, duties, pay, and benefits. You will know if important considerations have been omitted from the ad and can bring them up in your letter of application. Most importantly, you can tailor your letter to the needs implied as well as to those stated openly. This letter of application, or *cover letter*, makes your initial impression on a prospective employer and should utilize all your skill in organization, development, and attention to audience. In fact, in the process of responding to an employer's ad, four of the five basic steps involve the use of your writing skills. Let's take a look at these five steps:

> résumé,
> cover letter,
> interview appointment letter,
> interview,
> follow-up letter.

The Résumé (sometimes called a *vita*)

The résumé is a written summary of your experience and accomplishments to date. It provides the basic information on which employers will judge whether you meet their specific needs. Your résumé is important. The six rules listed below are an efficient summary of the key points:

Composing the first draft can be a dispiriting moment of truth. There you are, all the accomplishments in your life reduced to one page. Would you hire you? Maybe not, but take heart.

A résumé is nothing less than an advertisement for yourself. And as in any commercial, it makes sense to play up the good and play down, or leave out, the bad. Often it's the way you phrase things that makes the difference. Ask any advertising copywriter which is better, "Was made foreman in June, 1975," or "Promoted to foreman in less than six months."

As to the form of your résumé, there are no firm rules. Any number of guidebooks can fill you in on the details. But there are some invariables you should bear in mind:

1. *Make it flawless.* Type it without a single typo, strikeover, or spelling error. Reproduce it by offset, not on an office copier. Offset reproduction costs only a few dollars a hundred.
2. *Keep it brief, two pages at most, and leave out the pronoun "I."* Instead of, "I handled all of the company's dealings with members of the press," write, "Responsible for contacts with the press."
3. *Use action verbs wherever possible and polish the truth* a little. Instead of saying, "Was assigned to production and shipping departments," say, "Coordinated functions of production and shipping department."
4. *List your accomplishments as well as your duties.* And use numbers if they make a particularly good point, such as: "Reduced waste in department by 70 percent," "Tripled yearly billings," "In charge of accounts valued at $75,000,000."
5. *If you are just beginning your career, list your summer jobs* no matter how unimportant they look. If an interviewer sees you've spent time where business was conducted (you were a waiter in a restaurant) or that you supervised people (you were a camp counselor), you will be that much ahead of people who haven't had much experience. If you're just out of college, list your major extracurricular activities.
6. *Never list your references.* Just say, "References on request" at the bottom. That way fewer interviewers will get in touch with them, and you'll be less likely to wear out their goodwill. The exception to this rule is if you have a file of references available from your college placement service that can be copied and sent out repeatedly. In this case, list the names of your references and note that they are available on request. (Adapted from "Nuts, Bolts and Directions," *Esquire*)

You may wish to prepare more than one résumé. For example if you are trained in both commercial art and drafting, you might wish to prepare two separate résumés, each one emphasizing your accomplishments in one or the other field.

Résumés are exercises in classification. The applicant creates categories that best highlight his or her accomplishments. The first sample résumé that follows was prepared in application for a job as a recreation director at a summer camp. It emphasizes the applicant's athletic skills and musical abilities. Notice that the information under each category is arranged in reverse chronological order, with most recent experience first.

RÉSUMÉ

Frederick B. Hayward
50 Wicket Boulevard
North Hollywood, California 91605
Telephone: (716) 637-2444

EDUCATION
1980–Present	University of California at Los Angeles
1978–1980	Northridge High School North Hollywood, California (Senior: HPA 3.59)
1976–1978	Interlochen Academy Interlochen, Michigan

SPECIAL TRAINING
1978	Soccer Clinic, UCLA
1976–1978	Studied Music (clarinet) at Interlochen Academy

HONORS AND AWARDS
1980	Offered full soccer scholarship to UCLA
1977	Voted "Outstanding Musician" at Interlochen Academy
1976	Partial tuition scholarship to Interlochen Academy

ATHLETIC ACTIVITIES
1978–1980	Varsity Soccer, Northridge High School (Second team All-State)
1976–1978	Varsity Soccer, Interlochen Academy

RELATED WORK EXPERIENCE
1978–Present	Assistant Soccer Coach, Greenhaven Elementary School

1976–1978   Service Station Attendant
              During summer months.
              Appointed assistant manager, June, 1977.

REFERENCES
Available on Request

This sample résumé was written by a young man with fairly limited work experience. Writing an effective résumé becomes a more demanding task as your experience and background increase. The arrangement of the résumé will change as you change and grow. People with a strong educational background—those just completing college, for example—will put their educational background first in the résumé. People with extensive work experience will probably present work experience first. The following example emphasizes the writer's work experience. Notice that this résumé requires fairly careful reading. The information is presented as a narrative, but in reverse chronological order. The heading "Career Objectives" describes the type of position the person wants, and the résumé should offer support that the person is qualified for that position.

RÉSUMÉ

Wanda B. Stover **Phone: (804) 932-7599**
1319 Kirkland Drive
Bayshore, VA 23237

CAREER OBJECTIVES
    Executive position in advertising agency.

SUMMARY OF EXPERIENCE
    Advertising editor, advertising layout, advertising sales for three years. Director of innovative educational programs. Experience in art-graphics with various companies.

EMPLOYMENT HISTORY
1975–Present: *Advertising editor for Bayshore Weekly News, Bayshore, Virginia.*
    Duties: Prepare advertising copy for weekly newspaper. Sell advertising space. Layout ads. Manage advertising accounts. Current salary: $14,500.

1974–1975: *Coordinator of Volunteer Arts Program* for The New School in Hullsport, Tennessee.
Duties: Development of volunteer run arts program, scheduling of volunteer hours and duties, budgeting, ordering and purchasing of supplies, publicizing of the program, soliciting parent and community support.

1972–1974: *Director of Arts-Crafts Program*, Hullsport, Tennessee.
Duties: Development and maintenance of an arts-crafts program for children ages 6 through 14; supervision of four full-time and four part-time employees; budgeting, purchasing, and ordering of supplies; publicizing the program and directing citywide art competitions for children.

1969–1971: *Director of Graphic Arts*, The Accent Agency, Knoxville, Tennessee.
Duties: Illustration, layout, silk and photo screen printing, photography and photo processing, copywriting for newspaper, magazine, and radio accounts. Ordering and purchasing of supplies, direct supervision of three full-time employees, budgeting, maintenance of filing system.

1967–1968: *University of Tennessee Press.* Dual position in editorial and graphic arts department.
Duties: Proofreading and correcting galleys, editing of works in progress, layout, stripping, photography and photo processing, typing, operation of office machinery, etc.

EDUCATION

University of Tennessee, Knoxville, TN. Attended 1965–66.

Aspen Writer's Workshop, Aspen, Colorado, Scholarship student, Summer, 1966.

REFERENCES

Available on Request.

Here are some additional points to consider in working up your résumé:

1. Many people include height and weight, social security number, military experience, state of health in a category labeled *Personal Data*. This information is probably unnecessary since it will be required on a formal application form if the applicant gets through the screening process.
2. The *Career Objective* should match the stated objective of the job for which you are applying. The cover letter will expand on your objectives. Keep the objective broad enough to avoid restricting yourself, but it should accurately reflect your interests and abilities.

3. The *Summary of Experience* provides a concise statement of your background and accomplishments. It resembles the topic sentence to a paragraph. The data that follows will provide the detail. Make sure the summary supports your career objective.
4. The *Employment History* is presented with your most recent job first. Name each position you held and identify the company you worked for and its general location. Underline the job title you held. This makes the résumé easier to read.
5. Stress *Duties* and responsibilities. Try to be specific about the job you held; emphasize those duties that support your career objective.
6. In listing *Education* don't mention a high school diploma if you have a college degree. Mention honors or scholarships. If your educational background is less impressive than your work experience, then list education toward the end of your résumé as is done in the second sample.

EXERCISE

Write a résumé for yourself. Decide on a career objective and organize categories of the résumé accordingly. Try at least two different arrangements. Find the format that shows you to the best advantage.

The Cover Letter

The cover letter accompanies your résumé. The cover letter should always be an original, typed letter—never a reproduced copy. If you don't type well enough to produce a flawless letter, pay a professional typist. Cover letters follow a basic form, but each one should vary in response to the particular ad you are answering. The cover letter should do two things: (1) stress that the employer is the one with the need (after all, he or she is the one doing the advertising); and (2) show how you are the one person best-suited to solve the employer's problem.

Look back at the hypothetical ad from *Advertising Age* (p. 196). Before examining a cover letter in response to Billings, Drexel, and Smith, let's spend a little time analyzing the ad itself. The key to tailoring your cover letter to an employer's needs is learning to read between the lines of the ad—to discover what hidden needs may be implied. What needs do you find implied by the ad for a copywriter? Begin by making a list of the key points:

1. experienced copywriter
2. additional skills, if possible (layout and accounts)
3. someone innovative
4. the business is growing

What does each of these suggest? Let's examine them one by one.

1. The fact that they want an *experienced* person suggests that they need someone who can be productive right away. There's no time for training; they need someone *now*.
2. The request for additional skills suggests that what they really need is a *generalist*, someone with varied experience who can handle a variety of things that come up. Combined with #4, that the business is *growing*, the ad suggests a small, recently established firm not yet handling enough business to afford specialists in each area.
3. The emphasis on innovation and departure from the traditional reinforces the idea that this is not a well-established operation.

The ad implies a picture of a small business, still struggling to establish itself in a competitive field, needing someone right away who can do a variety of jobs and offer fresh ideas that might bring in more business.

With this picture now in mind, the writer can decide the best way to approach the audience, using the information in his or her prepared résumé. A good cover letter should follow this basic pattern:

1. Begin with a reference to the employer's need; for example, "Your ad in the May issue of *Advertising Age* states your need for an experienced copywriter."
2. In the body of the letter, draw from your résumé and highlight the one or two accomplishments that will most impress the employer, best reassure him or her that you are the right person to meet the implied needs.
3. Conclude your letter by *suggesting*, not asking for, an interview. Perhaps something like this: "I will be in the Washing-

ton area the week of the 25th and would be happy to discuss your need for a copywriter. We could review my qualifications in greater detail then."

Remember that the cover letter should be concise (less than one page). Study the following sample carefully:

1319 Kirkland Drive
Bayshore, VA. 23237
May 10, 1981

Mr. Jason Billings
Billings, Drexel, and Smith, Inc.
341 Indiana Avenue, N.W.
Washington, D.C. 20202

Dear Mr. Billings:

Your ad in the May issue of Advertising Age *states your need for an experienced copywriter. Because my experience fits your description so well, I am applying for the job.*

At present, I am advertising editor for a weekly newspaper with a circulation of 17,000. Running the advertising for a small town weekly means I am responsible for everything—from selling ad space to writing and laying out the final ad. I supervise three people, manage accounts, and see to it that we sell enough advertising to make a profit. During my six years here, we have doubled advertising sales. With a limited number of advertisers available, doubling sales meant coming up with a lot of new ways to convince the same people to advertise more heavily. I introduced bold graphic designs for local ads and built a sense of competition among local merchants desiring the flashiest ad. The flashier they got, the bigger they got, and we were on our way to doubling advertising space.

Over more than a dozen years, I've worked in jobs that demanded a combination of writing, art, and management skills. I like the idea that I could put my experience in all these areas to work for you at Billings, Drexel, and Smith, Inc. I will be in the Washington area the week of May 25th and would be happy to discuss your need for a copywriter. We could review my qualifications in greater detail then.

Sincerely yours,
Wanda B. Stover

EXERCISE

Go back to the résumé you prepared for the preceding exercise.

1. Select one of the job ads you located in your research for the exercise on page 196.
2. Analyze the ad, then write a cover letter applying for the job and highlighting the parts of your résumé best-suited to this job.

The Interview Appointment Letter

This letter is an apparently minor but actually very important step in the job search. Whenever you receive a request for an interview, either by phone or by mail, be sure to confirm in writing. A simple two-line letter will do:

> *Thank you for your letter of May 17. I shall be happy to meet with you in your office at 11:00 A.M. on May 27.*
>
> *Sincerely yours,*

or,

> *This is to confirm our telephone conversation today. I shall be happy to meet with you in your office at 11:00 A.M. on May 27.*
>
> *Sincerely yours,*

The Interview

Now comes the task of selling yourself in person as well as you have sold yourself so far on paper. The voice projected in your cover letter and résumé suggested self-confidence and competence. You must emphasize these same characteristics in an interview. Don't try to tell the interviewer that you are confident and competent; show these qualities in action. Careful dress and a relaxed, confident manner are more impressive than self-conscious bragging.

Every guide to successful interviewing stresses the need to dress carefully. Clothing should be generally conservative and of the best quality you can afford at the time. Hundreds of personnel directors tell over and over again that they reject candidates all the time for apparently minor reasons: short socks that show a man's ankles (even worse, white socks), or too strong a perfume worn by a woman. Consider that most interviewers are looking for excuses to reject people, to screen out a large number of candidates quickly, and narrow the field to one or two. Don't make their job easy for them. Don't forget that participating in a job interview is quite literally playing a role with a built-in script. Particular social situations call upon people to play specific roles for a few minutes. For example, graduation speakers always talk about the challenge of the future—it's part of the role. Everyone expects it. Similarly, for the few minutes you are cast in the role of an interviewee, you are expected to behave confidently and to assert that you are a positive, team-playing, loyal, above-average person who has a take-charge attitude and will get the job done. To admit that you are actually rather insecure, sloppy, a bit lazy, and not at all sure you can handle the job may be honest, but it will violate the rules of the game, disturb the interviewer, and provide an easy excuse to eliminate you.

Remember that during these few minutes little real knowledge is going to be gained by either side. *Style* must dominate because you do not really have a fair chance to demonstrate the substance of your character and abilities. Only months or years on the job will do that. We don't mean that you should be phony and pretend to be a different person. We just mean that you should concentrate *only* on your good qualities and on presenting *only* them to the interviewer.

The Follow-Up Letter
(after the interview)

Writing a follow-up letter is often cited by both job counselors and personnel directors as the most important step in the whole job-hunting process. No matter how many times this advice is given, most job seekers still don't bother to write a follow-up letter after an interview. Those who do frequently get the job. The letter itself is extremely simple: thank the interviewer for your having had the opportunity to discuss your background and remind him or her of your unique qualifications for the job at hand. End on a positive note.

Study the following example:

> *Dear Mr. Billings:*
>
> *I enjoyed talking with you yesterday and appreciate the opportunity for reviewing my qualifications. I am particularly pleased by the fact that my background in both copywriting and the production of ads meets your need for someone who can handle a variety of jobs within the agency. I look forward to hearing from you.*
>
> *Sincerely yours,*
> *Wanda B. Stover*

We have discussed at length the procedures involved in answering an employer's ad because the steps are virtually the same in the other two methods of finding a job. If you advertise yourself and get a reply, you must then submit a written application or cover letter, a résumé, and so on. Actually, most people find that placing ads announcing their qualifications and desire for employment doesn't work very well. Instead of getting responses from potential employers, they are deluged with rip-off schemes, wild offers, and ads for expensive job-counseling services. There is one way of "advertising yourself," however, that is frequently recommended. This approach relies on advertising yourself in person. Select a company, study it carefully, learn all about it including the problems; then try to make an appointment with someone higher in the organizational hierarchy than the personnel department staff. Impress that person with your detailed knowledge of the company—including some well-thought-out solutions to important problems—and perhaps you will gain access to someone who will hire you on the spot. It's a good theory, at least.

The final way of obtaining employment relies on a third party, a broker in effect who brings the mutual needs of the applicant and the employer together. Employment agencies abound in every city. Study the list carefully to determine which ones specialize in your field or in closely related fields. These will be your best bet. Local agencies are generally more helpful than national ones, especially if they have been in business a long time and have established close ties with local firms. Above all, avoid any agency that makes you pay a fee in advance. These usually refer to their service as "career counseling" and offer a package deal of a jazzy résumé written for you, an all-purpose cover letter, and some guidance on choosing a career. You can do as well on your own with the guidelines we've given you here and the aid of a good job-hunting book from the library to fill in the details. Actually, one of the best employment agencies is your own school's placement office. Many companies interview widely at colleges and hire large numbers of applicants through these placement-service arranged meetings. Don't overlook this possibility—stop by and talk with the people at the placement service well before you are near the end of your program.

SUMMARY

1. Job hunting is a two-way proposition. There are mutual needs to be met, and you have as much to offer as you have to get.
2. Use every avenue open when looking for a job; keep in touch with people in the field, read the journals and ads, get out and promote yourself, use your school placement service.

3. Keep a well-prepared, up-to-date résumé handy.
4. Write careful cover letters when applying; match your experience and training to the employer's needs.
5. Don't forget to acknowledge interview appointments and to send an interview follow-up letter!
6. At the interview, concentrate on your good qualities and present a positive image; dress carefully; don't apologize for yourself or your lack of experience—stress what you have to offer.
7. SEND A FOLLOW-UP LETTER AFTER THE INTERVIEW!!

WRITING ASSIGNMENT

Go back to the research you did for the exercise on page 196. Select the one job that most appeals to you.

1. Write a letter to the employer telling him or her that you are not looking for a job yet, but that you are preparing for a career in this field and would someday like to get a job like the one advertised.

2. Describe *briefly* the program you're in now, and ask for advice on how you might best prepare yourself for the kind of job you want. Edit the letter carefully, prepare a perfect copy, and mail it to the employer.

12
WRITING LETTERS, MEMOS, and INSTRUCTIONS

Résumés and letters are important in job hunting, but just how important are they? How important is writing skill once you've landed a job? Students often seem convinced that writing well has little to do with job success, especially if they are in a technical area—data processing or medical lab technology, for example. Every student knows somebody who is making $40,000 who never writes anything—at least that's what every student tells writing teachers. But a strange thing happens when you stop talking to students and go out to the businesses and government agencies that hire college graduates. Here you find a different story. Over and over, employers told us that writing skill was the most important ability a person could bring to a job, frequently that it was more important than the specific technical skill the job required. A candidate had to have the required skill, of course, but in choosing between two candidates, the employer would take the one whose résumé and letters showed greater writing ability. Once employed, the worker needs to be good at the job, but inevitably a worker who communicates well in writing will be promoted over one who is technically better at the job but who cannot write well.

For example, we interviewed a city manager and asked him about the importance of writing ability. Remember, local governments hire people trained in business, engineering, health services, police and fire sci-

209

ences, social work, education, planning, recreation, computer science, and many other areas. This city manager responded that "writing skill is just tremendously important. If we can get someone who has that skill already we're way ahead." He went on to say that for all but the lowest-level jobs, writing skill is "the primary criterion for selection." And that for *all* jobs "good writing is the primary criterion for promotion." Writing—for example, letters, memos, or instructions—makes up a regular, sometimes daily, part of many jobs indeed.

Letters

Business letters are written for a number of standard reasons: to get or to give information, to ask for correction of a problem or to respond to such requests, and to place orders, among others. As you can see, the purposes for business letters are specific versions of the general purposes for writing: to inform, to explain, to persuade.

Format

Whatever their purpose, the format for business letters remains the same. There are six parts to the form:

>Heading
>Inside address
>Greeting
>Body
>Closing
>Signature

The way these six parts are laid out on the page determines the style of the format: *full block, modified block,* or *semiblock.* If you are using company stationery with a printed letterhead, you do not need to bother about the heading except to type the date of the letter. Ordinarily, all parts of a business letter are single spaced.

Heading

The heading gives your address and the date. In the full-block format, it is set against the left margin; in modified or semiblock formats, the heading begins in the center of the page:

1021 Novitiate Road
Eugene, OR 97403
May 1, 1981

Inside Address

The inside address gives the name, and title (if any) of the person to whom you are writing, the company name (if any), and the address. The same information appears here that will go on the outside of the envelope:

Mr. David Jenkins, Director
Customer Relations
Chrysler Motors Corporation
P.O. Box 40
Detroit, MI 48231

In all formats, the inside address begins at the left margin.

Greeting

Two lines below the inside address at the left margin, you begin the letter with "Dear _____:"

Dear Mr. Marion:

Dear Ms. Abernathy: (use Ms. to indicate gender without considering the woman's marital status or if you do not know whether the woman addressed prefers Miss or Mrs.)

Dear Senator Barnum:

If you do not know the individual's name, only the title, the first line of the inside address would be that title and the greeting would be by title also:

Dear Director of Customer Relations:

If you know only a last name, do not include it in the inside address or the greeting. Use an "attention line" instead:

Customer Relations
Chrysler Motors Corporation
P.O. Box 40
Detroit, MI 48231

Attention: Mr. Jenkins

Body

The body of the letter contains the information, request, order, and so forth. In full- and modified block format, all lines begin at the left margin. In semi block format, indent five spaces for the first line of each new paragraph. In all formats, double space between paragraphs. Keep paragraphs short, perhaps to five or six lines. Be clear, concise, and direct. Avoid a distant, formal voice, but do not be too casual and chatty either. Be friendly and polite.

Closing

The closing introduces your signature. The most common closings are:

Yours truly,

Sincerely yours,

Sincerely,

Best regards, (for a somewhat warmer, more personal touch)

Note that only the first word is capitalized and that the closing is followed by a comma. In full-block format, this too is lined up with the left margin; in the other two formats the closing begins in the middle of the page, directly below the heading.

Signature

Your name should be typed four spaces below the closing and aligned with it, at the left margin for a letter in full-block format, in the center for the other formats:

Sincerely,

John Josephson

If you have an official title, it would go immediately below your name.

Additional Elements

When a *secretary* types a letter, an initialed reference will be included two lines below the signature and always at the left margin. The writer's

WRITING LETTERS, MEMOS, AND INSTRUCTIONS | 213

initials are given in capitals, the secretary's in lower case, separated by a slash:

JJ/ch

When materials are enclosed with the letter, an *enclosure notation* appears on the line below the secretarial reference:

JJ/ch

Enc.

Finally, if *copies* of the letter are sent to other people, this fact and their names should be included. Use the abbreviation "cc:" (for carbon copies)

JJ/ch
Enc.
cc: William Hanson
  Marylynne Singer

If there were no enclosure, the copy notation would, of course, come immediately below the secretarial reference. Study the following letter carefully:

329 Atlantic Avenue
Big Rapids, MI 49307
March 8, 1981

Mr. David Jenkins
Director
Customer Relations
Chrysler Motors Corporation
P.O. Box 40
Detroit, Michigan 48231

Dear Mr. Jenkins:

   This letter is to make you aware of a serious manufacturing defect in the automobile I purchased on October 15, 1979. I realize one person's problem may not be significant to a corporation as large as Chrysler, but I was sold a defective product that required major transmission repair as a direct result of factory error. The wrong drive line was fitted on the car at the factory and this error has caused excessive wear to engine, transmission, and differential components.

I purchased a new Plymouth Valiant from March Chrysler Plymouth in Big Rapids, Michigan. Early in the warranty period I mentioned to the service manager that the automatic transmission sometimes stuck in second range and seemed to shift erratically. The dealer's explanation that these symptoms often occurred during the break-in period seemed reasonable, and I was assured that the transmission functioned normally. The problems did not become serious until February 28, 1981, when the transmission stuck in low range while I was traveling in New England.

I took the car to Hampshire Chrysler Plymouth in Easthampton, Massachusetts, for what I assumed would be a minor transmission tune-up. The service manager showed me large pieces of metal in the transmission pan that indicated extensive internal damage. The cause of this damage was not discovered until the mechanic tried to reinstall the drive line, which did not fit the car. He cut 1-1/2" from the drive line to make it fit. The service manager and the mechanic who worked on the car told me that the drive line installed by the factory caused the transmission failure and pointed out how the damaged parts were affected by the excessive pressure the wrong drive line put on them.

Mr. David Jenkins
March 8, 1981
Page 2

My request to Chrysler is simple and reasonable: replace the automobile with one that will give me what I paid for. Reimbursement for the cost of repairing the transmission will not compensate for the inevitable future problems caused directly or indirectly by the malfunctioning transmission and improper drive line. My anger has subsided somewhat (thanks in large part to the courteous treatment I received at Hampshire Chrysler Plymouth). May I point out, however, that for seventeen months I have been paying a high price to drive a defective product, and the anxiety I now suffer while transporting my family in this car goes beyond economic loss.

Chrysler sold me a defective product. I do not want to own this automobile any longer. I understand that my experience is unique *and the Chrysler products have a fine reputation; this car is a blight to that reputation and should be replaced. I am enclosing copies of my original sales agreement and of the service receipt from Hampshire Chrysler Plymouth.*

Sincerely,

John Josephson

JJ/ch
Enc.

Notice that this letter is presented in semiblock form, probably the most common for business correspondence. Modified-block form would be identical, except that the first line of each paragraph would not be indented; all lines in the body would begin at the left margin. Full-block form would place the heading, closing, and signature at the left margin as well. Most business letters should be held to one page or less, but in a complicated letter such as the preceding one, the body may run on to additional pages. Notice that any pages after the first should be typed on plain stationery, not company letterhead, and should have the name of the person addressed, the date of the letter, and the appropriate page number at the top. As in any business letter, abbreviations are not used here except for the standard ones for gender ("Mr." and "Ms.," and "Mrs.," where appropriate), the postal service two-letter abbreviations for states, and the abbreviations used in additional notations at the end of the letter.

Claim and Adjustment Letters

The preceding letter is an example of a *claim* letter (sometimes called a *complaint* letter). A claim letter does just what the name suggests—it makes a claim against the party being written to. Essentially, it is an attempt to persuade the party addressed to respond favorably to the claim being made. Therefore, it is important when writing claim letters to remember the advice in Chapter 9 about *persuading an involved audience* (pp. 167–168).

Adjustment letters are the responses to claim letters; here you are telling the claimant what you will or will not do to satisfy the claim. In writing adjustment letters, remember the *good news, bad news* strategy.

An adjustment letter telling the reader you are going to grant the claim is good news—open with the good news up front, then provide details or explanations:

Dear Mr. Josephson:

Thank you for informing us about your difficulties with your Chrysler product. We will be happy to replace the car as you requested.

(The body of the letter would explain the details of how the replacement will be handled.)

On the other hand, adjustment letters often reject the claim—here you must persuade an involved audience to accept your opinion. Don't hit the claimant with the bad news right off. Restate his position without judging it, and try to establish some common ground before launching into the bad news. When you do get to it, state the rejection clearly and simply, but follow it with a statement of what partial adjustment may be possible and an offer of future help. Above all, avoid judgmental words that seem to attack the claimant, phrases such as "you claim," "you state that ... but ... ," "we cannot accept," "faulty maintenance," and the like. Instead of saying, "You claim that Chrysler installed the wrong drive shaft," the effective adjustment letter would say, "Thank you for telling us about the difficulties you experienced with your car."

A bad news adjustment letter might read like the one below. (Note that modified block format is used in this letter.)

Mr. John Josephson
329 Altantic Avenue
Big Rapids, MI 49307

Dear Mr. Josephson:

Thank you for informing us about the difficulties you experienced with your car. We appreciate how distressed you have been by the inconvenience and expense involved.

As you know, many thousands of cars come off Chrysler production lines daily, and, as in any sophisticated technological work, there is an unavoidable margin of human error. However, mass production makes it possible for us to deliver advanced automobiles at a reasonable price. To minimize the problems of mass produced cars, we maintain strict quality control procedures and a strong warranty program to correct the few difficulties that come to light after a car has been purchased. Obviously, to replace every car that experiences such difficulties would undercut the cost benefits to everyone that come with mass production. We cannot replace your car, but will gladly reimburse you for the cost of correcting the drive shaft. Our engineers assure me that you need not *worry about future problems, but out of consideration for your concern we will extend you new car warranty an additional 12,000 miles or twelve months. I am enclosing your certificate of extended warranty and a check for the amount of repairs on the service invoice you submitted.*

We certainly appreciate your telling us about your situation and expect that you will have no further problems with your car. If I can be of any future assistance, please do not hesitate to contact me.

Best regards,

David Jenkins, Director
Customer Relations

DJ/al
Enc.

EXERCISES

1. Write a claim letter about a product or service you are dissatisfied with. It may be to a private company or to a government agency. Be sure to specify what you want done about your claim.
2. Exchange claim letters with one of your classmates. Now write an adjustment letter in response to his or her claim in which you reject all or most of the claim.

Inquiry Letters and Responses

Many letters are written to get or to give information. A common form of inquiry letter is sent when a company has advertised its willingness to provide additional information about a product or service. When inquiring in response to an ad, you should keep the letter short, identify the ad, and mention the specific information sought. Unsolicited inquiry letters need to be a bit more developed:

1. State the information needed
2. State why it is wanted
3. Provide a list of specific questions
4. Express appreciation

In replying to inquiry letters, enclose material such as brochures if possible, and refer to the enclosures in the letter without repeating what's in them. If you must refuse a request for information, remember this is bad news. Begin by stating your appreciation to the inquirer for his or her interest and be sure to explain why the request must be refused. If at all possible, suggest another possible source and offer to be of service in the future.

EXERCISES

1. Look through magazine ads for offers of additional information on some product or service of interest to you. Write a letter of inquiry in response to the ad.
2. Write an unsolicited inquiry letter to the Chamber of Commerce of some city you would like to visit. Request information that would be helpful to you in planning a week-long vacation to that city.

Order Letters

Order letters are a straightforward form of business correspondence, but one that must be carefully written to avoid costly errors. Order letters should do the following:

1. Specify the exact catalogue (by date) or other source of your information about the products or materials being ordered.
2. Identify the product by correct manufacturer's or catalogue code numbers.
3. Specify the number or amount desired for each item ordered.
4. Specify the unit price for each item and the total price if more than one item is being ordered.
5. Give any shipping directions necessary (to whom the order should be addressed, at what location, and the like).
6. Specify any deadlines for delivery.
7. Specify how payment will be made.

Ordinarily, the body of an order letter is set up as a numbered list of the items being ordered.

EXERCISE

Borrow an equipment catalogue. It may be equipment precisely related to your job or field of study, or simply an office-products catalogue. Write an order letter to request several items.

SUMMARY

1. Letters are written for all the reasons people need to write: to inform, to explain, to persuade.
2. Letters follow a standard, six-part format: heading, inside address, greeting, body, closing, signature. These parts may be laid out in Full-Block, Modified-Block, or Semiblock form.
3. Claim and adjustment letters should use the principles of persuading an involved audience; inquiry and order letters should concentrate on being clear and direct.

Memos

Memos That Inform

Memos are, in effect, the letters written within a company. Although memo formats vary slightly from company to company, the strategies used to write the contents of those memos rely on the writing techniques you have been practicing. Memos are used to distribute information to employers, colleagues, or employees. This information can take many forms. A typical example would be a follow-up memo that makes a record for the files of information first passed on by phone.

In the following memo, someone has encountered a problem, called the supervisor, and has been asked to describe the problem in a memo.

To: Gary Miller
From: Fred Hecking, Shipping Foreman
Subject: Damage to bats stored in warehouse
Date: May 15, 1981

We are having a problem in the shipping department. As I explained during our phone conversation yesterday, the new egg crate box for softball bats works well for those customers who order bats by the box. Our policy has always been to ship exactly the number of bats ordered; this means some of the boxes have to be broken open to fill orders. Some of the bats are removed from the carton and stored in the warehouse.

When these bats were in a plastic sleeve they remained in good shape. With the new egg crate boxes, however, we don't use a plastic sleeve. As a result, the bats take quite a beating if they are stored out of the box. Not only is the finish affected but the white tape on the softball bats soon becomes very dirty. The taped handles on the baseball bats stay fairly clean, but their finish is anything but improved.

Notice the simple heading placed at the left margin. With minor variations, this "To-From-Subject-Date" heading is standard. Like the majority of memos, this sample is short—only two paragraphs long. As most memos are only one or two paragraphs, a review of paragraphing in Chapter 2 would be helpful.

Memos That Explain

Memos are also used to interpret or evaluate information and help a supervisor or colleague establish policy or make a decision. The amount of information necessary in the memo depends, of course, on the reader's prior knowledge of the situation. This type of memo is often organized according to the strategies discussed in the chapters on analysis. The evaluation memo provides a concise evaluation of information or data. This evaluation will have a specific purpose depending on the assignment.

Mr. Georgetown, the owner of a newly founded manufacturing company, wants to establish guidelines for hiring prospective employees. New employees will go through a training program before they begin work. Mr. Georgetown asks Mr. Perkins, who will be the personnel manager, to evaluate data to determine whether "years of education" should be an important factor in hiring new employees.

WRITING LETTERS, MEMOS, AND INSTRUCTIONS | 221

To: Mr. Frank Georgetown, President
From: Frank Perkins, Personnel Manager
Subject: Years of education as a condition for hiring
Date: February 15, 1982

I have read the reports you received from HHS on the relationship between years of education and a person's potential success in technical training programs. Following is my interpretation of this information:
    A. Years of education are:
        1) a poor predictor of a person's potential success in a technical training program;
        2) unrelated to measures of an employee's ability to perform on the job.
    B. Further research seems to show that educational institutions:
        1) promote children from grade to grade in terms of their age rather than their level of achievement;
        2) adjust curriculum offerings to suit the ability of the students.
    C. Completion of high school does not seem to be a valid or useful standard for selecting employees.

The thinking process that results in the cause-and-effect writing strategy is evident in this memo. Mr. Perkins examined the information for a direct cause-and-effect relationship between graduation from high school and performance on the job. He found that such a relationship does not exist. Section B of the memo summarizes the factors in the educational process that cause the circumstances summarized in section A. Mr. Perkins gives his evaluation of the information in section C.

    Mr. Perkins' memo presents an evaluation based on reading and studying published information. Many memos that provide evaluation of information are based on direct observation of a situation. In these cases the people reading the memo cannot duplicate the writer's observations. Often memos are used to provide a written evaluation of an employee's performance on the job. The following memo evaluates an employee. Classification is used to give an overview of the employee's performance.

To: Alma T. Bytonski, Vice-President for Personnel Administration
From: Robert Fenchley, Office Manager
Subject: Performance Evaluation: Michael Herring, Assistant Office Manager
Date: June 30, 1981

SUPERVISION: Mr. Herring takes his role as supervisor seriously. During the last eight months, Mr. Herring has gained confidence in his supervisory skills and has become an effective supervisor. Mr. Herring is able to recognize problem areas and correct them promptly.

TECHNICAL JOB KNOWLEDGE: Mr. Herring has a high degree of technical knowledge. He can answer most questions asked by the staff. He is able to assist the programmers with their problems; when he is unable to answer a question, he is quick to refer the question to the proper administrative unit.

TRAINING: Mr. Herring is aware that proper training of our staff is necessary to maintain the high degree of efficiency maintained in this office. He supports our constant efforts to train and retrain our staff.

EXPENSE CONTROL: Mr. Herring lacks experience in preparing the office budget and salary package. He needs to develop in this area. Mr. Herring does a good job ordering supplies, and he works hard to keep expenses at a minimum.

GENERAL COMMENT: As assistant office manager, Mr. Herring is often required to perform a variety of duties. He is always willing to take on extra work and produces high quality results. He relates well to both staff and customers and is able to make intelligent decisions.

The techniques of classification organize this memo. The memo classifies the various jobs performed by the employee; this method allows a comprehensive evaluation of his work. The method of classification allows the writer to emphasize Mr. Herring's strengths as well as specify areas that need improvement. The memo puts the categories in bold headings for easy reference.

EXERCISES

1. Write a memo to your instructor informing him or her about a problem with the course.

2. Your college has been losing enrollment and the president wants to know what factors cause students to leave school. You have been asked to provide a summary of reasons why students drop out of college. Use cause-and-effect strategies for analysis in a memo to the college president.

Memos That Persuade

Information and evaluation lead directly to conclusions or recommendations for action. An employee might be asked to recommend a solution to a problem once information has been gathered and evaluated. Recommendations and conclusions must be based on awareness of factual information and its implications. The memo format, however, does not leave much room to review all the necessary information. The assumption of the writer is that the person or persons reading the memo are thoroughly familiar with the facts. In offering a recommendation you are trying to *persuade* an involved audience to accept your ideas.

The following memo, part of a correspondence between two people, one of whom asked for the advice of the other, responds to a previous memo requesting recommendations. The writer has been asked to express his opinions and judgments. In a more formal report this would be out of place unless supported by facts. Notice that the various topics covered in the memo are clearly indicated. This memo is longer than our other samples and contains much more detail.

To: Frank Blaster *From:* Robert Douglas
Subject: Re your June 2 memo on improving sales of new bat line *Date:* June 5, 1976

You asked for suggestions on overhauling the "Bigstick" line. Some of this should come at once and some as years pass and we learn the tricks of putting out good looking bats.

First, branding:
The H & B people, I think, have the most appealing logo. We should try to keep previous Bigstick customers while trying to introduce our own brand name. I suggest a compromise: call the line "Bigstick by Blaster."

Second, pricing:
I can only tell you that Bigstick was high priced compared to some other lines that were on the market. I see too few Bigsticks on the local market to make any valid price comparison. Despite Bigstick's policy to sell to any one who wanted the line, the bats were not very popular in this area. Perhaps the price cut down orders.

Third, the product itself:
There is a tendency back to three types of bats:
(a) Natural finish
(b) Flame treated
(c) Very highly polished finish (which both Blasters and Bigsticks seem to lack).

Dark finish bats are a dandy way to cover up flaws and many people are aware of this fact. I suggest we abandon the dark finish on Bigsticks and use one of the three finishes listed above.

Fourth, autographed models:
These are a good selling feature and I would think that the cost of printing is worth it in the long run. Use more modern names like Rusty Staub, Fred Lynn, or Reggie Jackson. Lou Gehrig, Babe Ruth, and Al Kaline are not big names with the present generation.

General:
I have been in touch with our good friend Doug Frye and he confirms the views I have expressed here.
- (a) Offer at least a 4 percent quantity discount.
- (b) Bigstick prices were better than Blaster but not quite as good as H & B and Wally Enterprises.
- (c) H & B and Wally offer a better price on quantity orders (10 percent below Bigstick).
- (d) We should maintain the Bigstick name while introducing our own.
- (e) We should abandon the dark finish.

This memo uses the strategies discussed in the chapter on analysis. The various aspects of the problem are identified and described. This memo represents a "breakdown" of the problem ("overhauling the 'Bigstick' line") into its component parts. Notice that each section of the memo concludes with a suggestion or recommendation. These recommendations—the main points made in the memo—are pulled together and summarized at the end.

EXERCISES

1. You work in the shipping department of a company that makes pretzels. By the time the bags of pretzels reach the shelves in the grocery store, most of the pretzels are broken. Write a memo suggesting a solution to your boss.

2. You are supervisor for a department of thirty people. You notice that some of your employees are regularly late for work. Write a memo to the employees that will correct this situation.

3. You work on the staff at a large hospital. You notice that the nurses do not refer to patients by name but by room number ("number twenty-two needs a bedpan"). Write a memo to a supervisor suggesting that this practice be discouraged. Explain why it should be discouraged.

Memos That Instruct

A memo can describe a change in procedure and instruct personnel how to use the procedure. The techniques you practiced in process analysis organize the following memo.

The memo begins with a statement of purpose (a topic sentence). The procedures follow in sequence with a specific example to illustrate an important step. The memo also explains why it is necessary to follow a certain procedure.

October 12, 1981

HI-WAY EXPRESS, INC.   cc: E.D. Ryan
Los Angeles Terminal—821   R.E. Tolbert
                                       R.L. Cavanaugh

TO: CASUAL DOCK EMPLOYEES
FROM: Ronald T. Pryor, Personnel
SUBJECT: DOCK CASUAL
            CALL-IN
            PROCEDURE

States the purpose of the memo

We have established the following call-in procedures to make better use of our casual personnel and to allow all of our casuals an equal chance to work on the dock.

Specific instructions spaced for easy reading

You will be required to call 213-589-7635 on the days that you are available to work.

If you are available for the day shift: Call between
                5:00 A.M. and
                8:00 A.M.

If you are available for the night shift: Call between
                4:00 P.M. and
                5:00 P.M.

Specific procedures with example

Call between these times *only*. To save time give your full name and tell us the number of days you have worked since Sunday of the particular week during which you are calling.

    EXAMPLE: Ronald T. Pryor—Worked (3) days this week.

Explains why a step is necessary

    NOTE: Use your full name because we have many casuals with the same last name.

> For weekend and holiday work *only:* Call between 3:00 P.M. and 4:00 P.M. Friday and we will book you for weekend or holiday work.
>
> Call in between these times *only.* If the shifts are full for that day or time, we may be able to prebook you for another day or time.

This instructional memo has characteristics common to most memos.

1. It comes directly to the point. People in the same company usually know each other and are aware of the circumstances the memo concerns. The writer can come directly to the point without elaborate introductory comments.
2. The memo can use fairly informal language, but must remain precise and courteous.

EXERCISE

You work in a police department or county sheriff's office. During the past six months, two police officers have been severely injured by colliding with other police vehicles rushing to the same accident scene. Organize the following information into a memo to the patrol officers. Add any other instructions you think would be helpful.

1. Close windows tightly and lock all doors.
2. Cars called to the same location must keep in radio contact with each other.
3. Collisions have occurred at intersections and access roads.
4. Collisions have occurred between patrol cars that are both operating sirens.
5. Neither driver could hear the siren of the other.
6. Wind noise can make it difficult to hear the radio.

SUMMARY

1. Memos are the lifeblood of most companies. They are the internal mail that keeps everyone informed.
2. Memos are written to inform, explain, persuade, and instruct.
3. Keep the form simple: TO, FROM, SUBJECT, DATE
4. Memos draw on all the skills studied in the strategies section of this book. Because most memos are only one or two paragraphs, review the skills in paragraph building presented in Chapter 2.

Giving Instructions

Actually, writing instructions often calls for a more fully developed form than the brief memo allows. Frequently the processes for operating machinery or the procedures involved in various work tasks are quite complex and require detailed written instructions to make sure that they are carried out properly.

The thinking process and the writing strategies associated with description and analysis are important in giving clear instructions. Description gives the reader precise details or landmarks. The spatial order often used in description organizes many sets of instructions, and time order puts instructions in sequence. The techniques of process analysis also contribute to clear instructions. For example, the activity of a job must be broken down into specific steps or stages before someone else can perform the task.

The following example uses description and analysis to present a set of instructions for lifting heavy objects.

LIFTING AND HANDLING

Lifting and handling material, books, boxes, cleaning gear, and furniture have been a major source of injuries to school district employees. From July 1, 1980 through March 31, 1981, careless lifting and handling techniques have caused

116 handling accidents and 47 lifting accidents. So far, the cost of the district has been $228,158. To help reduce the number of accidents, here are a few hints on proper lifting and handling techniques.

1. *Analyze* the job, observe the position of the object, look over the surroundings and check the route you will be traveling. If you need help, get it before you attempt the job.
2. Try to tip the object with one hand, if you can; then you can probably lift it safely.
3. When two or more persons are carrying the same object, designate one as the leader; he will use voice signals to coordinate the actions.
4. *Check* the object to see if there are any sharp edges, protruding nails, splinters, and the like.
5. *Face* the object. Plant you feet firmly near the base. Stand close to the object, and spread your feet for a good balance.
6. *Bend* down with your knees, keeping your back straight. You should be slightly bent at the waist.
7. *Grip* the object firmly with your whole hand, not just with your finger tips.
8. Push straight up with your legs (avoiding sudden jerking), keeping the object close to your body. If you must turn with the object in your hands, turn using your feet and not your upper body.
9. When you have to walk carrying an object, make sure you can see where you are placing your feet.
10. Make two or more trips when you have a large number of objects to be moved. Do not try to move too much at one time.
11. To lower the object to the floor reverse Step #8.

Remember, you only have one back and it is very easy to cause either temporary or permanent back damage. Think before you act. Use the proper lifting methods. Don't become a statistic in the Worker's Compensation file.

Guidelines

Here is a set of guidelines for writing instructions:

1. Make sure the reader knows why it is necessary to follow the procedures. People need to know what a set of procedures is intended to accomplish. This allows them to adapt to unusual circumstances and gives them a feeling of confidence.

2. Show your own confidence in the instructions. Write with a tone of command. Say: "Remove the hatch cover with a medium sized screwdriver," not "You can try to pry the cover off the hatch."
3. Set your instructions up on the page so that they are easy to read. Leave lots of space between each step. Use caps or underline for especially important procedures.
4. Number each step in sequence. If this is not appropriate, then use clear headings to separate each step in the process.
5. Explain why a specific step or procedure is necessary and why it is important.
6. Tell the reader precisely what equipment or tools are necessary for each step in the process.
7. Use the fewest words necessary to get your point across.

The following example illustrates the guidelines. It is meant for police officers, who will be glancing at the instructions while carrying out the procedures to test an arrest subject for intoxication. While the test is taking place a videotape record will be made. The instructions must be set up on the page in a way that allows the officer to read them at a glance:

The following procedures will result in an accurate picture of the condition of the arrested subject. Simple tests performed at the request of the arresting officer will show how much the person has been influenced by alcohol.

Follow these procedures, keeping in mind that they are designed to show the true mental and physical condition of the subject.

REMEMBER. ... THE ARRESTED PERSON IS THE STAR OF THE SHOW

Give him sufficient leeway to display his true condition. If the person wants to talk at any time. ... KEEP QUIET AND LET HIM TALK.

The entire "on camera" time should be about 10 minutes.

Repeat your questions or explanations until you are satisfied that the offender has demonstrated the inability to understand or to follow simple instructions.

We are trying to avoid making the officer appear to be overbearing, thereby creating sympathy for the arrested subject.

PLEASE READ THE FOLLOWING PAGE VERY CAREFULLY. ...
it emphasizes points that are vitally important to the success of this program.

BE PROFESSIONAL
Do not laugh at or make fun of the subject at any time. Be fair, firm, patient, and polite—not patronizing. Do not obviously try to hurry the procedures.

REMEMBER THAT YOU ARE <u>ON CAMERA</u> TOO.
    Take your jacket off.
    Take your cap off.
    Don't smoke on camera.

This booklet has been prepared to ensure uniformity in the procedures. Follow the various test directions as closely as possible.

Now begin the actual testing. . . .

test #1

Bring suspect into room and have him stand near the center of the camera shooting area with his feet together. A mark on the floor will be provided for accused and officer.
<u>DO NOT PERMIT HIM TO LEAN AGAINST ANYTHING.</u>

The officer should first of all identify the accused and state the traffic ticket violation number.

Ask him the following questions:
1. <u>Do you know where you are?</u>
2. <u>Do you know that you have been arrested for driving while under the influence of intoxicants?</u>
3. <u>I am going to ask you to perform a series of simple dexterity tests. It should only take about 10 minutes.</u>
4. <u>Would you like to talk to your attorney before we start?</u>

If he wants to call his attorney, let him. Hand him the telephone book and let him find his attorney's phone number. When it is obvious that he is unable to locate the number, the officer may assist. Keep recording his actions until he begins the actual conversation with the attorney. The camera should be shut off at this time because this conversation is not admissible.

As soon as he hangs up the telephone, turn the camera back on and go right on with the testing.

If he refuses to cooperate any further, ask him to perform the following:
1. To write his name, etc. . . .
2. To walk the square. . . .
3. To recite the alphabet. . . .

His refusal to cooperate with something as simple and as reasonable as the above will show his uncooperative attitude to the jury.

test #2

Ask the person to step over by the large paper hanging on the wall.

QUESTION. . . . <u>Can you read and write?</u>

Hold the <u>felt pen</u> in your hand as you say . . . "Write four things on this large piece of paper in this order";

Your name
Your address
The date
The time

Give him the felt pen and SAY NOTHING ELSE . . . if the person is unable to complete the above . . . then you will say: "Do you remember what I asked you to write?" . . . and repeat the instructions.

Don't repeat this so often that you appear to be overbearing. Repeat the instructions just enough to demonstrate that the suspect is unable to understand or to follow simple instructions.

Save the paper. Fold it and put it in one of the big envelopes. The prosecutor wants it as evidence at the trial.

EXERCISES

1. Point out instances of each of the seven guidelines for giving instructions used in the preceding example.
2. How many of the guidelines for giving instructions does the following example use? Point out examples of the use of these guidelines.

   When threading the film, follow the threading diagram that is usually supplied by the manufacturer. It is often attached to the projector. Here are a few items that deserve attention:

   a. Before threading the film, make sure that the television film projector is on local control, rather than remote control. If you leave it on remote control, it may be accidentally started by someone from a control room, and you may get your fingers caught in the projector mechanism.

   b. Be sure to thread the film *firmly* over the sound drum, and to adhere to the prescribed loops. Otherwise your film will be out of lip-sync.

   c. Even if you are in a hurry, thread the film carefully. A careless threading job may result in severe film damage.

   d. Once you have threaded the film, start the projector and run the film for a little while to make sure that you have loaded the projector correctly. Back up the film again to the number 4 (or whatever cue you have designated) of the academy leader.

   e. Just in case your film should break, have the splicing equipment close at hand. Usually, a simple splicer and high-speed rewind equipment are located right next to the film islands.

   f. If your projector does not have an automatic switchover from optical to magnetic sound, make sure that the sound pickup device on the projector corresponds to the film sound track.

g. Treat all film gently. (Herbert Zettl, *Television Production Handbook*)
3. Write a set of procedures that would improve the efficiency of a situation you have experienced: a grocery store's check-out procedures; the registration process at your school; crowded traffic conditions on local streets.

SUMMARY

1. Well-written instructions can be crucial to both safety and job performance.
2. Observe the guidelines when writing instructions:
   A. Tell the reader *why*.
   B. Use a confident voice.
   C. Use a layout that will aid the reader.
   D. Number or use headings for each step.
   E. Explain the need for each step.
   F. Describe tools or equipment precisely.
   G. Keep instructions as simple as possible.

WRITING ASSIGNMENTS

1. Write a letter of inquiry seeking detailed information about an industrial process or a research project you have read about recently in a general news magazine or newspaper. For example, you may have read about a medical research discovery that might relate to the allied health area you are training for. Write to the researcher named in the article.
2. Write a claim letter about a billing error. This might be either a business problem, a personal account for which you have not been properly billed, a payment that has not been properly credited, and so on.
3. Write a memo summarizing the results of a meeting or a phone call during which one or more problems were discussed.
4. Write a memo announcing a meeting. Set the time and place, list the items on the agenda for the meeting, and request that those people

attending be prepared to discuss them. The meeting might be for a business, school, or social group about to begin some new project.

5. Address a memo to a supervisor suggesting that certain procedures at school or work be changed.
6. Write a set of safety instructions for some potentially dangerous activity such as riding a motorcycle, riding a horse, or doing home wiring, among others.

13
WRITING REPORTS and PROPOSALS

Reports

Purpose and Audience

Only a small handful of people ever write formal essays after leaving school, but people in all professions do write reports. Reports range in form from a one-page memorandum, to a policeman's report on an accident, to a massive report on the financial condition of a multinational corporation.

Most companies establish their own report format, but the principles we present here can be adapted to most of the circumstances you encounter on the job. This section provides guidelines for writing short reports like those required every day in business and industry. In general, reports are written for one of three purposes:

1. *To give information.* This purpose relies on the techniques of description and classification to provide an audience with factual information.
2. *To evaluate information.* This purpose explains information for the audience. Analysis, cause and effect, and comparison

are important strategies in organizing a report with this purpose.
3. *To make recommendations.* This purpose requires presenting and evaluating information to make recommendations or draw conclusions. In addition to the strategies used to evaluate, this purpose uses the strategies of persuasion.

Each of these purposes can take on different forms within a company. Generally, reports fall into two large categories distinguished by audience and format: *Informal reports* make up the day-to-day communication tasks, often in the form of memorandums or letters. *Formal reports* follow established procedures and are the basis for decision making within a company. This chapter examines the following types of short formal reports:

1. Reports that inform
2. Reports that interpret
3. Reports that recommend

A written report becomes a permanent record of a job, explaining why certain decisions were made or procedures established. A reader has time to study a written report and get to know the information in a way impossible when listening to someone report orally. Written reports complement an oral presentation and allow the speaker to emphasize the most important points and rely on the written report to fill in the details. A report reflects the writer's ability to think clearly, analyze information, and get the job done. Often, a written report provides a permanent record of how a job was accomplished—a model—so that someone else can use the same procedures to solve a similar problem.

Creating a voice and understanding your audience bear directly on writing an effective report. Knowing the audience for a report helps answer some important questions before you begin to write:

1. How much information does the reader already have about the problem?
2. What level of technical knowledge does the reader have?
3. What is your relationship with the reader?

Many times a report will provide specific information on which someone will base a decision. The audience does not know certain things; otherwise the report would not have been requested. Try to establish where the information gap lies and work to fill that gap rather than telling the reader about things he or she already knows. Present information in language the reader will understand. Displaying your knowledge of technical terms to someone who doesn't know what you are talking about accomplishes nothing. Determine whether the reader wants your inferences and judgments. Is your relationship with the reader such that you can speak bluntly or offer an opinion without sounding as if you are trying to make decisions? A police report, for example, gives the facts; it is out of place for the officer to act as judge and jury.

Reports That Inform

Progress Report

A *progress report* is filed while a project or job is under way; it answers the question, "How are things going?" Progress reports are required in situations ranging from pure scientific research to the progress of a construction project. A telephone call can keep company executives up to date on how a job is going, but a written report on the project's status is also essential to provide a permanent record of job progress. A written report includes much more detail than any set of notes made after a telephone call can ever hope to do.

Progress reports provide important information. For example, J & K Construction Company bids for a job in a neighboring state and the bid is accepted. J & K has a dozen crews working in different places on different jobs throughout the year. Progress reports from each construction site are vital to the company in several ways:

1. They inform executives when a crew will be ready to take on a new project.
2. They are vital when a customer calls the company to find out how work is progressing and whether the schedule is being followed.
3. They provide records of how each type of job was handled so that similar jobs in the future can be evaluated in terms of cost and profit.
4. They help the company evaluate the efficiency of a particular crew or a particular supervisor.

The format of progress reports may differ from company to company, but all progress reports follow basically the same pattern. No matter what the circumstances, common sense can tell you that the reader of a progress report will want to know (1) what the report is all about; (2) what work has been done during the period covered in the report; (3) and what is going to happen in the immediate future. These purposes can be carried out by dividing the progress report into an *introduction*, a *body*, and a *conclusion*.

Introduction. The *introduction* identifies the job. If other reports have been filed, the current report is related to earlier reports by mentioning the period this specific report covers and by numbering the report ("This is the second of five progress reports on the Echo Hill project.") The introduction reminds the reader of important facts: how long the job was supposed to take; reference to problems outlined in a previous report; perhaps even a reminder as to who you are and what your role is in the project.

Body. The body of the report contains detailed information on current progress. The organization of the body itself will depend a great deal on the circumstances of the job and the needs of the readers. Often the body can be organized chronologically with specific dates highlighted:

November, 1981:	Our best supplier of oak was purchased by ROHO Manufacturing. We were immediately cut off from this supply. We contracted with Siskiyou Lumber Products to supply us with oak.
January, 1981:	Siskiyou Lumber did not live up to its commitments. Production of oak tables fell off by 30 percent. We began looking for a new supplier.
February, 1981:	James McCoy has arranged to purchase the surplus inventory of Merit Manufacturing. We will sand off the "Merit" name and silk screen our own brand names on this supply. This will help us meet our commitments until production returns to normal.

Progress reports can also be organized topically, using the techniques of classification and division. A construction job may be broken into its various components:

> Survey
> Underground
> Foundations
> Roads

Clearly the nature of the job will influence the organization of a progress report. You may want to describe problems that will delay completion of the project or to mention obstacles that you have overcome successfully. The body of the report could be divided into a section on "Work Completed" and a section on "Problems."

Conclusion. The conclusion of the progress report will usually look ahead to work left to be completed and may look back to offer recommendations for avoiding future problems. The reader will want to know when the project will be completed. Make realistic forecasts. If you promise rapid progress, then fail to deliver, your readers might be placed in an embarrassing position.

In general, keep the progress report as brief and concise as possible. Keep the language nontechnical. Don't exaggerate your accomplishments in an attempt to convince the reader you are doing a good job. The facts will speak for themselves. Here is an example of a typical progress report:

Date: February 12, 1982
To: Bill Becker, General Contractor
From: Marvin Gaines, Site Foreman
Subject: Progress Report #1 on the construction of Echo Hill apartment complex

Introduction: This report is submitted in accord with your instructions of December 1, 1981. The Echo Hill project (job number 03125-15) is located in the NW 1/4 of Section 24, Green Township, Maribosta County, Minnesota. This report covers the first phase of the project. The first phase was planned to take fifteen months to complete.

Work Completed: The mild weather during December and January allowed us to begin work on aspects of the job we didn't expect to begin until spring.

The outline survey by Plumber Engineering has been completed. The sewer lines and water lines are now at 95% completion.

Work was started on the roadways leading to the apartments and all the roadways have been cut out. Manson Company had to pull off the road job when frost set in during late December.

Raymond and Mattoon Co. completed the foundations and basement walls for the seven apartment buildings on December 29, 1981.

Problems: Raymond and Mattoon had a problem with unit number 5. This was the last basement completed and required heating to prevent the cold weather from freezing the fresh concrete.

We discovered a problem with unit number 4. The sub-grade for the basement was too high compared to the surrounding topography. Plumber Engineering approved lowering the floor grade by three feet.

Construction of the parking area has been delayed due to problems with final grades. We have accepted bids from four companies for the job and have forwarded that information to you on January 5, 1981.

Work to Be Completed: Manson Co., has promised completion of the roadways by May 15, 1982.

Rough carpentry has begun on all units. Ramsey Construction promises completion of the rough carpentry by April 17, 1982, and the completion of fine carpentry work by October 30, 1982.

The plumbers (Hanson Bros.) have moved their equipment to the site and are due to begin work March 1, 1982, with the expected completion date of November 1, 1982.

Work is proceeding faster than we anticipated last August. Completion of phase one can be reasonably expected by December 1, 1982.

EXERCISES

1. Write a progress report on your education so far. Address it to your advisor.
2. Pretend you are the captain of a spaceship from another galaxy. Your assignment is to create problems for the inhabitants of planet earth so that the conquest of earth will be made easier. Write a progress report to the superiors who sent you and your crew to carry out the mission.

Occurrence Report

A second type of report that informs is the *occurrence report* that answers the question, "What happened?" An occurrence report may be a routine record of information, for example, about a visit to a client by a social worker. Or an occurrence report may be called for by a special incident; for example, if a sexual-harassment charge is filed, the immediate supervisor of the people involved might be asked to gather the facts and file a noninterpretive report on the incident. Occurrence reports follow the same general pattern as progress reports: introduction, body, and conclusion. Study the following example of a routine occurrence report filed by a police officer:

Initial Information: At 4:10 P.M., Saturday, May 19, 1981, Officers HAYES and KELLEY received a radio run: "See the woman, 101 Avon St., Apartment 13."

Investigation: Upon arrival at the above address (4:30 P.M.), the officers were met at the door by the Complainant, Mrs. John HILTON. She told the officers that someone had stolen several articles of her clothing from the bedroom closet of the apartment while she and her husband were away on vacation.

Officer KELLEY examined the apartment, which was on the second floor of the building and overlooked a courtyard. She discovered that all windows were still locked from the inside. Mrs. HILTON told KELLEY that the door, which was the only one to the apartment, had been locked when she and her husband returned home. KELLEY noted that there were no pry marks nor was there any evidence of forced entry on any of the windows or the door.

Interview with Complainant: Mrs. HILTON told Officer HAYES that she and her husband had left on vacation for San Francisco, California, at approximately 10:00 A.M., Tuesday, May 1, 1981. They returned at 3:00 P.M. on May 19. She began to unpack; while placing clothes in the bedroom closet, she discovered that several articles of her summer clothing were missing. Nothing else in the apartment had been touched, as far as she and her husband could determine. Mrs. HILTON added that she had asked the Apartment Manager, Ms. Dorothy BONN, who lived in Apartment 1, to keep an eye on the apartment while the HILTONS were away. Mrs. HILTON further stated that BONN had previously admired several articles of Mrs. HILTON'S clothing. One outfit in particular that BONN had admired, a red sleeveless dress, was among those articles missing.

Mrs. HILTON added that she and BONN were approximately the same size and build.

HAYES asked Mrs. HILTON if she knew anything about BONN'S background. Mrs. HILTON replied that she did not.

Further Investigation: While Officer HAYES cataloged the missing items, Officer KELLEY went to Apartment 1 and was met at the door by Mr. T. S. MATTE. MATTE said that BONN had been fired as apartment manager on May 11 because of "too many complaints by tenants that she was going into unoccupied apartments." MATTE stated that he was the new apartment manager and that BONN had left no forwarding address with him. MATTE further stated that Robert BROWN, 211 W. Pippa St., owned the apartment complex and would have any forwarding address.

When asked if he knew anything that might help locate BONN, MATTE said that he knew nothing of her background, but that he could give a description of her car. (Ref. *Additional Information*)

KELLEY asked which apartments on the second floor were occupied from May 1 through May 11. Matte said only two, Apartments 12 and 14, and those people still lived there.

Officer KELLEY then rejoined Officer HAYES in Complainant's apartment.

KELLEY went to Apartment 12, occupied by Donald B. SHAW. SHAW said he had seen BONN enter Apartment 13 on Wednesday, May 9, but he did not see her leave the apartment.

HAYES, meanwhile, went to Apartment 14, occupied by Mr. and Mrs. Art MILLER. The MILLERS said they had seen BONN enter Apartment 13 on either the 3rd or 4th of May, but they could not remember the exact date. They did not see her leave the apartment.

Officer HAYES attempted to telephone Mr. BROWN but received only a recorded message that "Mr. Brown will be in at 8:00 Monday morning. Please call then."

Based on the above information, it appears that Ms. Dorothy BONN, using her pass key, entered the HILTON apartment on at least two occasions between 10:00 A.M. May 1 and 3:00 P.M. May 19, 1981. She could have removed several articles of clothing belonging to Mrs. HILTON.

Stolen Property:
The Complainant reported that the following articles of clothing were missing from her closet:

One (1) red, sleeveless, knee-length dress, size 10	$62.00
One (1) yellow, slipover sweater, medium size	25.00
One (1) pair of light blue dress slacks, size 10	36.00
One (1) navy blue, short sleeve shirt, medium size	24.00
TOTAL	147.00

The above values are those assigned by the Complainant.

Additional Information:
MATTE gave the following description of BONN'S car: Datsun 210, 1979 two-door, baby blue, small dent in passenger door, one "I Brake for Animals" sticker on the rear bumper. License check run at Dept. of Motor Vehicles. Plate number MPX-882 (Nevada)

Officer will contact Mr. BROWN at 8:00 A.M., Monday, May 21, 1981.

Status of Case:
Open, pending further investigation.

Signed: Mary Kelley

EXERCISES

1. Select a recent incident from work, school, or your personal life. Write an occurrence report to someone who might need to know about the incident.
2. Read a newspaper article about a crime, fire, meeting, or some other incident. Write an occurrence report from the details given in the story.

Reports That Interpret and Evaluate

This type of report explains the meaning of the facts and figures related to a specific problem. People in a position to make decisions may have all the facts at their disposal but lack the background or the time to interpret the meaning of factual data. Reports that interpret information have a definite purpose; selecting information and interpreting that information are guided by that purpose.

These reports vary in format, but all contain certain elements.

1. A report interpreting information begins with a *summary* that explains the purpose of the report and its findings.
2. The report presents the important factual information classified into definite areas.
3. The report explains the significance of the information in terms of the purpose of the report.

In organizing this type of report, you first summarize the information, then in a separate section explain or interpret that information.

Formal reports are similar in many ways to school research papers;

that is, they involve gathering evidence and examples, organizing and interpreting these materials, and making clear to the reader the sources of the information. Unlike research papers, however, reports may be addressed to several different readers with very different needs. A state government agency, for example, might prepare a report that would be read by legislators, by their staff members who might need more detailed information, by technical people in engineering or some such field who will be affected by the report, and by general interest reporters who will write news stories about the report. In other words, one report must often serve several different audience needs. In the informative report the audience is reading for the information contained, but in the report that interprets or evaluates one or more of the audiences addressed may be reading only for the evaluation, with no concern for the information it is based on. To solve this problem of different audience needs, a general format for reports has developed:

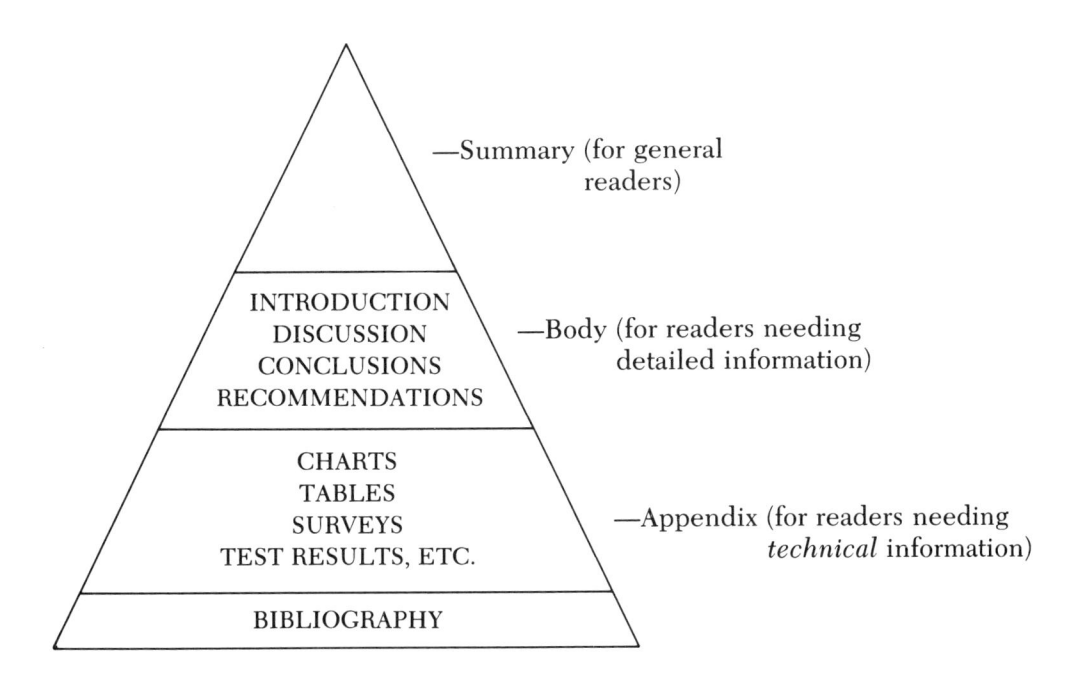

```
                    /\
                   /  \
                  /    \ —Summary (for general
                 /      \      readers)
                /--------\
               / INTRODUCTION \
              /  DISCUSSION    \ —Body (for readers needing
             /   CONCLUSIONS    \      detailed information)
            /  RECOMMENDATIONS   \
           /----------------------\
          /        CHARTS          \
         /         TABLES           \ —Appendix (for readers needing
        /         SURVEYS            \       technical information)
       /     TEST RESULTS, ETC.       \
      /--------------------------------\
     /           BIBLIOGRAPHY           \
    /------------------------------------\
```

Summary. A short version of the whole report, the summary identifies the most important points.

Body. The body of the report contains a full *introduction*, outlining the situation being reported on and the purpose for the report. In addition, there is a *discussion* presenting how the author investigated the situation and provided the information gathered. Next are *conclusions,* the interpretation or evaluation of the information. Finally, there may be *recommendations,* what the author suggests should be done based on his or her conclusions.

Appendix. This section provides all the supporting material of a technical nature such as copies of survey instruments, explanation of the statistical method used to interpret results, discussion of laboratory procedures and test results, technical specifications for materials or equipment, and the like.

Bibliography. The list of references is the same as in a research paper. It provides the information necessary for a reader to find all the research documents used by the author.

Other elements. Depending on the length and formality of the report, there may be a formal cover, title page, and table of contents.

The following report is a possible version of one prepared at the request of a zoning commission in a small suburban community.

Rapid growth of rental housing (apartment complexes and residences) in this "bedroom" community had created concern among long-time residents that the community would develop run down, slum areas. The report gives the results of a survey conducted among the owners of rental units and explains the implications of the information to the zoning commission. (The report does not make recommendations and, because it is very simple, has no appendix or bibliography.)

REPORT TO THE ALVIN COUNTY ZONING COMMISSION:
PROPERTY OWNERSHIP PATTERNS, 1954–1970
Prepared by the Office of the County Manager

Summary

This report presents data gathered on rental unit ownership patterns between 1954–1970 in Alvin County. The report supplies data in three main areas: (1) the types of unit purchased during this time; (2) the reasons for purchase of rental units; (3) the amount of time landlords spend maintaining rental property. The data shows a significant increase in purchase of type 5 rental units (apartment complexes) for the purpose of investment income during the past five years. The data indicates the need for concern regarding the maintenance of type 5 rental units.

Introduction: ownership patterns, 1954–1970

The average landlord in Alvin County purchased property in 1965. Purchasers of residence units have owned their property an average of ten years. Purchasers of apartment complexes have owned their property an average of three years. Since 1965, purchases of residences for rental purposes have increased 10 percent; purchases of building sites for apartment complexes have increased 75 percent. This report will evaluate these changes in ownership patterns.

Reasons for purchase of rental property

Seventy percent (70 percent) of the landlords surveyed purchased property for investment purposes. Of those who purchased property prior to 1965, forty percent (40 percent) did so for investment purposes. Of those who purchased property during and after 1965, ninety percent (90 percent) did so for investment purposes. Owners of three or more units were investors by a ratio of 5:1.

The reasons given by those surveyed for investing in rental property were as follows:

1. for current income (40 percent)
2. for capital gains (30 percent)
3. for current income plus capital gains (30 percent)

Owners of apartment units sought such investment advantages five times more often than landlords of residences. Tax shelters motivated only 11 percent of apartment complex owners but they offered this reasons nineteen times more often than landlords who owned one rental purchase.

Maintenance time on rental property

Corporate landlords do not spend much time working on their property. Thirty-two percent devoted one hour or less per week to maintenance. For all corporate landlords the median number of hours per week spent in maintaining property was two.

On the other hand, landlords who owned one residence unit spent a median of four hours per week in maintenance.

Conclusions

1. The figures show a definite shift in the pattern of rental unit ownership in the past five years.
2. Apartment ownership is becoming a big business in Alvin County. Among those who own the majority of the apartment complexes 82 percent are non-residents of the county. Forty percent (40 percent) of these represent cor-

porate interests. Land ownership in Alvin County is dominated by nonresidents.
3. The insignificant amount of time devoted to maintenance by corporate landlords suggests that the rental units they own will deteriorate fairly rapidly.

EXERCISE

You have been given the job of writing a report for your college administration interpreting the facts about the growing number of older students enrolling in a certain program. The college needs to assess the impact of an increasing older student population on the nature of that program. Select a program and interview faculty in it to gather information about the increase of older students. Write the report.

Reports That Recommend

In general, reports that offer recommendations are organized around three questions:

>Why?
>What?
>How?

To illustrate the report writing process let's create a hypothetical situation. Sally Biggs, an engineer who designs engine modifications for the Road King Truck plant in Ypsilanti, Michigan, receives an urgent phone call from A. J. Heller, vice president in charge of production. It seems the plant is about to run out of engines for the C-500 Fleet Van, the year's best selling model. Heller tells Biggs that his office has decided to consider the possibility of installing some other engine in the C-500. Can it be done? What engine will work? Biggs is asked to investigate the possibility and to make a recommendation.

Format and Strategies

The report format outlined below can be adapted to the needs of both plant manager or engineer (and to a multitude of other professions and circumstances).

WRITING REPORTS AND PROPOSALS | 247

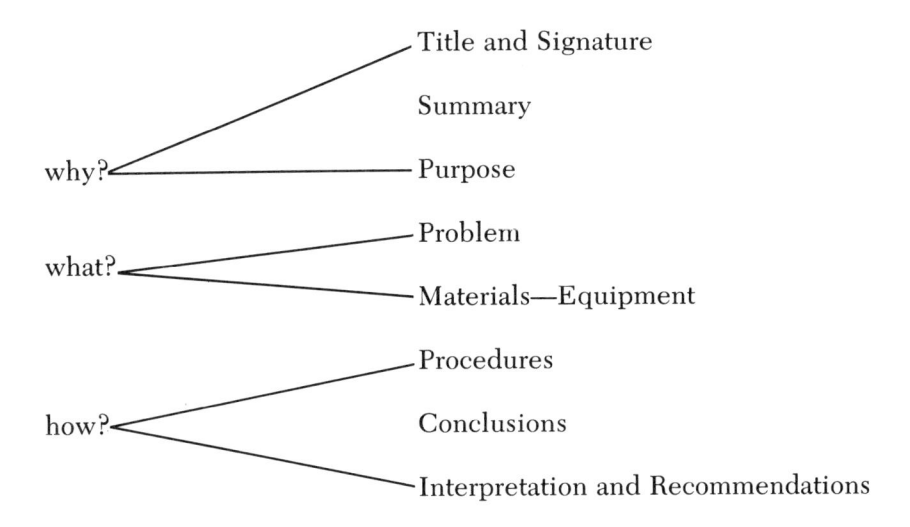

```
why? ─────────── Title and Signature
                 Summary
                 Purpose

what? ────────── Problem
                 Materials—Equipment

how? ─────────── Procedures
                 Conclusions
                 Interpretation and Recommendations
```

The general report format we outlined provides a functional organizational pattern for many different types of work-related writing. Here is a possible version of the report Biggs filed.

ALLEVIATING THE C–500 ENGINE SHORTAGE

Prepared by Sally R. Biggs, Division of Engine Design and Modification

Summary

The shortage of 1982 C-500 engines can be alleviated by substituting the 210 cubic inch Road King engine in 1,000 C-500 models. Substituting the 210 engine will require modifications to the linkage, motor mounts, and bell housing on the C-500. No noticeable difference in performance and economy results from the substitution.

A. Purpose

This report was requested by A. J. Heller, vice president for production, Road King Motors. The purpose of the report is to determine whether a substitute engine can be mounted in the 1982 C-500 and, if so, determine what engine can be substituted most efficiently. Mr. Heller also asked for an evaluation of the costs involved in the substitution and the costs involved in having to recall the vans at a later date.

B. Problem

This project was undertaken to find a reasonable solution to the shortage of C-500 engines. The steelworkers' strike of 1980 caused extensive layoffs at the Ypsilanti plant and depleted the on-hand supply of 1982 C-500 engines. In addition to this, projections for the 1982 model year did not anticipate the increased demand for the C-500. In September 1981, production was already running far behind dealer demand for these models. It was estimated (memo #A-20018) that the anticipated slowdown caused by lack of suitable engines for the C-500 will result in a profit loss of approximately $500,000 by December 1, 1981.

The problem has four dimensions: (1) find an engine that will fit the C-500 engine compartment; (2) select an engine that performs like the original when placed in a C-500; (3) determine what modifications must be made to the C-500 to accommodate the new engine; and (4) evaluate the costs involved.

C. Materials—equipment

The choice of possible substitutes was restricted on the basis of initial engine cost to the following engines:

Ford	220
GM	220
Road King	189
Road King	210

Installing the Road King 210 cubic inch engine requires least modifications to the C-500 and demands no retooling on the production line. Materials required for the adaptation of each C-500 to accept the new engine are as follows:

- 2 #G 300016B engine mounts
- 1 #TB 60058-7 throttle linkage
- 1 (modified) #SB798200-G bell housing

D. Procedures

The following procedures were followed to determine which engine was most satisfactory:

1. *Dimensions* Although the standard C-500 engine has 220 cu. in. displacement, the two equal engines (Ford and GM) were eliminated because installation required enlarging the C-500 engine compartment.

The Road King 210 and 189 both fit the C-500's dimensions.

2. *Performance* The Road King 210 engine gave the C-500 performance characteristics similar to those with the normal engine. The Road King 189 was noticeably sluggish and would result in customer dissatisfaction.

3. *Economy* The 210 is not as efficient in fuel consumption as the normal C-500 engine, but the difference in economy is small enough not to be a major factor.

The following modifications must be performed on the C-500 to accommodate the Road King 210:

1. Weld support plates to left front and right front frame members (see fig. 1 in "Appendix").
2. Fasten engine mounts to support plates.
3. Remove existing throttle linkage from firewall.
4. Replace throttle linkage with unit #TB 60058-7. This requires enlarging the access hole at bottom left of the firewall.
5. Remove bell housing from C-500 transmission unit. Replace with modified bell housing #SB 798200-G.

The following procedures should be followed to facilitate substitution of the 210 cubic inch engine in the C-500:

1. Ship 1,000 210 cubic inch engines from the Dearborn plant to the C-500 assembly plant in Ypsilanti.
2. Ship 2,000 #G 300016B engine mounts to the C-500 plant in Ypsilanti.
3. Ship 1,000 #TB 60058-7 throttle linkage units to the C-500 assembly plant in Ypsilanti.
4. Modify 1,000 #SB 798200-G bell housings as indicated in fig. 2 (Appendix).
5. Put John Foster of the Dearborn plant in charge of making necessary modifications to the C-500 and to the bell housings (he has the specifications and has been briefed).

E. Conclusions

1. Substituting the Road King 210 cubic inch engine in the C-500 results in no noticeable difference in performance and only minor variations in fuel economy.
2. The cost of the necessary modifications is $100 per unit. This takes into account assigning a crew to make the necessary modifications.
3. The procedures outlined above will avoid the production slowdown and profit loss anticipated by J. M. Reese in his memo of October 1, 1981 (#M-39876).

F. Interpretation and recommendations

1. The cost factor analysis in the Appendix shows that even if we eventually have to replace the substituted engine ($300 per unit) or reimburse consumers, the profit loss from delayed production far outweights future costs.

2. It is unlikely that every customer who receives the modified C-500 will notice the difference. Regular warranty maintenance procedures are routine enough that most mechanics will probably not notice the substitution.

3. We recommend that customer complaints resulting from the discovery of the modifications be satisfied with the offer of an extended (5 year) warranty on the drive train of the car in question.

4. We recommend dispersing the modified C-500 to the largest number of dealers possible. We do not recommend notifying the dealers of the modifications.

Appendix

(The Appendix would contain the detailed technical data relevant to engine tests, modifications recommended, cost analysis, and so forth.)

Notice that the engineer uses an outline form for her report. One reason for this is easy reference to the appropriate section of the report ("Sally, would you elaborate on section E, point three?") The outline format also adds to the clarity and readability of the report. The interpretations and recommendations should not go beyond the scope of the report's purpose. The "voice" is determined by the writer's working relationship with the principal audience for the report.

EXERCISES

You can practice writing reports by working on the hypothetical situations included here. Feel free to add details in the cases before working on them.

1. You supervise truck-loading operations for a small manufacturing firm. The company manufactures fragile glassware items. The products are packed in boxes for shipment to distributors throughout the region. The company pays five full-time men $5 an hour to load carts with boxes of glassware and wheel the carts onto waiting trucks. You are asked to decide whether the company should replace the loading crew by purchasing two lift trucks ($4,000 each) and pallets (flat boards that enable the lift trucks to lift a large number of boxes at a time) that will cost a total of $1,000. Write the report to your immediate supervisor. Decide what this person is like before writing to him or her.

2. You have been asked by a student association to evaluate the course you are enrolled in and to write a report recommending changes. Write the report for a course guide that the association is publishing.

Proposals

Proposal writing is a very serious business. Because some companies depend on winning competitive bids for contracts, great effort is put into preparing the best proposal possible to compete with other companies for a specific contract. Individual employees also rely on proposal writing to convince others within the company that there is a better way to do a certain job or that certain circumstances must be changed. A proposal is a sales pitch. Using the techniques of description, process analysis, and persuasion, you must describe what needs to be done and what you will do, including the equipment you will use and the procedures you will follow. You must also persuade readers that your idea is the best way to get the job done.

Other reports generally grow from activities or work you have performed, but in a proposal you are speaking about a situation that has not yet occurred and your reader may not be aware that the present situation needs changing or needs improvement. As with many other reports, proposing a new idea usually demands research of some sort. This research may consist of careful observation and record keeping, or it may require digging out facts in a library. But you must thoroughly understand the way things are now before you can propose to change them.

If a proposal is being written to gain a published contract, two other vital research steps come into play. You must study the specifications in the "invitation to bid" and find out all you can about the organization issuing the invitation. You must also investigate the competition. Who else or what other company is likely to bid on this project? How do your company's products and performance compare with those of another company? Is the competition strong in one area and weak in another? What are the strengths and weaknesses of your own company? In competitive bidding situations, proposal writing requires a collaborative effort from various personnel in the company.

Format

In general, a good proposal will be organized around the following outline:

Abstract

(A brief overview of the proposal.)

Objectives

(A list of what the proposed idea or process will accomplish.)

Need

(Establish the need for the process or idea. This is where research comes in.)

Procedures

(Exactly what will happen if the proposal is accepted and approved and how it will be done.)

Cost

(A breakdown of costs necessary to carry out the idea. This section might also contain a list of necessary equipment.)

Personnel

(You often have to demonstrate that the personnel involved have the qualifications to carry out the project.)

Our example shows you a proposal designed to sell a service. This proposal is aimed at boards of commissioners, prosecutors, and judges to convince them to subscribe to the services of Legal VTR, Inc. The proposal begins with an *Abstract* that tells the readers the purpose of the proposal. This is followed by a statement of *Need*. A *Description of Services* shows what the company will do and the type of services it will provide. Included here is a statement of cost. In some proposals cost breakdowns may be much more complex, requiring a separate section to themselves. The final sections list equipment and materials used by Legal VTR in providing the services. The cost list here is a persuasive point since the subscriber will get the use of this equipment free of charge.

Abstract:

Legal VTR Productions, Inc., is offering its services to counties and municipalities to videotape persons accused of driving while intoxicated (DWI). This service can be offered at a minimal cost and result in considerable time savings to the prosecutor's office, police officers, and the courts.

Objectives:

1. To provide an accurate record of a DWI offender's condition at the time of arrest.
2. To provide a visual record for the arresting officer.

3. To encourage guilty pleas in DWI cases.
4. To eliminate the costs of jury trials in DWI cases.

Need:

Various counties, municipalities, and prosecutors in the past have considered videotaping persons accused of DWI. This has not been practical because of the expense of purchasing and operating the equipment or the lack of trained personnel.

A recent Michigan Court of Appeals decision holds that an individual's refusal to take the Breathalyzer test is inadmissable at his trial. This decision creates problems in prosecuting a person charged with DWI. The jury can conclude that the officers never offered the Breathalyzer test and could lean toward finding the accused innocent.

Videotaping DWI offenders avoids the problems created by a refusal to take the Breathalyzer test and shows accurately the individual's condition at the time of arrest.

Procedures:

DWI Videotaping:

1. VTR will provide trained technicians available 24 hours a day. If a DWI is arrested, the arresting officer contacts his department head who, in turn, telephones VTR's paging service. A trained technician will be on the premises to videotape the individual within 15 minutes of any call.
2. VTR will provide all equipment, including camera, recorder, microphones, tape stock, monitor (for immediate viewing), and time/date generator. See Equipment List for total cost of unit provided by VTR.
3. VTR will assume all maintenance of equipment.
4. The charge for each DWI will include the initial taping, subsequent viewings of the tape (including trials), and any editing necessary (for inadmissable evidence).
5. VTR will charge $75 per individual charged with DWI. MSA 9.2325 (c) provides as follows:

Any person who is convicted of a violation of Paragraph (a) or (b) of this section shall be punished by imprisonment in the County jail or Detroit House of Correction for not more than 90 days or by a fine of not less than $50 nor more than $100 or both such fine and imprisonment in the discretion of the court, *together with costs to prosecution.*

> According to this Statute, the charge of $75 per individual charged with DWI is a cost of prosecution and therefore can be assessed against the individual as part of costs.

> Not all costs can be collected from an individual, because a certain number of indigent cases will arise. The County will be responsible for payment of those expenses. In the majority of the cases, however, the VTR charge can be collected from the individual.

254 PRACTICAL APPLICATIONS

County responsibility:

The County will have no responsibility for equipment or maintenance, except that the County will give VTR space to store the equipment necessary for DWI tapings.

Equipment list:

Sony Camera (B&W) AVC 3260	$1,065.00
Davis-Sanford Tripod DGW-H4	180.00
Sony VTR (B&W) AV 3650	1,250.00
Sony Monitor (B&W) 18" CUM 194U	750.00
Data-Vision Time Date Generator DTI	850.00
Smith-Victor Light Kit K-33	300.00
Wheelit Carts C402	145.00
Carrying Case for AV 3650 LC100	45.00
Shotgun Microphone Electro Voice DL42	360.00
Sony Non-Directional ECM 220	42.00
Sony Microphone Cable EC5M	7.00
Sony Microphone Cable EC10M	8.60
CCJ5 Extension Cable	58.00
Sony Audio Mixer MX300	65.00
Videotape Scotch Brand 100 reels	1,900.00
Sony ECM 16 Microphone 4 at $35	140.00
Total Cost for One Black and White Unit	$6,790.00

Personnel:

The organizers of Legal VTR Productions, Inc., consist of an attorney with numerous years of experience and a television expert with extensive experience in video tape productions, including fifteen years as producer-director for NBC affiliate, WWJ-TV, Detroit. Legal VTR's staff consists of trained television technicians to operate and maintain the equipment.

EXERCISES

1. The following information can be organized into a proposal to a hospital administrator. You might have to create additional facts. Write the proposal.

    There is no education or orientation for patients placed in isolation at Memorial Hospital in Farwell, Michigan. Talking with various staff members at the hospital, one learns that patients placed in isolation are not given any explanation of the reasons for isolation, or how their care will differ from the care of a nonisolation patient. Isolation technique was being broken by family and visitors due to lack of explanation. Patients were irritable when doors were kept closed until they realized why this was necessary. The *In-*

structions for Patient Manual explains isolation techniques for the patient with an infectious disease. An article in *Nursing,* May, 1975 ("Isolation: Precise Procedures for Better Protection") described safe isolation procedures and techniques. *Medical-Surgical Nursing* by Brunner explains isolation procedures, the needs for isolation, and the different types of isolation. *Fundamentals of Nursing* by Fuerst and Wolff covers the principles of infection control, isolation techniques, and types of sterilization. An orientation sheet could be given to the patient when he or she is admitted to the hospital for isolation care. This sheet could also be given to those who are already patients in the hospital and require isolation. This orientation sheet will give patient and family a better understanding of isolation techniques and care.

2. If there is not an internship as part of your major program, write a proposal that one be added. (If there is an internship already, write a proposal for a new course you would like to see available in the program.)

SUMMARY

1. Proposals are, of course, similar to reports, but they initiate action instead of reviewing an existing situation.
2. Proposals are *always* intended to persuade.
3. Proposals are *always* addressed to an involved audience.
4. The format for a proposal will cover every aspect of the job to be done by analyzing the idea and providing a separate section for each component such as Objectives, Need, Procedures, Cost, Equipment, and Personnel.
5. A proposal begins with an Abstract (summary) to give the reader a general overview of the idea and the benefits if adopted.

WRITING ASSIGNMENTS

1. You have been put in charge of making a significant change in procedures for your job. This change may involve new equipment, new personnel, and so forth. The changeover is now half completed. Write a progress report for your supervisor.
2. Write a progress report on an activity you are engaged in at school, work, or in a social and/or community group you belong to.
3. Investigate a local issue that affects you. It might be a proposed tuition

increase at your college, a local tax issue, plans to open or close an industrial plant in the area, or some other issue. Write an interpretive report showing how this issue will affect people in your situation. It should be addressed to a person or group that has some responsibility for what will happen (plant manager, school board, county board of supervisors, and the like).

4. Analyze the program you are majoring in. Write a full report addressed to the president of the college, the appropriate dean, the department head and members of the department recommending an overhaul of the program. Consider that this report may also go to the board of trustees and to the local news media.

5. Review your skills, abilities, and interests. Decide on a profitable part-time service you might offer. Write a proposal pitching your service to potential customers.

appendixes

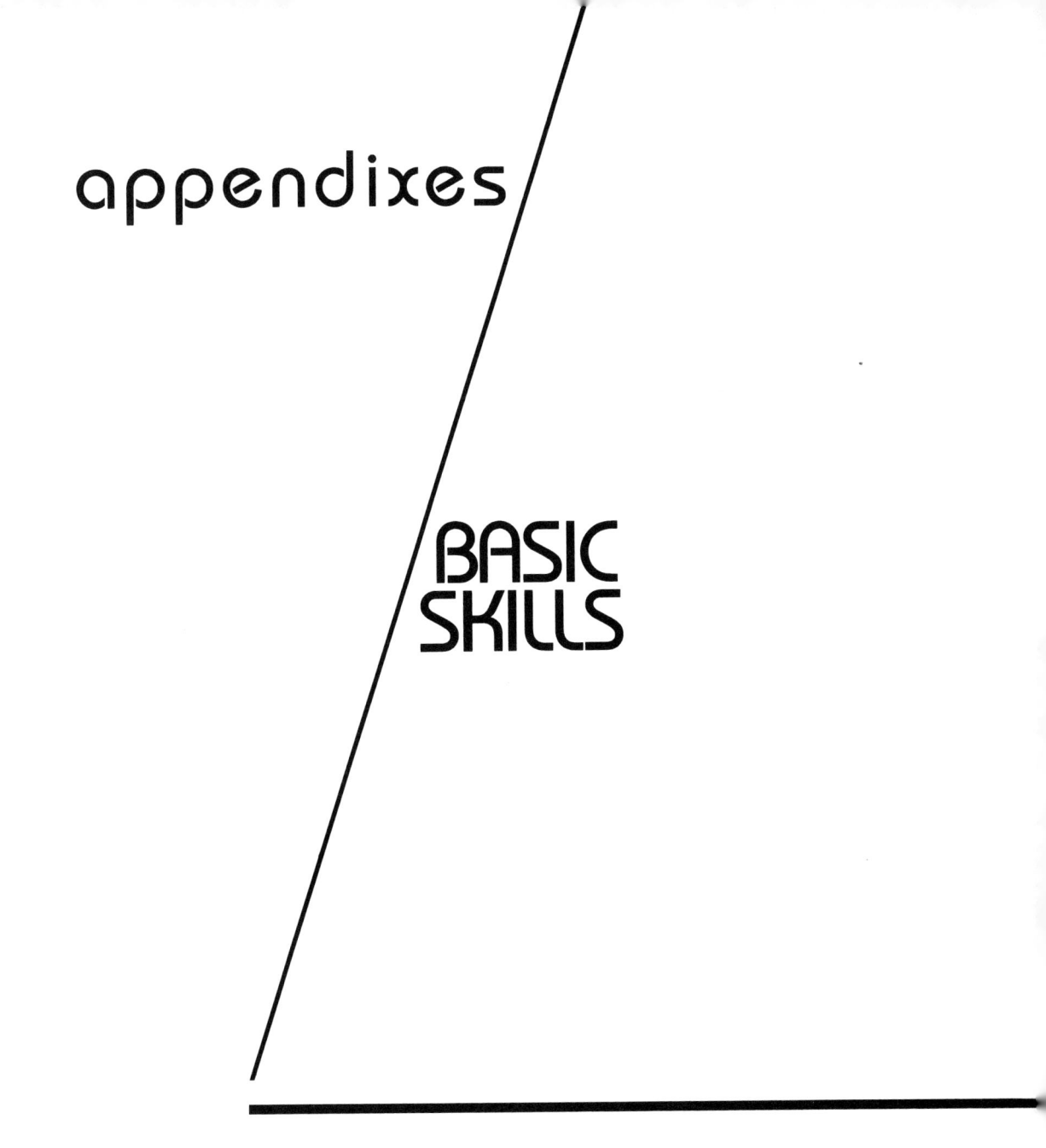

BASIC SKILLS

UNDERSTANDING SENTENCES

You have been creating English sentences since the age of two or three, so you already know a great deal about how sentences are formed. You know more grammar right now than you realize. With very little effort, you can write a sentence which no one has ever written before. Language is not really something you have to "come up to." It's yours already. Although the nonsense sentences following have no meaning, your intuitive knowledge of grammar will lead you to recognize something familiar about them.

EXERCISES

1. Try to figure out what is familiar in the following sentences. Then select any four of these sentences for comparison. Which "words" from one sentence can be substituted for which words in the other three sentences?
    A. The mean strath was swallowing snubs in the smield when the lunter came along.
    B. Smelling the lunter, the strath glopped for the closest thwicket.

C. The flish's foat is the rouchest of them all.
D. The guiches were tribbing while the flishes laksed.
E. Zonk zonked the marbs.
F. Their tramotion kelmed slurkly.
G. They rowked vobally over the kelm.
H. He forbatized the sampic.
I. The slurker's wampability difled.
J. The lean lambers pibbled over the pasture.

2. Write ten standard English sentences to match the preceding ten. For example, to match "The slurker's wampability difled," we could write:
   A. The programmer's responsibility changed
      or
   B. The owner's liability increased.

If you can't explain why these two sentences match the nonsense sentence, simply trust your ear in making your own match.

Word Groups

Think for a moment about what happens when you listen or read. When you listen to someone speaking, you automatically sort the sounds into "chunks." These chunks consist of words, of several words in phrases or clauses, and of longer groups of words. Sorting out these chunks of language enables you to understand what the other person is saying. Listen to someone speaking another language—Japanese or Italian or Spanish. If you don't know the language, you hear an uninterrupted flow of sound all run together with only an occasional pause. You can't hear the chunks.

Phrases and Clauses

The basic word groups in English are: phrases and clauses.

Phrases

A *phrase* is a group of words that does *not* have *both* a *subject* and a *verb* (we'll define these shortly):

The young *woman* (a noun phrase—no verb)
arrived for work (a verb phrase—no subject)
before nine o'clock (a prepositional phrase)

Clauses

A *clause* is a group of words that has both a subject and a verb:

The young *woman arrived* at work.

There are two kinds of clauses: *main* (or *independent*) and *subordinate* (or *dependent*):

1. Main clauses make sense by themselves. They can be set apart as complete sentences: "The young woman arrived at work."
2. Subordinate clauses do not express full meaning by themselves; they must be attached to a main clause in order to make complete sense:

   Because she did not come to work

   Dependent clauses must always be attached to an independent one:

   Because she did not come to work, *the young woman missed the president's visit.*

   Notice how the main clause (italicized) could have been set apart as an *independent* clause.

Obviously, phrases (which lack the combination of subject and verb) must also be attached to independent clauses.

What Is a Sentence?

Sentences range in length from one word ("Fire!"; "Congratulations.") to several thousand words. But between these extremes there are a few basic sentence patterns that will serve your writing needs in school, at work, and in the community. A simple working definition is that:

A SENTENCE IS A WORD OR GROUP OF WORDS EXPRESSING A MEANINGFUL MESSAGE.

The word "Hello," for example, makes a meaningful message by itself, but "She says hello to. . . ." is meaningless. The two words "I do" are meaningful, but the five words "Before they said I do...," are meaningless. The rest of this chapter explains the basic elements of grammar that you need to know to write clear, meaningful sentences.

Subject Groups and Verb Groups

The basic structure of all English sentences can be described by a very simple formula:

SG + VG (Subject Group + Verb Group)

The subject group tells your reader what you are going to talk about by naming it. It may also tell how big it is; how small it is; what color it is; what kind it is; where it is; which one of many other things it is. Here is a subject group:

> The President of the United States

This phrase names what we are talking about (the President) and what kind it is (of the United States). But the message is meaningless by itself. It needs a verb group. The verb group tells what it is you want to say about that subject group. The verb group is the power source, like the engine in a car or the batteries in a flashlight. The verb group either puts the subject group into action or it tells what the subject group is in itself, is going to do, or has done; it may tell how it is doing what it does, where it is taking place, at what time it is taking place, and why it is taking place, or it may tell us who or what the action is done to. Here is a verb group:

> lives in the White House.

The verb "lives" tells us what the President is doing and the phrase "in the White House" tells us where he does it.

Remember, sentences are built from groups of words, not from one word added to another. Try to see sentences as groups of words in systematic relationships to each other.

The formula SG + VG shows that the subject usually stands in front of the verb: you usually tell someone what you are talking about before saying what it does. Ordinarily we don't say:

> *South in the winter fly birds.

> *Is on the table the brown cup.

The simplest SG + VG sentence is rarely used in English, but knowing this pattern enables you to gain better control of your own writing. Two-word sentences such as these exemplify this pattern:

*An asterisk is used to mark sentence constructions that do not conform to standard English patterns.

SG	+	VG
He		works.
She		won.
Birds		fly.

We can begin adding new words to expand our meaning and yet keep this basic structure intact.

SG	+	VG
The *birds*		fly.
All the *birds*		fly.
All the *birds* of one color		fly.
All the *birds* of one color that landed in my yard		fly.

Here we have expanded only the subject group, giving more information about the subject of the sentence, birds. To expand information about the verb, add words, phrases, and clauses to the verb group part of the sentence. Begin to look and listen for words, phrases, and clauses commonly used to expand sentences (the "that" group in the preceding example is one of them). More important, look and listen for the two "halves" of the sentence, the subject group and the verb group. In this type of sentence, where the SG ends, the VG begins.

SG	+	VG
These birds		probably fly south.
These birds		usually fly south.
These birds		probably fly south for the winter.
These birds		usually fly against the wind for faster lift.
These birds		probably fly south for the winter at the same time each year.

Dividing the sentence into these parts, SG+VG, makes it easier to spot the specific word (sometimes several words working together) that is the subject of the entire sentence and the word (or words) that is the main verb.

Adverbials

The verb group in a sentence often contains a word or group of words that adds more specific information about the action being performed. These words, phrases, or clauses are called adverbs, because they *add* information to a *verb*. An adverb will usually tell one or perhaps several of these five types of information:

1. TIME or FREQUENCY: now, then, yesterday, tomorrow, never, occasionally . . .
2. PLACE or DIRECTION: here, there, everywhere, up, down, around, in and out . . .
3. MANNER: slowly, quickly, fearfully, courageously . . .
4. DEGREE: little, much, very, too, almost, quite . . .
5. CAUSE: why, for this reason, because, in order to . . .

With these qualifier adverbs, you can build from the simple sentence: "The compressor broke down," to give important information.

TIME: The compressor broke down *yesterday.*
PLACE: The compressor broke down *in its rotor assembly.*
MANNER: The compressor broke down *very quickly.*
DEGREE: The compressor broke down *beyond repair.*
CAUSE: The compressor broke down *because of a faulty bearing.*

Although many adverbs end in *ly*, some do not, and some words that end in *ly* are not adverbs. So the best way to find adverbs is to look for words that qualify verbs, adjectives, and other adverbs by answering the questions: When? Where? Why? How? To what degree? Notice above that "quickly" is an adverb of manner (tells how); "very" is also an adverb because it modifies "quickly."

EXERCISE

Complete the following sentences using adverbs as indicated.

Time: The contractor examined _____.
          The insurance adjuster filed _____.
Place: The production manager wants _____.
          The personnel department moved _____.
Manner: Stainless steel bearings wear _____.
          Microsurgery has developed _____.
Degree: Anodized aluminum resists _____.
          The project coordinator must inform _____.
Cause: The impeller blades were damaged _____.
          The patient's death resulted _____.

We have described the basic structure of the sentence in terms of groups of words. Sentences are built by combining smaller groups of words into a larger structure. Many problems with writing disappear as soon as a writer sees the sentence as a structure built from word groups rather than from isolated words.

REVIEW EXERCISES

1. From the following list, combine as many subject groups, verb groups, and adverb groups as you can; that is, any one subject group will combine with more than one verb group or adverb group to form separate sentences. For example, the SG's *he and she* can combine with each of the VG's *ran,* and *jumped* to make: "He ran," "He jumped," "She ran," "She jumped." You may change verb forms to make subject and verb agree.

SG	VG	AG
The supervisor	try to do good work	most of the time
My friends	is asking for help	without pay
A stranger	have been in court	before noon
Most of the lawyers	has graduated	as quickly as possible
All the nurses	want to go	within the past five years

2. Divide the following sentences into their SG, VG, and AG.
   A. An extension spring shackle provides space to adjust the spring.
   B. Gasoline is pumped into the carburetor bowl by the fuel pump.
   C. A horse costs fifteen dollars in Cheyenne.
   D. Juan owns an apartment house in Missoula.
   E. The gloves protect his hands from the heat.
   F. The supervisor ran across the plant toward the loading dock.
   G. The doctor couldn't believe her son was still critically ill.

3. Rearrange the following strings of words into SG and VG so as to form sentences. For example:

   *by students most success highly motivated are. Most students + are highly motivated by success.
   A. *young trees apple in the grow spring rapidly
   B. *your by July 21 down payment be must available
   C. *waiting me saw lawyer the
   D. *stands he upright of the flying boat in the tossed bow
   E. *at he the whale levels the lance

4. Now write five sentences of your own and label the SG and VG in each.

Nouns and Verbs

The bases of subject groups and verb groups in sentences are words that name (nouns) and words that show action (verbs).

Finding Nouns

Nouns are a large class of words that name persons, places, things, or ideas. You probably have no trouble recognizing *proper* nouns such as *Ronald Reagan, George Washington, General Motors, Boston, Barberton Memorial Hospital. Common* nouns such as *apple, field, plant, water, dishes, tulip,* and *oak* are easily recognized. But if you're not sure whether *forgetfulness* or *beautification* are nouns or not, the following noun-finder hints will help.

Determiners

One small group of words, called determiners, signals that a noun will follow. These words are almost always used with a noun; their basic function is to say, "Look! Here comes a noun." On rare occasion, they may be used with a pronoun instead of a noun.

a	the	my	our
an	every	your	their

A few examples of determiners pointing to nouns follow:

a drill press *a* heliarc welder
an American Pace Maker Lathe *the* South Bend Lathe
every machine in the shop *your* AC-DC arc welder

Quite often, descriptive words will come between the determiner and the noun, but you'll have no trouble distinguishing nouns from descriptive words if you apply all these noun-finder hints. A noun will always answer the question "What?" after a determiner. For example, in "a beautiful old carpet," we ask, "A what?" The only answer is "A carpet"; "a beautiful" and "a old" can't stand alone.

Demonstratives

The words *this, that, these,* and *those* usually signal that nouns will follow: *This* man, *these* women, *those* tools, *that* job. These words may also be pronouns substituting for nouns: "This must be done," "Those must go," and "That will not do."

EXERCISES

1. Make a list of all the determiners and demonstratives you could write in the following blanks.
   _____ truck hit _____ father's mailbox.
2. Using the determiner test, underline the nouns in the following sentences:
   A. People live longer today than ever before.
   B. These advances in medicine have prolonged life.
   C. A cure for cancer remains to be found.
   D. The truck caused the accident.
   E. After the game, some friends came to my house.
   F. My forgetfulness cost me a promotion.

Number

Another method for recognizing nouns is to look for words that change number. Almost all nouns have a *singular* (one) form and a *plural* (more than one) form. One student, but two student*s*; anxiety, but anxiet*ies*; one child, but two child*ren*. You can often identify a word as a noun simply by checking to see if it has a singular and a plural form.

EXERCISE

Which of the following words can be identified as nouns by using this method of checking for words that can change in number?

man	children	generous
job	already	student
woman	rabbit	work

hurry	safely	worker
kind	home	book
word	raised	read

Prepositions

A certain group of words called prepositions also are noun signals. These are words like *of*, *to*, *with*, *into*, *over*, *after*, and *before*. We usually go *to* somewhere, or we think *about* something, or we fall *into* something. The "something" is a noun or a word doing the work of a noun; prepositions and their noun objects (italicized below) make up prepositional phrases:

from the *field*	in the *beginning*
of the *frost*	before the *dawn*
into the *lake*	after *work*

EXERCISE

Identify the nouns in the following prepositional phrases:

against all possible odds	into a difficult period
up the wall	over the top
to Baltimore	with Joe

Possession

Most nouns can be made to show possession by adding *'s* or *s'*.

Bill's wheelbarrow	the cat's fur
the tree's limbs	the houses' windows
the woman's beauty	the cars' engines

EXERCISE

Try to identify words that could be nouns in the following list of words by making them possessive:

carburetor   hygiene
book   law
look   valuables
sit   energy
blow   handles

EXERCISES ON FINDING NOUNS

1. Using a variety of "noun-finders," underline the nouns in the following sentences:
   A. Taxpayers have shelled out $72 million.
   B. Taxpayers paid $12 million to build a highway that goes nowhere.
   C. Now an additional $1 million is being spent on an environmental study.
   D. The state government is trying to determine whether the road should be completed.
   E. Natural gas will be in great demand this winter.
   F. Supplies of natural gas are dwindling.
   G. Certain sections of the country will have blackouts and shortages during the winter.
   H. Wood-burning stoves are a hot item in cold climates.
   I. Some of these stoves can burn for twelve hours without adding fuel.
   J. Natural gas prices are expected to rise by 15 percent next year.

2. Write ten sentences, underlining all nouns. Be prepared to explain what test or tests you used to identify each noun.

Finding Verbs

There are three types of verbs:

1. verbs of physical action (e.g., *kiss, hit, throw, run, jump, explode*)
2. verbs of mental or emotional action (e.g., *think, hope, fear, hate*)
3. verbs of being or linking verbs (e.g., *is, are, was, becomes, gets, seems*)

To find verbs, simply look for words that take *-ed* for the past tense, or an internal vowel change to make the past tense or the present tense: talk–talk*ed*; walk–walk*ed*; work–work*ed*; sing–s*a*ng; ring–r*a*ng; bring–

brought; teach–taught. The verbs *be, go,* and *have* are exceptions to this rule: *be* changes the entire form of the word from *is, am,* and *are* in the present to *was, were,* and *been* in the past; *have* and *has* change to *had; go* becomes *went* and *gone.* Only verbs change to show tense or time.

This verb-finding method works also for finding words that are doing the work of verbs in any particular sentence. The word "house," for example, is usually a noun; but like many other nouns, it can also be a verb: "They house the team at the Colonial Inn." To test words that you think might be functioning as verbs, add, one at a time, the words "yesterday," "today," and "tomorrow" to the beginning of the sentence. If the word changes its form to show time changes, it is functioning as a verb:

"Yesterday, they hous*ed* the team at the Colonial Inn."

"Tomorrow, they *will house* the team at the Colonial Inn."

A second method for finding verbs is to try adding *-ing* to a word. Only verbs (or nouns that can act as verbs) can have an *-ing* form: add–add*ing;* work–work*ing;* run–runn*ing;* study–study*ing* (but *not:* boy–boy*ing;* grass–grass*ing;* sky–sky*ing*). The combination of the *-ing* test and the "yesterday, today, and tomorrow" test should enable you to identify all the verbs, and nouns acting as verbs, in any sentence.

EXERCISE

Underline verbs or words functioning as verbs in the following sentences:

1. General Dynamics will hire twenty college graduates.
2. The Tanned Hide Shoe Company uses several trade names.
3. They trade sales districts.
4. Tensile strength decreases with age.
5. Antioxidants, properly applied, preserve rubber.
6. The Fireman's Casualty Company issues monthly reports.
7. She reports the news sensitively.
8. Twelve ships are docked because of the strike.
9. Consolidated Freight ships by truck.
10. Consolidated Freight trucked continuously during the strike.
11. Machines are becoming more complicated every year.
12. Roller bearings are machined to precise specifications.
13. Timken specified the size of its bearings.

14. They will buy the plant by the river.
15. At $500,000, it was a good buy.
16. Vaccines have been developed against polio and influenza.
17. Heart disease accounts for more than half the deaths in the USA.
18. To keep her accounts in order, she bought two new files.
19. New accounts must be filed immediately.
20. Before it expires, we must renew our account.

Finding Main Verbs

From finding nouns and verbs in sentences, there are only a few more steps to enable you to find the grammatical *subject* and *main* verb.

Once you have identified all the verbs in your sentence, narrow your search for the main verb by following these three principles:

1. The *-ing* form of the verb can never by itself be the main verb; it must have helpers.
2. The word "to" plus a verb can never by themselves be the main verb.
3. Verbs in *dependent* clauses can never be the main verb.

The -ing Form of the Verb

The *-ing* form of the verb without a helping verb is usually working as an adjective or as a noun, but never as a verb. Even though it expresses the sense of action or being that verbs do, when it is by itself it cannot be working as a verb.

1. *-ing* form as adjective: (Here the *-ing* forms describes a noun.)
   A. A *rolling* stone gathers no moss.
   B. Most houses today have *running* water.
   C. The *Leaning* Tower of Pisa is famous.
   D. The village smithy stands under the *spreading* chestnut tree.
2. *-ing* form as a noun: (Here the *-ing* forms name an activity, just as nouns do.)
   A. *Jogging* and *swimming* are fun.
   B. *Studying* requires self-discipline.
   C. He spends too much time *sleeping*.
   D. *Thinking* requires much energy.
   E. *Loving* your neighbor is sometimes difficult.

3. *-ing* form as a verb: (This always requires a helping verb and it expresses the action or state of being of the subject of the sentence.) Memorize these helping verbs: am, are, is, was, were, be, been, has, have, had, do, does, did, shall, will, should, would, may, might, must, can, could. Whenever you see these helpers, look for a verb to follow.
   A. I *am* read*ing*. (but not: * I reading.)
   B. You *are* driv*ing*. (but not: * You driving.)
   C. She *might be* leav*ing*. (but not: * She leaving.)
   D. They *should* not *be* liv*ing* here.
   E. You *must have been* expect*ing* us.

A WARNING: Forms of the words *have, be, get,* and *do* can be either main verbs or helpers; but all other helpers tell you a verb is following:

   Main Verb: Hal *has* a houseboat.
   Helper: Hal *has written* his report.

   Main Verb: She *did* her assignment.
   Helper: She *did enjoy* college.

   Main Verb: Emily *was* in class.
   Helper: Emily *was studying* sign language.

   Main Verb: Sharon *got* better quickly.
   Helper: Sharon *gets started* early.

The Infinitive Form of the Verb

The word "to" plus a verb (the *infinitive* form) can never by themselves be the main verb. "To" plus a verb is used to name an activity or to describe something just as *-ing* can.

To succeed is better than *to fail.*

To err is human.

To forgive is divine.

His father told him *to get* a job.

There is a time *to mourn* and a time *to dance.*

In fact, notice that *-ing* words can sometimes be substituted for the infinitive; so can nouns:

Succeeding is better than *failing.*

Success is better than *failure.*

There is a time *for mourning* and a time *for dancing.*

EXERCISES

1. Write ten sentences in which you use *-ing* words. Use some as nouns, some as adjectives, some as verbs. Mark above them with an "N," "Adj," or "V." For example:

      N   V   Adj
   Typing was becoming boring.

2. Use the verb tests to pick out and underline the main verb in the following sentences:
   A. A rolling stone is gathering no moss.
   B. Most houses today are being equipped with good insulation.
   C. The Leaning Tower of Pisa is being painted.
   D. Jogging is going out of fashion.
   E. Studying is becoming easier for me.
   F. He is spending too much time sleeping.
   G. To be or not to be is the question.
   H. His father told him to try looking for a job.
   I. The director of the agency is expecting the full report soon.
   J. She told us to do a better job of detailing client contacts.

Dependent Clauses

Verbs in *dependent* (subordinate) clauses can't be the main verb. Being able to distinguish dependent from *independent* (main) clauses enables you to avoid two of the worst errors: *fragments* and *run-on sentences*.

We have defined a sentence as a word or group of words that express a meaningful message; an independent clause can be defined the same way. It can stand alone because it conveys a meaningful message. Notice the difference between these independent and dependent clauses:

> He isn't going to be coddled.
> If he learns he isn't going to be coddled. . . .
>
> He needn't expect a lot of free food.
> Although he needn't expect a lot of free food. . . .
>
> He earns them.
> Unless he earns them. . . .
>
> The country needs workers who will produce, produce, produce.
> Because the country needs workers who will produce. . . .

In each of these examples, the independent clause is made dependent by simply adding a word or two. Although dependent clauses have a subject and verb relationship, they can't stand alone. They begin with words called *subordinators*, which make the entire clause logically dependent on another clause. For example, notice how all the following independent statements are easily made incomplete by adding just one word at the beginning of each.

> He wants to be promoted.
> *If* he wants to be promoted.... (another clause is needed)

> The superintendents failed to tabulate results.
> *When* the superintendents failed to tabulate results....

> Our company wishes to avoid complaints.
> *Because* our company wishes to avoid complaints....

Memorize the following subordinators. They stand at the beginning of a group of words, usually a dependent clause, and they connect that clause to an independent clause. Do you feel the sense of incompleteness that these words create?

after	how	unless	while
although	if	until	who
as	in order that	what	whose
as if	since	whatever	whom
as long as	so	when	whoever
as soon as	so that	whenever	whomever
because	that	where	
before	till	which	

DON'T LOOK FOR THE MAIN VERB IN ANY GROUP OF WORDS ATTACHED TO THE INDEPENDENT CLAUSE BY ANY OF THESE SUBORDINATOR WORDS.

Dependent clauses contain both a subject and a verb, but the subject of the whole sentence and the main verb are always in the independent clause. Notice also that dependent clauses usually come at the very end or the very beginning of your sentences and are usually separated from the main clause by a pause in speech. In writing, separate a dependent clause with a comma when it comes at the beginning of the sentence. For example:

While you were working, I painted the kitchen.

The street will be wet if it rains.

After she graduated from college, her salary increased.

EXERCISE

In the following sentences, we have bracketed the dependent clauses. Underline the subordinator once and the main verb of the sentence twice.

Notice that a comma usually separates the independent and dependent clauses, except when the dependent clause comes at the end.

1. [After she graduates next spring], she will begin working.
2. [Although she graduates next spring], she will not begin working.
3. [As she had planned for years], Karen became a hospital dietitian.
4. [As long as we have known her], Karen has wanted to be a dietitian.
5. She handled her responsibilities well, [as if she had done them for years].
6. [Because you need to know more about office management], you should take a few more business courses.
7. [Before you start applying for jobs], take a few more business courses.
8. The technician explained [how the gas exploded].
9. [If you start applying now], you should have a job by graduation.
10. Eileen has planned to be a computer programmer [since she was a child].
11. Eileen is taking more business courses [so she can be a computer programmer].
12. Eileen is taking more business courses [so that she can be a computer programmer].
13. Ralph was an emergency medical technician [until he graduated].
14. [Unless résumés are sent now], they cannot be processed.
15. [When Kevin finishes his course work], he must take a licensing exam.
16. Kevin, [whose course work is finished], is taking his licensing exam.
17. Kevin, [who finished his course work], is taking his licensing exam.
18. Jeff studied at the commercial art school [that his father attended].
19. This is the school [that his father recommends].
20. The Simpson program, [which we discussed last week], is still available.

Finding the Subject

Who + Verb; What + Verb

Once you have located the main verb in the independent clause, apply this simple subject test to see if you, in fact, have a subject.

THE SUBJECT ANSWERS THE QUESTION "WHO+VERB?" OR "WHAT+VERB?"

Bob Gladding sold the most merchandise last month.

"Sold" is the verb because it is the only word that changes to show time. The vowel *o* changes to *e* to make the present tense, *sell* (future: *will sell*). Now ask "Who sold?" The answer is *Bob Gladding*.

EXERCISE

Underline the main verb and then the subject of these sentences:

1. A sales quota was established for the department.
2. They will honor two employees at the banquet.
3. Loyal to whomever serves his need, Babbitt outsells them all.
4. After school he planned to drive to Chicago.
5. Whenever he sees poor workmanship, he gets very angry.
6. In five minutes, the machine should be repaired.
7. For three days, the work was halted because of the strike.
8. Living in the suburbs requires her to drive thirty-five miles to work.
9. You may have to write a brochure to advertise a new product.
10. Jack and Jill were clumsy.

Prepositional Phrases

Another very important principle to keep in mind while checking your sentences for subjects and verbs is that the subject can never be part of a prepositional phrase. As we noted earlier (p. 268), prepositions are words like *at, by, for, from, in, of, on, to,* and *with* (see p. 288 for a more complete list). A prepositional phrase is simply one of these words and a noun or a word doing the work of a noun:

at the office   on the desk
by the people   to the theater
for the people   with the intention
from the shop   during the class

UNDERSTANDING SENTENCES | 277

    in the beginning   behind the house
    of the boys   over the rainbow

Frequently the prepositional phrase comes between the subject and the main verb. To avoid mistaking the noun in the prepositional phrase for the sentence subject, mentally remove the phrase before trying to match the main verb and subject.

    The memos [on the desk] are mine.

Removing the prepositional phrase shows that *are* is the verb and *memos* the subject. Here are two more examples:

    X-ray *technicians* [at Temple Hospital] are on strike.

    Agricultural *production* [in the New England states] is declining.

EXERCISE

Put parentheses around the prepositional phrases in each of the following sentences. Then underline the subject of the sentence once and the main verb twice.

1. The tires for the truck seem very expensive.
2. Each of the employees must belong to the union.
3. Some of the new transformers shorted out.
4. Sound-level meters at major intersections registered above 70db.
5. Sound levels above 70db are considered objectionable.
6. The drills against the wall have been inspected.
7. Steel wires around a cylindrical sheath protect the phone cable.
8. Tests at a laboratory in New York determined that the manufacturer met all specifications.
9. The control valve behind the boiler leaks.
10. Profits in the oil industry during the first quarter doubled.
11. Actual labor costs for the job will be posted.
12. Nursing majors from eleven colleges were interviewed Monday.
13. Charts in the manager's office show that our productivity is improving.
14. Job opportunities of various types are listed in the classified pages.
15. Emotional stress on psychiatric nurses is difficult to measure.

Agreement

Verb forms change to match their noun subjects; singular nouns take singular verbs; plural nouns require plural verb forms.

We will discuss agreement more thoroughly in Appendix C (pp. 299–320), but many, if not most, agreement problems are caused by making the verb agree in number (either singular or plural) with a nearby noun in a prepositional phrase rather than with the actual subject, which is farther away from the verb. Ordinarily, if the subject of your sentence is singular, it will not end in *s* for the plural, so the verb takes the *s*:

> The car_ seems expensive.
>
> The house_ sits on the hill.
>
> The boy_ tries to study while watching television.

On the other hand, if the subject is plural, it will usually have an *s* but the verb won't.

> The cars seem_ expensive.
>
> The houses sit_ on the hill.
>
> The boys try_ to study while listening to Bartok.

Words that show the plural by a change of spelling rather than with -s also follow the -s rule.

> The man dresses expensively.
> The men dress_ expensively.
>
> The mouse sits on the still.
> The mice sit_ on the still.
>
> The goose flies.
> The geese fly_.

Because of this rule, you automatically add or withhold the *s* of the verb depending on whether your subject is singular or plural. But agreement problems arise when, in constructing longer sentences, you place nouns between the subject and verb. Your ear will catch the *s* sound or the lack of it of the noun closest to the verb and cause you to make the verb agree with the wrong noun. In proofreading your own writing, first cover up all prepositional phrases (and, of course, dependent clauses), then do the subject test. For example:

> The tires for the car seem expensive.
> The tires for the car seems expensive.
>
> One of the boys tries to study while listening to Bartok.
> One of the boys try to study while listening to Bartok.

Your ear might tell you that the second and fourth sentences above are correct because *car seems* and *boys try* sound correct. The problem is that *car* isn't the subject of *seems* and *boys* isn't the subject of *try*. Both the subject test and the prepositional phrase rule tell us that neither *car* nor *boys* are subjects. Therefore, the first and third sentences are correct.

EXERCISE

In the following sentences, underline the subject and main verb; change any verb forms that do not agree in number with the subject.

1. Neither of the parachutes opened in time.
2. Each of the employees pay union dues.
3. One of our teachers dislike using class time to show films.
4. That fellow in the brown mackintosh appearing in various places is unknown to us.
5. Thousands of household products are potentially dangerous.
6. In the future, people will have a great deal of leisure time.
7. My cousin, who has lost many jobs, were fired this time for drinking at work.

REVIEW EXERCISES

In each of the following sentences, put brackets—[ ]—around subordinate clauses and parentheses—( )—around prepositional phrases. This helps emphasize the technique of mentally removing these groups from sentences when checking for the subject and main verb. Underline the subject once and the main verb twice.

1. The engineer who was assigned the Balsam River project mysteriously disappeared after work.
2. The plumber who installed our sink in the kitchen did a good job.
3. After the officer made the arrest, she had to write a detailed report for the captain.

4. Because of some confusing sections, she was asked to rewrite it.
5. The builders in our area continue to plan projects as if land were unlimited.
6. As long as they are permitted, monopolies will control the market.
7. Before consumer protection groups developed in recent years, the buyer had little recourse.
8. When it is time for a new contract, support for the union increases.
9. During the negotiations, the National Labor Relations Board was brought in.
10. Whatever their personal preference may be, they are bound to advise objectively.
11. When he leaned over the engine, the fan blade nearly hit his arm.
12. Because the boss did not know who was to blame, he accepted the responsibility himself.
13. Taxpayers have shelled out $72 million to build a highway that goes nowhere.
14. Now an additional $1 million is being spent on an environmental study to determine whether the road should be completed.
15. The current environmental impact study is being prepared by a private consulting firm hired by the state.
16. The price has increased from $500,000 to $1 million in a little over two years.
17. The rough draft currently weighs about ten pounds.
18. Four small segments of the highway, totaling thirteen miles, have been built.
19. One of them, a 2.5-mile stretch completed in 1970 at a cost of $3.7 million, is used once a year as a parking lot during a tournament at the Radnor Valley Country Club near suburban Rosemont.
20. In one case, homeowners were forced to sell, then the state rented their houses to other people when it became apparent the properties would be sitting idle for quite some time.

B

COMBINING SENTENCES

Why Combine Sentences?

As children we all began speaking with one-word sentences, then expanded these into two- and three-word sentences such as "My ball," "Give me," and "Give me ball." The fact that you no longer speak nor write such simple sentences is evidence of your unconscious sentence-combining ability. Most of the sentences that you write have already gone through that process. Through years of using language, your sentences develop into longer, more precise, more varied forms. And yet you or your instructor or employer may find your writing too wordy, too repetitious, unclear, or monotonous. If so, you need to face up to the fact that your sentences must be revised with these points in mind. Simply starting all over again, hoping it will turn out better, won't help either. Nearly every piece of good writing goes through an extensive process of revision.

This section explains five basic methods of expanding and combining your sentences to improve the following characteristics:

1. economy
2. clarity
3. variety
4. emphasis.

Economy

Economy here means combining several sentences into one to express the same ideas in fewer words. It sounds ridiculous to say: "Birds fly. They fly south. They fly south in the winter. Birds fly to a warmer climate." To avoid the needless repetition here, we simply combine all the facts into one sentence. We can do this because all the facts relate to the same subject, which needs to be mentioned only once. Instead of seventeen words, we use only ten: "Birds fly south in the winter to a warmer climate."

Your own writing is advanced well beyond sentences like "Birds fly. Birds fly south." But the same type of problem is found in more advanced levels. Consider the following example:

> Sheila works for General Motors. She works the graveyard shift. She doesn't like the work.

Notice that these sentences use the same basic sentence pattern SG + VG. *They also have the same subject*—Sheila—which means that the rest of each sentence states additional information about her. For the same reason that we combined all those sentences on birds, we can combine these three. We don't need to repeat the subject that often. One possible combination of these is:

> Sheila doesn't like her work on the graveyard shift at General Motors.

We left out no details yet used fewer words. This is economy. This section introduces you to techniques for combining sentences in this way.

Clarity

You know that the meaning of your sentences depends on using the right words. But clear meaning is also controlled by the relationship of one sentence to the next. No matter how carefully you choose words to state facts in each particular sentence, your meaning will not be clear if you don't indicate exactly how the sentences relate. For example, someone says:

> "The road was covered with five inches of snow. Jack ran into the back of a truck."

The meaning of each sentence seems clear enough. The meaning of both sentences together might be obvious. But the message seems clear only because we *assume* that the snow was the cause of the accident. Should we assume this? Notice that the word *cause* is not mentioned in either sentence. There could have been a number of other reasons why Jack hit the truck. Remember the difference between *sequence* and *causality* from Chapter 8. Jack could have fallen asleep at the wheel or swerved to avoid a deer. A careful writer clarifies the relationship between sentences so the reader doesn't have to assume anything; and, in this case, the best way to do this is to combine the two sentences, being careful to *use connecting words and phrases that clearly point out the relationship:*

> *Because* the road was covered with five inches of snow, Jack ran into the back of a truck.

Combining these sentences makes the meaning clear; it takes the guessing out of reading. Here is another example:

> Jack has problems with his boss. He isn't getting along well with his girlfriend.

What is the meaning of these two sentences together? Are the troubles with work and those with his girlfriend at all related? Is, perhaps, the trouble at work caused in some way by the troubles with the friend? Or is it the other way around? Or are they both the result of some other cause entirely? We don't know. These sentences could be combined in a number of ways to show exactly what the relationship is:

> Jack's troubles with his girlfriend are creating problems at work.
>
> Because of Jack's problem with his boss, he isn't getting along with his girlfriend.
>
> Jack's problems with his parents have caused troubles with his boss and his girlfriend.

Combining sentences to show relationships makes our meaning clear.

Variety

Combining sentences for economy and clarity usually achieves a third objective—variety. Sometimes, your sentences may be economically constructed and clear, but in rereading your work you notice that too many of the sentences seem to *sound* the same. This is caused by overusing one sentence pattern so that it becomes monotonous. Listen to and feel the repetitive rhythms of this paragraph.

> McMurphy was a savior. He came to the asylum boisterous and full of fight. The men pictured him fearless as he bravely saved them from the Big Nurse's actions. They pictured him as a deliverer as he helped them to escape the asylum in their own way. They pictured him as a martyr. He died helping the men.

Using a few of the combining techniques you will soon learn these sentences can be restructured to avoid the repetitive use of one pattern (SG +

VG). Notice that the subject of each of these sentences is right at the beginning. Several of them even have the same subject and the same verb:

McMurphy was

he came

men pictured

they pictured

they pictured

he died

Compare the original paragraph to this one after combining:

McMurphy was a savior, coming to the asylum boisterous and full of fight. The men pictured him a fearless deliverer as he bravely saved them from Big Nurse's actions and helped them escape the asylum in their own way. When he died helping the men, they honored him as a martyr.

The difference between these two passages is not the result of "talent." The five techniques of combining we are about to explain will help you rewrite and revise your own sentences just as effectively.

Emphasis

Anything done habitually, repeated too often, becomes dull. And the mind soon turns away from dullness. If you want to make your writing interesting and increase the clarity, you'll need to know how to emphasize whatever particular word or idea in a sentence you want to. You'll also want to know how to avoid emphasizing points that shouldn't be emphasized. During the war in Vietnam, on several occasions we heard radio and television news announcers give reports such as this:

Today in Vietnam four American F105 fighter bombers were shot down at a cost of $24 million and all four pilots have been reported lost.

Although it's difficult to say exactly why, the sensitive listener is offended by listening to someone who talks first about "fighter bombers," then about "dollars," then finally adds, like a footnote at the bottom of the page, the most important point of all, the loss of the pilots.

There's no rule saying that the first position in a sentence is always the most emphatic; sometimes the last is. But in general follow these three principles:

1. Emphasize by placing the most important point first.
2. Emphasize by varying your sentence structures.
3. Emphasize by careful word choice; avoid lifeless words.

For example:

> The question is whether or not to commit suicide.

The meaning is clear enough; but compare:

> Suicide—that is the question.

Ways to Combine Sentences

The units most useful in sentence combining can be classified in five main types:

1. Independent (coordinate) groups
2. Prepositional groups (phrases)
3. *Wh-* groups (relative clauses)
4. *-ing* and *-ed* groups
5. Dependent (subordinate) groups

Let's take a closer look at each of these and practice using them in sentence combining.

Combining Independent (Coordinate) Groups

Using Coordinating Words

This technique of sentence combining brings two sentences into an equal and parallel relationship with each other. It relies on the use of "joining" words (conjunctions) that signal an *equal relationship* between two groups of words:

> and   or   but
> nor   yet   for

Basically, these coordinating words add one unit to another, or *contrast* one equal (but opposite or conflicting) unit with another. We can't gain economy, clarity, and variety by inserting *and* between any or all our sentences. But try to combine those sentences that make two closely related statements about the same subject. The easiest way, shown in the sentences below, is to simply insert the *and* or other coordinating words preceded by a comma.

1. The house is well-built. It is reasonably priced.
   The house is well-built, *and* it is reasonably priced.
2. Sally is looking for a job. She has been promised five interviews.
   Sally is looking for a job, *and* she has been promised five interviews.
3. The contractor promised completion of June 1. The lumber yard couldn't deliver the material in time. (The relationship between these two sentences is very close, but the second one suggests opposition to the first so join them with a comma and *but*.)
   The contractor promised completion by June 1, *but* the lumber yard couldn't deliver the materials in time.
4. You must come up with the balance of the payment. You will lose your deposit. (Combining these two sentences is not only desirable to avoid the choppy style, but this is necessary to clarify the relationship between the two.)
   You must come up with the balance of the payment, *or* you will lose your deposit.

Notice that wherever *and, but, yet, or, nor* are used to join two sentences, they are preceded by a comma. The comma and the coordinating word take the place of the period. On the other hand, don't use a comma before these words when they are used to connect words *within* an independent clause. It's easy to see the difference.

Jack_ and Jill should have been more careful. (*and* connects two nouns to make a compound subject; no comma)

Jack fell down_ and broke his crown, *and* Jill came tumbling after. (The second *and* connects two independent clauses—two complete messages that could stand alone as sentences—so the comma precedes the *and*.)

Don't write one independent clause after another without punctuation (called a *run-on* sentence). Use one of these three forms of punctuation:

Independent clause.   Independent clause. (a period)

Independent clause;   independent clause. (semicolon)

Independent clause, { and but / or for / nor yet } independent clause. (comma + coordinating word)

COMBINING SENTENCES | 287

Don't use the comma by itself (without a coordinating word) to separate independent clauses; this produces the infamous, the nefarious comma splice!

> Jack suffered a fractured skull, Jill had multiple contusions.

EXERCISE

Combine these sentences using coordinating words; remember the comma:

1. Nursing provides a service to the community. It is interesting work.
2. Recreation leadership is not a well-established program at many colleges. It offers an occupation with great potential for growth.
3. Real-estate management is demanding work. It provides a flexible schedule.
4. Would you prefer to work in a large city? Are you more interested in rural areas?
5. Farm management is not limited by geographical opportunity. It is not an overcrowded occupation.

Avoiding Repetition

As you may have noticed by now, combining with coordinating words helps smooth the choppy style and makes relationships clearer. You may also have noticed that some of the combinations you have just made could be changed to save repeating words needlessly. In fact, excessive repetition of words is a signal for the need to combine. Trust your ear to detect needless repetition by reading your rough draft aloud.

Going back to the first example on p. 286, we found that adding a comma and the word "and" to combine the two simple sentences reduced the choppy rhythm. Yet if you listen closely, you'll detect a repetition in: "The house is" and "it is." Look at the following sentence combinations and note how repetitions are eliminated:

1. The house is well-built, and it is reasonably priced. (There is nothing wrong with this sentence. It emphasizes by repetition. But if you have too many repetitions of this sort, combine them even further.)

    The house is well-built, and *it is* reasonably priced.
    The house is well-built and reasonably priced. (Because *and* is now con-

necting only two small parts of a sentence, the comma doesn't precede it as when *and* joins two independent clauses.)

2. Sally is looking for a job, and she has been promised five interviews. (The word group immediately following *and*—"has been promised five interviews"—can't stand alone as a complete message, so *and* doesn't require the comma.)

EXERCISES

1. Reread the sentences in the last exercise and listen for repeated words. Then combine them as we have just demonstrated.
2. Read the following sentences as though they were part of your rough draft. Combine them when necessary or leave them as they are. Remember the comma and coordinating word if you simply join two independent clauses.
   A. I had a contract to survey a route for a great mining ditch in California.
   B. I had only three weeks to get there by sea.
   C. There were a good many passengers.
   D. I had very little to say to them.
   E. Reading and dreaming were my passions.
   F. I avoided conversation to indulge in these appetites.
   G. There were three professional gamblers on board.
   H. They were rough, repulsive fellows.
   I. I never had any talk with them.
   J. I could not help seeing them with some frequency.
   K. They gambled in an upper-deck stateroom every day and night.
   L. Their door stood a little ajar to let out the surplus tobacco smoke.
   M. It also stood ajar to let out the profanity.
   N. They were an evil presence, and they were a hateful presence.

Combining Sentences with Prepositional Groups (Phrases)

Prepositional groups begin with prepositions. Those that you learned on page 268 are the most frequently used. Here they are again with others:

about	at	for	under
above	back of	from	up
according to	before	in	upon
across	behind	inside	with

after	beside	into	within
against	beyond	near	without
along	by	of	
among	down	on	
around	during	to	

These groups usually present us with additional information about something in a sentence (e.g., about how, where, or when something was done). Prepositional phrases can often be removed from one sentence and added to another. Remember, repeated words signal the need to combine. Note the prepositional phrases in the following sentences and their use in the combined sentence:

1. The recreation director fired the tennis coach. The tennis coach was fired *on Monday*. (Because *fired* and *the tennis coach* are repeated, we eliminate needless words and combine those left over).

The recreation director fired the tennis coach. ~~The tennis coach was fired~~ on Monday.

The recreation director fired the tennis coach on Monday.

2. The tennis coach found a new job. He found his new job *on Tuesday*. (Listen for repetition; combine the sentences without repetition.)

The tennis coach found a new job. ~~He found his new job~~ on Tuesday.

The tennis coach found a new job on Tuesday.

In reviewing for emphasis keep in mind that prepositional groups, *wh-* groups, *-ing* and *-ed* groups, and dependent clauses are flexible units; they usually can be placed at the beginning or the end of the sentence. And, depending on the sentence, they may be placed within the sentence. For example:

The director fired the coach without giving any reason. (most common order)

Without giving any reason, the director fired the coach.

The director, without giving any reason, fired the coach.

Notice how the second and third sentences provide both variety in structure and a change in emphasis. The second sentence emphasizes that the firing was done without giving any reason. Like the first sentence, the third one emphasizes the director again, but this time with more stress on the lack of a reason than on the firing itself.

Look at the placement of the prepositional phrase in each of the following sentences. How does moving the prepositional phrase affect emphasis in each?

Recreation leadership is not offered *at many colleges*.

At many colleges, recreation leadership is not offered.

Recreation leadership, *at many colleges*, is not offered.

EXERCISES

1. Combine the following sentences to avoid needless repetition and to retain the information provided by the prepositional phrases.
2. As soon as you have combined one group, rearrange the prepositional phrases to make sentences patterned like each of the sentences in the two preceding examples.
3. Be prepared to explain how each revision of the basic sentence achieves greater economy, clarity, variety and/or emphasis. Note if any of the revisions change the meaning of the sentence.

   A. (1) The computer is an IBM-360.
      (2) The computer is in the next room.
   B. (1) The Holmans live in a nice house.
      (2) The house is in a suburb.
      (3) The suburb is near Detroit.
   C. (1) The show is boring.
      (2) The show is on television.
      (3) The show is about education.
   D. (1) The welder carried the tank.
      (2) The tank was on his shoulder.
   E. (1) The old barn was painted red.
      (2) The old barn was on a hill.
      (3) The hill was in Pennsylvania.
   F. (1) She worked two months drawing up the plans.
      (2) The plans were drawn according to government regulations.
      (3) The plans were for a transit system.
   G. (1) His father worked twenty years on the docks.
      (2) The docks ran along the East River.
      (3) The docks were at the south end of the city.
   H. (1) Rick and Mary manage an apartment.
      (2) The apartment is on East Fourth Street.
      (3) The apartment is across town from us.
   I. (1) Audrey went to Puerto Rico.
      (2) She went to look for work.
      (3) She went during her Christmas vacation.
   J. (1) The employees argued that they had a right to strike.
      (2) They argued that the right to strike is within every worker's rights.

Combining Sentences by Using *Wh-* Groups (Relative Clauses)

Wh- groups are clauses that begin with the words *who, whose, which, where* and *that* (obviously *that* doesn't begin with *wh-* and there are other words such as *while* which do, but the five words given above begin what we call *wh-* groups). These groups always provide some specific information about someone or something that has just been named in a sentence. *Wh-* groups enable us to insert information in sentences and avoid the needless repetition of words. They introduce a form of dependent (subordinate) clause, called a "relative clause" because the information in it is related to the someone or something just named.

As before, repetition is the signal to revise by combining sentences. You may have repeated a word itself or perhaps its pronoun substitute. Combine by dropping the repeated words and substituting a *wh-* word, as in the following example:

> The employee was fired for missing work. The employee's house burned.

Substitute *whose* for the repeated "employee's" and insert the added information directly after the word it refers to:

> The employee was fired for missing work.
>   whose
> ~~The employee's~~ house burned.
> The employee whose house burned was fired for missing work.

Obviously, the combined sentence helps us understand a significant relationship that is missing from the first pair of simple sentences by clarifying something specific about the employee named in the sentence. The *wh-* group in this example identifies which employee among many is being talked about. If the employee is named, the *wh-* group is no longer essential to identifying him or her. When the *wh-* group is *not* essential to the sentence's message, it is set off by commas:

> Bill Gardner, whose house burned down, was fired for missing work.

Here are some more examples:

> The engineer mysteriously disappeared.
>   who
> ~~The engineer~~ was assigned the Balsam River project.
> The engineer who was assigned the Balsam River project mysteriously disappeared.
> James Kelley, who was assigned the Balsam River project, mysteriously disappeared.

Avoiding *Wh-* Fragments

These word groups must always be attached to a complete sentence. The wh- groups might look like independent sentences but they are not.

BASIC SKILLS

Remember, *wh-* words (and other qualifying words) should be as close as possible to the words they are qualifying.

>*Fragment:* Richard Perry is an airline pilot. Which is a very rewarding profession.
>*Complete:* Richard Perry is an airline pilot, which is a very rewarding profession.

EXERCISES

1. Check your dictionary for the correct usage of these *wh-* words; then,
2. Combine the following sentences using *wh-* groups.
   A. (1) The plumber did a good job.
      (2) The plumber installed our sink.
   B. (1) The police officer typed the report.
      (2) The officer made the arrest.
      (3) The officer typed slowly.
   C. (1) The flowers were planted by a landscape crew.
      (2) The flowers grew near the sidewalk.
      (3) They were colorful.
   D. (1) The accountant placed the tax forms in the drawer.
      (2) The accountant was tired.
      (3) The tax forms were her client's.
      (4) The forms would be safe in the drawer.
   E. (1) The truck arrived last night.
      (2) The truck delivered the load.
      (3) The load was of automotive parts.
   F. (1) Drop me off at the gate.
      (2) You picked me up at that gate.
      (3) You picked me up yesterday.
      (4) It was after work.
   G. (1) The receiver is on the shelf.
      (2) The receiver is broken.
      (3) He must repair it.
   H. (1) A woman reported the incident to the police.
      (2) Her mailbox was smashed.
   I. (1) The doctor talked with the nurse.
      (2) The nurse was worried about the patient.
   J. (1) The nurse called the doctor.
      (2) She is the floor nurse.
      (3) She was shocked by the patient's condition.
      (4) The doctor was in the cafeteria.

Combining Sentences by Using *-ing* and *-ed* Groups

Word groups formed around *-ing* and *-ed* words provide many opportunities for combining. Look for any unnecessarily repeated words in the following examples:

1. A. He thought about Jeanne.
   B. He was/ walking down the street. /
   C. ~~He was~~ walking down the street, he thought about Jeanne.
      Walking down the street, he thought about Jeanne.

2. A. She was shocked by his behavior.
   B. She got out of the car.
   C. ~~She was~~ shocked by his behavior, she got out of the car.
      Shocked by his behavior, she got out of the car.

You can move the groups around when combining them into an expanded sentence, but what is the result?

He thought about Jeanne walking down the street.

Who is doing the walking now? Look what happens with the other example:

She got out of the car shocked by his behavior.

His behavior might have been shocking to his car, but that's not what we started out to say. Because one of the reasons for combining sentences is to make the meaning *clearer,* always test all the alternatives to see which one states your message most accurately. Remember the rule from page 292: *wh-* words and other qualifying words should be as close as possible to the words they are qualifying.

QUALIFY CLOSELY

*Dale Hilton was an Air Force fighter pilot, but now he's an airline pilot, which is a very dangerous profession.

The rule of closeness causes us to understand this sentence to mean that the profession of airline pilot is dangerous. The writer intended to mean that the profession of Air Force fighter pilot is dangerous. To convey that meaning, place the qualifying group immediately after the word it should qualify:

Dale Hilton was an Air Force fighter pilot, which is a very dangerous profession, but now he's an airline pilot.

*The technician bumped into the table carrying several test tubes.

Again by the rule of closeness, we understand the *-ing* group to be qualifying *table,* but the writer meant that the technician was holding the tubes. So the sentence should read:

> The technician, carrying several test tubes, bumped into the table.
>
> or:
>
> Carrying several test tubes, the technician bumped into the table.

Did you notice that these three versions of one sentence show the *-ing* group at the beginning, middle, and end of the sentence? Study them briefly to explain the differences in meaning, emphasis, and variety.

Avoiding Fragments with *-ing* and/or *-ed* Groups

Take care when structuring your sentences with *-ing* groups at the end to connect them to the independent clause. Don't write them as separate units.

> *She applied for the job. Knowing her chances weren't very good because General Motors prefers experienced help.

This entire clause beginning with *knowing* is dependent not independent; if it isn't connected to an independent clause, it's called a *fragment* (a part of a sentence). The *-ing* and *-ed* groups are always dependent. Don't be confused by the subject and/or verb relationship that makes the clause seem, at first, to make sense by itself. If you listen to "her chances weren't very good because General Motors prefers experienced help," you might punctuate the whole clause as a sentence. *But remember that placing the -ing, -ed, wh- and other subordinating words before the rest of the clause makes the entire clause subordinate or dependent* (see pp. 273–274).

If in reading for revision, you find that you have written a structure similar to the one in the preceding example, correct it by attaching the *-ing* group to the independent clause; a comma usually precedes the *-ing* group when the group is qualifying the whole clause or when it qualifies a word earlier in the sentence:

> She applied for the job, knowing her chances weren't very good because General Motors prefers experienced help.

But if the *-ing* group or other qualifier groups are qualifying the word immediately preceding them, don't use the comma:

> The technician bumped into the rack holding several test tubes.

EXERCISES

1. Combine the following sentences.
2. Revise your combined sentence by placing *-ing* and *-ed* words in the beginning, middle, and end positions wherever possible.

3. Be prepared to explain the difference in emphasis, variety, and meaning each placement makes.
   A. (1) The draftsman completed the plans.
      (2) He was working carefully.
   B. (1) The secretary picked up the papers.
      (2) The papers were lying on the desk.
   C. (1) The supervisor called to the man.
      (2) The man was marking the crates.
   D. (1) The fireman was trapped in the building.
      (2) The fireman began to panic.
   E. (1) The lab assistant swept up the pieces of the flask.
      (2) The flask had been broken by falling off the shelf.

The *-ing* form of words can often be used to add a greater sense of action to your writing. This is particularly true when you are discussing something that has already happened. Because the action is in the past, you will naturally begin to write past tense verbs:

The dog smell*ed* a stranger. It began to bark furiously.

By converting at least one past tense verb to its *-ing* form, the sense of action increases:

Smell*ing* a stranger, the dog began to bark furiously.

He smashed the window. Then he climbed into the house.
Smashing the window, he climbed into the house.

Avoiding Dangling *-ing* and/or *-ed* Groups

An *-ing* group "dangles" when it is tacked on to a sentence in the wrong place (like the donkey's tail on its nose, or when the writer fails to *name* whoever or whatever is doing the acting stated in the *-ing* word). The *-ing* form of the verb conveys the action *in progress* (called the *progressive tense*); where there's action, there must be an actor. You'll have no trouble with this construction if you remember this simple diagram:

(who or what is) _____-ing__ , _____ .

Ask who or what is doing the action; place the answer immediately after the comma. From the example above, ask "Who or what is smelling?" The answer—"the dog"—goes immediately after the comma:

Smelling a stranger, the dog began to bark furiously.

We would not write:

*Smelling a stranger, the man was frightened off by the dog's barking.

This sentence means that the man smelled a stranger.

EXERCISES

1. Mark a *D* in front of the following sentences that have dangling *-ing* groups. Correct these sentences.
   A. Diving into the surf, the waves threw him back to shore.
   B. Running down the street, his hat was blown off.
   C. Hoping to become vice president of Hughes Markets, the supervisor used people ruthlessly.
   D. Trying to become a congressman, the cost of the campaign forced him to claim bankruptcy.
   E. Sensing danger, the hunter pursued the fleeing deer.

2. Combine the following sentences by changing at least one of the past-tense verbs into its *-ing* form; don't dangle the *-ing* groups.
   A. The waves pounded at the sides of the ship. The waves broke the ship in half.
   B. They hiked thirty-five miles without resting. They found help for their injured friend.
   C. The girls laughed and danced and sang. They expressed their love of life.
   D. She got up earlier than usual. She rushed through breakfast.
   E. He felt torn by indecision. He recalled the plight of Hamlet.

3. Review the second exercise to see if the sentences can be changed from your first revision. That is, if you changed the verb in the first sentence, try leaving it in the past tense and adding the *-ing* form in the second sentence.

Combining Sentences by Using Dependent (Subordinate) Groups

Dependent (subordinate) groups commonly begin with the following words (subordinators):

if	when	after
as soon as	because	before
while	although	until
since	so that	where

These words indicate a specific relationship between two clauses in a sentence. Notice, for example, that a number of these words indicate a *time* relationship between two actions—*as soon as, while, when, after, before, until.* What kind of relationship would *because* or *since* or *so that* indicate? In each case, the relationship is of one action depending in some way on the other; that is, something will be done when something else is finished or will be done *because* something else was done. These words are different from those in the *wh-* groups, which substitute for part of one sentence in combining it with another. The subordinators are simply placed *between* two sentences (two independent clauses) to combine them, showing the relationship that exists between the ideas in the two groups of words. The sentence that has the subordinator at the beginning becomes a dependent (surbordinate) clause, as in the following example:

> Larry was at lunch. John covered for him.
>
> John covered for him / while / Larry was at lunch.
>
> John covered for him while Larry was at lunch.

Notice the alternatives that are possible by moving the groups or rearranging words slightly. Notice also that two of these alternatives are confusing. Why are they confusing?

> While Larry was at lunch, John covered for him.
>
> John covered for Larry while he was at lunch.
>
> While he was at lunch, John covered for Larry.

The normal position for the dependent clause is after the main sentence:

> The technician struck a match.
>
> The gas exploded.
>
> The gas exploded *when* the technican struck a match.

But the dependent clause is movable; it can be placed elsewhere in the sentence. If it is moved from the normal position, however, the word group is followed by a comma:

> When the technician struck a match, the gas exploded.

Avoiding Fragments with Dependent Clauses

Dependent clauses look much like complete sentences, and some people tend to write them as such. But these groups should be attached to a complete sentence; that is why they are called *dependent*. Your ear can hear that these groups of words are not complete:

> *Fragment:* *While* he was waiting for a bus.
> *Complete:* While he was waiting for a bus, the old man was hit by a car.
> *Fragment:* She has not gone fishing. *Since* she left Oregon.
> *Complete:* She has not gone fishing since she left Oregon.

EXERCISE

Combine the following sets of sentences by using subordinator words like *when, while, if, as soon as, since, because, although, so that, after, before, until,* and *where* to make one of the clauses dependent.

A. (1) Will she be promoted?
   (2) She finishes the report this month.
B. (1) Karen decided to become a hospital dietitian.
   (2) Her father was hospitalized last year.
C. (1) You will know more about business management.
   (2) You take some data processing courses.
D. (1) Start applying for jobs.
   (2) You know your graduation date.
E. (1) Sharon has planned to be a corporate president.
   (2) She was a child.
F. (1) Ms. Mathews became an emergency medical technician.
   (2) She wanted to help people in distress.
G. (1) Send your résumés now.
   (2) You will get an early interview.
H. (1) Mark completes the associate degree in nursing.
   (2) He must take a licensing exam.
I. (1) You should think about several occupations.
   (2) You commit yourself.
J. (1) Jeff wanted to become a real-estate agent.
   (2) He went to college.
   (3) He became interested in commercial art.

IMPROVING USAGE

Subject-Verb Agreement

None of us would write a sentence in which the subject group and verb group don't match up:

The red car eats apples.

We know that this is an impossible situation. Cars don't eat apples. Not quite so obvious but just as distracting to the reader is the following mismatch between subject and verb:

*Once Bill get a job he will have enough money.

The mismatch here is a mismatch in *number*. The subject and verb don't agree with each other. Bill is one person, but the verb "get" tells us that the subject has to be either "you," "I," or more than one person or thing. The subject and verb in a clause must agree with each other in number. If the subject of a clause is singular, the verb must also be singular. If the subject is plural, the verb must be plural.

Here are some nouns in both singular and plural forms:

SINGULAR	PLURAL
tree	trees
car	cars
boat	boats
airplane	airplanes

Here are some verbs in singular and plural form:

SINGULAR	PLURAL
grows	grow
runs	run
sails	sail
flies	fly

Put the nouns and verbs together:

A tree grows.   A boat sails.
The trees grow.   The boats sail.
The car runs.   An airplane flies.
The cars run.   The airplanes fly.

One simple rule is demonstrated here: *Most* of the time if the subject ends in *s* the verb doesn't. There are, of course, a few singular nouns that end in -*s:* "Chess is a challenging game."

The subject groups must show that either there is one thing or one idea or one person acting in a sentence, or there is more than one. The verb in the sentence also tells us how many actors are performing.

*Bill, Larry, and Tom swims out to the raft.

According to the verb in this sentence, there is only one creature named "Bill, Larry, and Tom" that is able to swim. But without too much thought we know that Bill, Larry, and Tom are three separate people, so the verb must also indicate that more than one actor is performing:

Bill, Larry, and Tom swim out to the raft.

A few suggestions can help you keep your subjects and verbs agreeing in number.

-*s* and -*es* endings

Nouns and verbs alike use -*s* and -*es* endings. The difference is that nouns use -*s* and -*es* to signal *more than one:* bushes, houses, wheels, boats . . . Verbs, on the other hand, add -*s* and -*es* to signal that *only one* person, thing, or item is acting. Verbs that end in the *s, x, ch,* or *sh sound* add -*es* to show singular number in the present tense. All others use only -*s*.

Note that the -*es* ending adds an extra syllable:

box	box*es*	lurch	lurch*es*
church	church*es*	lunch	lunch*es*

These endings—the -s, -es ending for nouns and the -s, -es endings for verbs—are never used together. If the noun that is the subject has an -s or -es plural ending, then the verb does not have that ending. If the verb has an -s or -es ending, the noun does not have the -s or -es ending. The word "ending" here means that the letter -s (or -es) is *added* to a word. Therefore the "s" in such words as "kiss," "miss," or "boss" is not considered an *ending*.

> WRITE: The boss__ kiss*es* her husband.
> The boss*es* kiss__ their wives.
> NOT: The truck*s* stop*s* at the light.
> The truck__ stop__ at the light.

EXERCISE

Choose the verb that agrees with the subject in the following sentences:

1. Jack Nicklaus (stand, stands) in the middle of the fairway.
2. He (calculate, calculates) the distance to the green.
3. His caddy (tell, tells) him the distance to the pin.
4. Jack (judge, judges) the wind.
5. He (ask, asks) for a club.
6. He (grip, grips) the club, (stand, stands) behind the ball, and (look, looks) toward the green.
7. The golfer (is, are) seemingly in a trance.
8. He (imagine, imagines) every shot.
9. In his mind, he (picture, pictures) himself hitting the ball.
10. He (watch, watches) the ball drop to the heart of the green.
11. Most professional golfers (has, have) learned, like Jack Nicklaus, to imagine their shots.
12. Nicklaus' many victories on the tour (demonstrate, demonstrates) the effectiveness of this technique.

Words Between the Subject and the Verb

Problems with subject and verb agreement occur when words and phrases (especially prepositional phrases) come between the subject and the verb.

Doctors in a small town (has, have) many advantages.

The verb must agree with "doctors" not with "town," which is the object of the preposition "in."

EXERCISES

1. Choose the verb that agrees with the subject in the following sentences:
   A. Small towns in the Midwest, for example, (find, finds) it difficult to attract doctors.
   B. As a result, citizens in a small community (offer, offers) a doctor many enticements.
   C. Doctors who decide to begin practice in a small town (is, are) often supplied with a brand new clinic.
   D. People in a rural area (need, needs) a doctor who can treat a variety of ailments.
   E. A small-town doctor, on any given day, (treat, treats) ailments ranging from measles to arthritis.
   F. Many doctors who have chosen to give up their specialties (enjoy, enjoys) the importance of their role in a small community.

2. Insert suitable verbs in the blanks in the following paragraph:

   Cities _____ changing. Downtown _____ once the center of activity in a community. Today, many people _____ doing their shopping in malls built on the outskirts of the city. Higher crime rates _____ contributed to this changing pattern.

Subjects—Singular or Plural?

Certain kinds of subjects can be confusing. Four of these problem situations are discussed below: (1) compound subjects; (2) either/or, neither/nor; (3) there is/there are; (4) "you"/"I."

Compound Subjects

A subject may be more than one word that names a person, place, thing, or idea. A subject of more than one element is called a compound subject. Compound subjects take plural verbs. For example:

  Portland and Eugene *are* cities in Oregon.

  A pine tree, a maple tree, and a cedar tree *grow* in my backyard.

Nuclear power and solar energy *are* alternatives to oil and coal.

George and I *work* in the same building.

Sometimes, however, an apparently plural subject refers to only one thing. In these cases, use a singular verb. Note how the context of the following sentence determines whether the subject is plural:

Macaroni and cheese is my favorite meal. (One dish is being discussed.)

EXERCISE

Beginning with these compound subjects, create a sentence by adding a suitable verb that agrees with the subject. Write an additional five sentences with your own compound subjects and verbs that agree.

1. Magazines and newspapers
2. A shirt and tie
3. Beer and pretzels
4. Flowers and shrubs
5. The block and tackle

"Either/Or"; "Neither/Nor"

The connecting word "or" creates a special situation. Look at these examples:

Either the boss or one of his secretaries *makes* coffee in the morning.

Either Susan or her friends *are* responsible for the damage.

Buses, trains, or an automobile *provides* transportation into the city.

As these examples illustrate, the verb agrees in number with the subject word that appears closest to the verb (after the *or*). The same holds for neither . . . nor constructions.

Neither his looks nor his money *impresses* me.

Neither Fred nor his teachers *know* who won the contest.

Test your agreement this way: first, break the either/or, neither/nor construction into its parts; then match the verb with the closest part. We would say, for example:

Fred know*s* who won the contest.

The teachers know_ who won the contest.

Because *teachers* is closest to the verb in the original sentence, we use *know*.

EXERCISE

Using the following subjects, create sentences by adding the preferred form of a present-tense verb. Use different verbs for each sentence.

1. Either Mary or her parents
2. Television or movies
3. Either the water or the food
4. Neither pipes nor cigars
5. Either private cars or a bus

"There Is"/"There Are"

Accurate use of "there is" and "there are" gives the beginning writers some difficulty. The problem is that the subject of such sentences appears *after* the verb. *There* is just a filler word; the verb does not agree with *there* but with the subject that appears later in the sentence.

*There *is* twenty officers at the accident scene.

The subject of this sentence is *officers,* which is plural, so the verb should be plural.

There *are* twenty officers at the accident scene.

Sentences beginning with "there is" or "there are" can be turned around so that you can see the difference more clearly.

Twenty officers are at the accident scene.

In fact, in your revision stage, check to see that you haven't overused the "There is . . ." or "There are . . ." pattern. Notice that the revised sentence above emphasizes "twenty officers" because it's at the very beginning of the sentence.

EXERCISES

1. Underline the preferred verb in the following sentences:
   A. There (is, are) one problem we can't solve.
   B. There (is, are) twenty employees in her agency.

C. There (is, are) no rules against this.
D. There (is, are) only one student getting straight A's.
E. There (is, are) one of his explanations possible.

2. Revise the preceding sentences for better emphasis. (You may decide that one or several of them are in their best form now.)

"You"/"I"

The pronouns "you" and "I" deserve special attention. "You" can be either singular or plural; it can refer to one person or to an entire group. The pronoun "you," however, always takes the form of the verb that agrees with the plural.

You *are* my friend. (one person—verb *are*)

You *are* all a great group of people. (a group—verb *are*)

You *work* to make a good home for your family. (speaking about one person)

You *work* better than any group. (speaking about a large group)

I is used with *am* (not *is* or *are*) and with the verb form without -s or -es, the form that ordinarily indicates a plural subject. So we write *I do*, not *I does*; *I have*, not *I has*. Remember: "I" is singular but matches with the plural form of most verbs, except "be" where it has its own form.

> WRITE: I *am* tired of paying taxes.
> NOT: *I *is* tired of paying taxes.
>
> WRITE: I eat in the company cafeteria.
> NOT: *I eat*s* in the company cafeteria.

EXERCISES

1. Match the *I* subjects with the correct forms of the verbs in the following sentences:
   A. You (gather, gathers) the materials before beginning.
   B. I (work, works) with too many clients.
   C. I (help, helps) them to file the necessary forms.
   D. (Is, Are) you going to do that alone?
   E. It's hard when I (get, gets) to see them only once a month.

2. Write five additional sentences using "you" or "I" as the subject, being sure to make the verbs agree.

Verbs: Mainly in the Present Tense

Even if you have decided correctly whether the subject is singular or plural, you may still have difficulty choosing the correct form of the verb. The verb "to be," for example, creates particular problems.

The Verb "To Be"

The various forms of "be" are sometimes confused. Here are some rules for "be":

1. Present Tense

    A. be → *am* when the subject is *I*. (I am fine.)
    B. be → *is* when the subject is *he, she, it,* a proper noun, or a singular common noun. (John is . . .; the box is . . .)
    C. be → *are* in all other cases.

2. Past Tense

    A. be → *was* with *I, she, he, it,* a proper noun, or singular common noun.
    B. be → *were* in all other cases (we, they, storm*s*)

Thus,

instead of writing:	*write:*
*I be working.	I *am* working.
*He be working.	He *is* working.
*You be working.	You *are* working.
*They is working.	They *are* working.

EXERCISE

Underline the preferred verb in the following sentences:
A. I (am, is, be) gaining confidence to do college work.
B. He (am, is, be) taking nine hours this semester.
C. Sharon (am, is, be) graduating this semester.
D. It (am, is, be) easy to pass if you study.
E. A good job (am, is, be) hard to find without training.
F. You (am, are, be) my best friend.
G. They (am, are, be) expanding the course offerings.
H. Good jobs (am, are, be) never easy to find.
I. But my friends who have graduated (am, are, be) fully employed.
J. Cats (am, are, be) the best friend of man.

"Have/Has"; "Do/Does"

The same rule (#1) for verbs ending in -s, -es can be applied to *have/has* and *do/does*. Have + s = has. So *has* is the singular form and *have* is the plural form. Do + es = does, so *do* agrees with the plural and *does* with the singular. These words frequently cause problems with agreement.

Problems related to *do* arise with the contractions for *do not*. *Don't* and *doesn't* are both contractions. "Don't" means "do not." "Doesn't" means "does not." "Don't" agrees with plural subjects, while "doesn't" agrees with a singular subject. If you need to check on these forms, change the contraction back to the two-word form.

WRITE: The person who works for many years *doesn't* always enjoy retirement.
NOT: *The person who works for many years *don't* always enjoy retirement.

WRITE: My employee *has* all the benefits of a partner.
NOT: *My employee *have* all the benefits of a partner.

WRITE: The furnace *has* caused some serious problems.
NOT: *The furnace *have* caused some serious problems.

WRITE: The need for specialized training centers in many fields *has* increased.
NOT: *The need for specialized training centers in many fields *have* increased.

EXERCISE

Supply the preferred form of have/has, do/does, or don't/doesn't in the following sentences:

1. His supervisor _____ all the characteristics of a good leader.
2. The welder _____ caused some serious problems in production.
3. The need for experienced workers _____ increased.
4. He _____ not have any class.
5. His reasons for leaving work _____ never been known.
6. The correct answer _____ mean a thing unless you understand the question.
7. His father _____ intend to retire.
8. Her uncles _____ intend to retire.

9. His uncle's car _____ have fenders.
10. Three factories in town _____ have pollution-control equipment.

All Other Verbs in the Present Tense

Rules for all other verbs:

1. Verb + "s" when the subject is *he, she, it,* a proper noun, or a singular common noun:

    He work*s* hard.
    The boy look*s* angry.
    Mabel cri*es* often.
    Everybody like*s* George.
    Father dress*es* the baby.
    The car lurch*es* ahead.
    It break*s* down often.
    She organize*s* well.

2. Verb + (nothing) in all other cases:

    They weigh __ the box.
    We run __ fast.
    Houses sell __ quickly now.
    I work __ hard.
    You need __ help.

EXERCISE

Rewrite the following paragraph, correcting problems with subject-verb agreement:

I is not sure of what kind of job I wants. My father think I should be a doctor. Doctors earns a lot of money, but hospitals make me uncomfortable. Entrance requirements is very high for medical school. My grades in math and science has not been very good in high school.

Verbs: Past Forms

Not using the correct form of a verb when you write about things happening in the past is a common usage problem. A fiction writer may even use this problem to indicate a character's lack of education:

> "Now you tell me how you *done* it," the tall man said. I thought about it for a minute, then decided it would be better to say nothing. I waited for him to say something more.
>
> "Look," he said, "I *seen* you over there. I *known* then you was the one that *done* it."

Forming the Past Tense

Regular verbs indicate the past by adding *-ed*:

> I work every day.
>
> I work*ed* at Amalgamated last summer.
>
> I have work*ed* for them every summer since I started school.

Certain forms of the past use a helping verb such as *be* or *have* to indicate more than just a simple past action. In the last example above, the use of *have* with the past form of the verb indicates an action in the past that continues to the present time in some way. The use of *had* would indicate an action totally completed in the past, before some other past action took place:

> I had worked there before they closed the plant.

But the main usage problem comes with *irregular* verbs, ones that change spelling instead of merely taking an *-ed* ending to show past tense: *sing, sang, sung; know, knew, known; forgive, forgave, forgiven*. The problem here comes when a writer uses the third form of the verb (called the "past participle") to indicate the simple past. Our author above deliberately made the "tall man" sound poorly educated by using the third form of the irregular verbs "do," "see," and "know" to indicate the simple past:

>   *done*
> "how you did it . . ."
>
> *seen*
> "I saw you . . ."
>
>   *known*
> "I knew then . . ."

With regular verbs this problem doesn't come up because the simple past form and the third form are the same: you say (or write) both "I wait*ed* for that delivery," and "I *have waited* for it." With irregular verbs, the third form (past participle) is used as a verb *only* with a helping verb—some form of *be* or *have*. Using those forms without a helping verb—that is, using the third form for the simple past—makes you sound like the tall character in the story.

To avoid this problem, you need to know whether the verb you are using is regular or not. If it's irregular, you need to know if the past form and the past participle are the same. If they are different, don't use the third form without a helping verb. To get the information you need, check the following alphabetical list of irregular verbs. When you are proofreading your writing, check every verb against this list if you have had problems with using the past participle for the simple past. The more you use this list, the more you will begin to remember the correct verb forms.

If the verb is not on this list, it is a regular verb. The only problem with regular verbs is *forgetting to put the -ed on to show the past*. We often don't pronounce the *-ed* in speech and must be careful to make sure it is added in writing.

List of Irregular Verbs

Because language is always changing, some verbs have several forms currently in use. We have listed in parentheses additional forms that are acceptable. For the past participle, *have* is used with *I, you, we,* and *they; has* is used with *he, she,* and *it*. To avoid cluttering the page, we have listed *have* only.

PRESENT	PAST	PAST PARTICIPLE
arise	arose	have arisen
awake	awoke (awaked)	have awaked
be	was, were	have been
bear	bore	have borne, born*
beat	beat	have beaten
begin	began	have begun
bend	bent	have bent
bid	bid	have bid
bid	bade	have bidden

*See a dictionary for two different uses.

PRESENT	PAST	PAST PARTICIPLE
bind	bound	have bound
bite	bit	have bitten (bit)
blow	blew	have blown
break	broke	have broken
bring	brought	have brought
broadcast	broadcast (broadcasted)	have broadcast (-ed)
build	built	have built
burst	burst	have burst
buy	bought	have bought
cast	cast	have cast
catch	caught	have caught
choose	chose	have chosen
cling	clung	have clung
come	came	have come
creep	crept	have crept
cut	cut	have cut
deal	dealt	have dealt
dig	dug	have dug
dive	dived (dove)	have dived
do	did	have done
draw	drew	have drawn
drink	drank	have drunk
drive	drove	have driven
eat	ate	have eaten
fall	fell	have fallen
feed	fed	have fed
fight	fought	have fought
find	found	have found
flee	fled	have fled
fling	flung	have flung
fly	flew	have flown
forbid	forbade (forbad)	have forbidden
forget	forgot	have forgotten (forgot)
forgive	forgave	have forgiven
forsake	forsook	have forsaken
freeze	froze	have frozen
get	got	have got (gotten)
give	gave	have given
go	went	have gone

BASIC SKILLS

PRESENT	PAST	PAST PARTICIPLE
grind	ground	have ground
grow	grew	have grown
hang	hung*	have hung
have	had	have had
hear	heard	have heard
hide	hid	have hidden (hid)
hit	hit	have hit
hold	held	have held
hurt	hurt	have hurt
kneel	knelt (kneeled)	have knelt
know	knew	have known
lay	laid	have laid
lead	led	have led
leap	leaped (leapt)	leaped (leapt)
leave	left	have left
lend	lent	have lent
let	let	have let
lie	lay	have lain
lose	lost	have lost
make	made	have made
meet	met	have met
pay	paid	have paid
put	put	have put
read	read	have read
rend	rent	have rent
ride	rode	have ridden
ring	rang	have rung
rise	rose	have risen
run	ran	have run
say	said	have said
see	saw	have seen
seek	sought	have sought
sell	sold	have sold
send	sent	have sent
set	set	have set
shake	shook	have shaken
shine	shone	have shone
shoot	shot	have shot
shrink	shrank (shrunk)	have shrunk (shrunken)

*See a dictionary for two different uses.

PRESENT	PAST	PAST PARTICIPLE
sing	sang (sung)	have sung
sink	sank	have sunk
sit	sat	have sat
slay	slew	have slain
sleep	slept	have slept
slide	slid	have slid
sling	slung	have slung
smite	smote	have smitten
speak	spoke	have spoken
spin	spun	have spun
spring	sprang (sprung)	have sprung
stand	stood	have stood
steal	stole	have stolen
sting	stung	have stung
stride	strode	have stridden
strike	struck	have struck (stricken)
string	strung	have strung
strive	strove (strived)	have striven (strived)
swear	swore	have sworn
sweat	sweat (sweated)	have sweated
sweep	swept	have swept
swim	swam	have swum
swing	swung	have swung
take	took	have taken
teach	taught	have taught
tear	tore	have torn
tell	told	have told
think	thought	have thought
thrive	thrived (throve)	have thrived
throw	threw	have thrown
wake	woke (waked)	have waked (wakened, woken)
wear	wore	have worn
weave	wove	have woven
weep	wept	have wept
win	won	have won
wind	wound	have wound
wring	wrung	have wrung
write	wrote	have written

EXERCISES

1. Group as many irregular verbs as you can under each of the six common rhyme patterns. For example, "*arise*," "*arose*," "have *arisen*" shows an "i," "o," "-en" pattern, which is like "smite," "smote," "smitten"; "ride," "rode," "ridden."
   A. b*ear*, b*ore*, have b*orne*
   B. begin, began, have begun
   C. blow, blew, have blown
   D. buy, bought, have bought
   E. break, broke, have broken
   F. drive, drove, have driven

2. Fill in the blank in each of the following sentences with the appropriate past form of the verb given in parentheses.
   A. Yesterday the storm _____ trees across the power lines. (blow)
   B. Lockheed _____ $4 million for the contract. (bid)
   C. The earthquake _____ only a few water pipes. (burst)
   D. The union members have met and _____ their votes. (cast)
   E. The foreman _____ the timecards across the room. (fling)
   F. The credit union has _____ all its funds. (lend)
   G. Mike started to say, "Take this job and . . . .," but instead he _____ out the door. (stride)
   H. Her patients have _____ daily for physical therapy. (swim)
   I. Levis usually _____. (shrink)
   J. An expensive drill was _____ from his locker. (steal)

Pronoun Problems

Pronoun Agreement

Pronouns are words that replace nouns, so they should agree with the nouns they replace. See if you can spot the problems in the following sentences:

*A person may not really like the job they are trained for.

*One can repair his own car, but you have to know what you are doing.

In the first case, "*a person*" means *one* person, but the pronoun "they" means *more than one* person is referred to. The reader is momentarily confused by the shift from talking about *one* person to talking about *many* people. Correct it by writing:

Some people may not really like the job *they* are trained for.

In the second case, the sentence shifts pronouns from *one* to *his* to *you*. The reader is never certain who is being spoken about. The reader is distracted from the message in trying to figure out who is being talked to or talked about. Use pronouns consistently:

You can repair *your* own car, but *you* have to know what *you* are doing.

Words that end in *-one* or *-body* are singular nouns; they take singular pronoun substitutes and singular verbs:

One of us needs to be responsible.

Nobody likes to fail a test.

Everyone asks what happened to him.

EXERCISE

In the following sentences, correct the faulty pronoun agreement; if you change the subject you may also have to change the verb to make it agree.

1. When a woman is pregnant, you may feel uncomfortable at times.
2. A person who tries to do right gets their reward in time.
3. Ultimately, everyone must take responsibility for their own actions.
4. Someone lost his direction.
5. Everybody wants his pay even if their work isn't done.
6. Most men don't work as hard as they could, because he isn't given enough say in decisions that affect his job.
7. Profits are the major goal of business even if it means unemployment and inflation.
8. Either the coach or the players will have to change his mind.
9. Neither the owner nor the employees wants their production halted.
10. The government should keep the antitrust laws as it is.

When you have something you want to say, the best procedure is to write it down as fast as you can. The trouble is that many people write down thoughts and ideas in a rush, then forget or don't take the time to make sure the sentences say what they want to say. In putting a sentence on paper, words and ideas that are clear to you may not be clear to someone else. Here are some sources of confusion you can check for in going over what you have written.

Indefinite References

Problems with clarity rise from relying on pronouns to fill places in the sentence that should be filled by nouns. Pronouns are useful words, but they can clutter and confuse an otherwise clear idea. Look at the following sentences:

> George had some conflicts with his boss. He used to give him the jobs he didn't want to do himself.

By the time we finish the second sentence we are a little puzzled just who *he* is. The message can be figured out, but the reader shouldn't have to pause to think about which person "he," "him," and "himself" refer to. This sentence can be revised in a number of ways to get rid of the confusion. Here is one way:

> George had some conflicts with his boss. George was given the jobs his boss didn't want to do himself.

The revision simply uses the nouns *George* and *boss* in places of the confusing string of pronouns. When editing your own writing, beware of several pronouns following one another; consider using nouns instead.

Another more economical way of avoiding the problem pronouns is to combine:

> George had some conflicts with his boss *who* gave George the jobs he didn't want to do himself.

EXERCISE

Change the following sentences so that the indefinite pronouns no longer cause confusion:

1. Mary spoke with her mother about her being promoted before she had her accident.

2. The whole division is ineffective because of outdated equipment. It simply fails to do the job.
3. John works hard to satisfy his supervisor, but he is never sure what he is doing.
4. Kate's life has centered around her father's company ever since her mother died when she was a child.
5. Inflation is a problem in the economy and its increase may cause it further problems.

Vague Pronouns

"This"

The word "this" often becomes a crutch word at the beginning of sentences. "This" should refer back to a specific word or idea. Note the vagueness in the following pair of sentences:

> Lucy is working in a mental hospital this summer.
> This may become her career.

The problem here is, of course, lack of information. What kind of work is Lucy doing? Is her career going to be working in a mental hospital during the summers? Specify this:

> Lucy is working in a mental hospital this summer.
> Psychiatric counseling may become her career.

"They"

Pronouns used at the beginning of sentences often substitute for more precise terms. In speaking, we often begin sentences with pronouns that don't really refer to any specific person or thing: "They towed my car away last night." The message is clear, but the accuracy and clarity necessary in much of the writing you will do requires that you avoid this kind of construction:

Unclear: They claim their product is the best on the market.

Clear: Biggs and Platton claim their toothpaste is the best on the market.

We simply replaced "they" with a specific name and instead of the vague "their product" we named the product.

"It"

The pronoun "it" is another crutch word. In the preceding example the sentences that came before could make clear what "they" referred to. But "it" is often used without anything definite to refer back to:

It is reported in *Business Week* that prime interest rates will fall.

The *it is* occupies the most important places in the sentence: the subject and the verb slots. "It" refers to nothing definite; the pronoun just takes up space.

Business Week reports that prime interest rates will fall.

EXERCISE

Get rid of the vague "it" in the following sentences:

1. It seems that the energy crisis was a hoax.
2. It never occurred to me to call for an appointment.
3. It is obvious that the fire was caused by faulty wiring.

"You"

Another common problem results from the indefinite use of the pronoun "you." When we are writing directly to someone, "you" establishes contact between writer and reader. But when "you" refers to no one in particular, a sentence can lose precision and clarity.

Muddled: You often make mistakes when you are a beginner.

Better: Beginners often make mistakes.

EXERCISE

Wherever necessary in the following sentences, cross out the vague or confusing pronoun and substitute the appropriate noun for it:

IMPROVING USAGE | 319

A. The train was waiting at the station. It contained thirty people.
B. The engineer told the conductor that he was supposed to take a ten-minute break.
C. The banker confessed to the police that he had embezzled company funds. This is when the problem began.
D. They say that it's going to rain this weekend. But sometimes they are wrong.
E. It says in the newspaper this evening that they are planning another space launch.
F. The car was parked beside the garage. It needed to be painted.
G. Thinking of their friends as they sat around the fire, the couple thought they were lucky.
H. It is snowing in the mountains, so they say.
I. Always keep track of your time while you're flying.
J. You should always plan ahead.

REVIEW EXERCISE

Each of the following sentences contains one of the writing problems discussed in this appendix. Revise the sentences to eliminate the problems.

1. Long hours and dedication is part of a nurse's job.
2. There is a fire station, a library, and a gas station in Remus.
3. I is not sure of the answer.
4. The drought during the winter months have caused crop damage.
5. After lunch, the supervisor of the crew don't work very hard.
6. Either the students or the teacher are in the wrong classroom.
7. George agreed with the customer that he was responsible.
8. Judy rung the doorbell again and again.
9. Deirdre has always been very fond of animals and enjoyed caring for them. This has influenced her thinking about a career.
10. Anyone who wants to may begin their job.
11. None of the singers have received any pay.
12. My father and brother doesn't care for baseball.
13. There are only one of the five brothers living in America.
14. Deciding whether or not to finish college or to get a job now is a difficult decision.
15. His uncles and he works forty-eight hours a week.

16. They say people have to look out for themselves.
17. You is the one who must do it.
18. It is believed by conservatives that the government has the right to dictate moral values.
19. When you put a plane into a steep dive, you get a thrill like nothing else I've ever experienced.
20. Rick drunk eighteen cans of beer at the picnic.

INDEX

A

Abstract, 177
  descriptive, 178
  proposal, 251
Adjustment letters, 215–217
  bad news, 216–217
Adverbials, 263–264
  information provided by, 264
Advertisements, 197, 206
  answering employers'. *See* Job search
Agreement
  possessive, 300–301
  pronoun, 314–317
  subject-verb, 278–279, 299–308
Analysis
  cause-effect, 117, 129–148
  defined, 83
  in evaluation memos, 220
  functional, 116, 120–123
  of parts or components, 115–116, 118
  steps in a process, 116, 123–124
    dividing operation into steps, 125
    functions of, 125
    necessary equipment or tools in, 124–125
    objective, 124
  surface details in, 113
  types of, 115
  understanding, 113–118
  written, 118–127
Analytic thinking, 113–114
Appendix, of reports, 244, 250
Appropriate voice, 11, 150, 188
  distant, 13
  formal, 11
  informal, 12, 150
  involved, 12
Arguments, kinds of, 151
Attitude toward subject, 8
Audience
  attitude toward, 8
  identifying, 167–168, 809
  persuasion of, 167–168
  writing to, 7–15

321

B

Bandwagoning persuasion, 162, 165
Bibliography, in reports, 244
Body language, 3
Brainstorming, 18
Breakdown strategy, in persuasion memos, 224
Business letters, 210–215
   addresses, inside, 211
   body, 212
   closing, 212
   copies, abbreviation for, 213
   enclosure notation, 213
   format, 210–215
   greeting, 211–212
   heading, 210–211
   initialed references in, 212–213
   sample, 213–215
   signature, 212
Business writings
   guidelines, 228–229
   instructions, 227–321
   letters, 210–219
   memos, 219–227
   proposals, 251–255
   reports, 235–250

C

Capitalization, 5
Career objectives, 200
Causal analysis. *See* Cause-effect analysis
Cause-effect analysis, 117, 129–148
   cause to effect, 138–140
   effect to cause, 141–142
   effect-cause-effect combination, 143–144
   evaluating, 136–137
   in evaluation memos, 221–222
   immediate and remote causes in, 131–133
   organizing, 144–147
   sequence vs. causality in, 129–130
   uses for, 133–135
Claim letters, 215–217

Clarity, sentence, 282–283, 293
Clarity of organization, 188
Class, 77
Classifications, 77
   analysis of, 83
   defined, 77
   and division, 77–78
   establishing principles, 78–82
   in evaluation memos, 222
   introductions to, types of, 85–86
   and resumés, 198
   transition statements, 87
   writing, 85
Clauses
   defined, 261
   dependent (subordinate), 261, 273–275, 294, 296–298
      normal position of, 297
      relative, 290–292
   independent, 273, 286–287
   main, 261
Closeness, rule of, 291, 293
College writing, 173–192
   critical reviews, 185–191
   essay exams, 174–175
   general essays, 175–176
   summaries, 177–185
Commas
   and coordinating words, 286
   with dependent clauses, 297
   and non-essential clauses, 291
Communication
   guidelines, 7
   persuasion and, 149
   system of signals in, 5, 6
   two-way, 3–4
   written, 5–6
   effective, 7
Comparison(s), 61–76
   and contrast, 61–62
   defined, 61, 62
   purpose of, 61
   significant differences, 62
   significant likenesses, 62
   standards of, 67–68
   types of, 63–66

advantages and disadvantages, 64–65
analogy, 65–66
preferences, 64
writing methods, 69–74
combination of methods, 74
point-by-point, 69, 72–74
whole-by-whole, 69–72
Complaint letter, 215
Component analysis, 113, 115, 118
Compound subjects, 302–303
Conjunctions, coordinating, 285–286
Connecting words, 303–304
Contractions, 307
Contrasts, 61
Controlling idea, 26–28, 29
repetition of, 30
Coordinating conjunctions, 285–286
within independent clauses, 286
Cover letter, 201–204
Critical analysis. See Critical reviews
Critical reviews, 185–191
author's effectiveness and, 186–188
appropriate voice, 188
clarity of organization, 188
general strengths and weaknesses, 188
quality of ideas, 187
support for ideas and, 187–188
author's purpose and, 186
author's thesis and, 186
comparative evaluation with other works in, 189
sample of, 189–190
usefulness to specific audience and, 189

D

Dangling word groups, 295
Deductive paper, organizing, 161–162
Deductive persuasion, 161–162
Definitions, 95–111
classification and division, relationship to, 95–96
comparing terms, 105

distinguishing term from others in class, 103–104
by characteristics, 104
by functions, 104
by parts, 103–104
examples, use of, 107
extended, 96, 100–102
developing, 101
and simple, difference between, 100
and negative examples, 108–109
placing term in a class, 102–103
problems in, 98–99
purpose of, 99
simple, 95, 97–98
Demonstratives, 267
Dependent clause, 261, 273–275, 294, 296–298
fragments with, 297
Description(s), 51–60
defined, 51
details, paying attention to, 53
general picture, 52–53
use of senses, 53–54
writing, 54–60
steps in, 57–58
words, 56–57
Descriptive abstract, 178
Descriptive elements, 51
Descriptive writing, 54
Details, observing, 16
Determiners, 266
Devil-words, 164
Division, 77
Do/does, 307

E

Economy, sentence, 282
Either/or, 303–304
Emphasis, in sentences, 284–285
Essay exams, 174–175
strategies for, 174
Essays, general, 175–176
Evaluation memos, 220–223
analysis in, 220
cause-and-effect in, 221–222

Evaluation memos *(continued)*
   classification in, 222
Evaluation vs. summary, 185; *see also*
   Critical reviews
   in reports, 235
Evidence, 152–153
   and critical review, 187
   expert opinion, 153–154
   facts
      historical, 153
      physical, 152–153
      scientific, 153
      statistical, 153
   sources of, 154
Examples, use of, 155–156
   and critical review, 187–188
Exams, essay, 174–175
Expert opinion, 153–154
Explain, writing to, 10
   in summaries, 179
Expressive writing, 10

F

Facial expressions, 4
Facts, 152–153
Flow charting, 18
Follow-up letter, to job interview, 205–207
Formal reports, 243
Fragment clauses, 291–292, 293–294
Free association lists, 16–17
Functional analysis, 116, 120–123
   basic tasks of, 120

G

General persuasion, 162, 164
Generalities, glittering, 164
Generalization ladder, 25, 42, 102, 107
Gestures, 4, 5
God-words, 164
Guidelines, writing, 228–231

H

Have/has, 307

I

Illustration, 34
Independent clause, 261, 275–276, 294
   punctuation with, 286–287
Inductive paper, organizing, 159–160
Inductive persuasion, 157–160
Infinitives, 272
Information, writing to provide, 10
   in reports, 235
Inquiry letters, 217–218
   responses to, 218
   unsolicited, 217
Instruction writing, 227–233
   analysis of, 227
   description in, 228
   guidelines for, 228–229
   thinking process in, 227
   writing strategies in, 227
Instructional memo, 225–226
   characteristics common to, 226
Interview appointment letter, 204
Interviews, 204–207
   appointment, 204
   follow-up to, 205
   see also Job Interview
Investigation, 151
Irregular verbs, 309–314
   list of, 310–313
   past tenses of, 309

J

Job interview, 204–205
   appointment letter, 204
   follow-up letter, 205–207
Job market, 194–195
Job search, 193–207
   advertisements and, 196
   cover letter, 201–204
   follow-up letter, 205–207

INDEX **325**

interview, 204–205
interview appointment letter, 204
job market and, 194–195
professional or trade journals and, 195
resumé and, 197–201
steps in, 196–201
understanding, 193–207
Journals
professional, 195
trade, 195
Judgment, 151
Judgmental words, 166

L

Language persuasion, 166
Letter writing, 209–233
additional elements, 212
adjustment, 215–217
business, 210–215
claim, 215–217
cover letter, 201
follow-up, 205
inquiry, and responses, 217–218
interview appointment, 204
order, 218–219

M

Memos, 219–227
cause and effect in, 221
evaluation, 220–223
explanatory, 220
informational, 219–220
instructional, 225–226
characteristics common to, 226
purpose of, 225
persuasion, 223–225
analysis of, 224
to-from-subject-date, 220

N

Name-calling, 162–164
Negative definition, 108

Neither/nor, 303–304
Nouns, 266–269
common, 264
defining of (main subject), 266
demonstrative, 267
determiners, 266
number and
plural, 267
singular, 267
possessive, 268–269
proper, 266
-*s* and -*es* endings, 300–301
Noun-finders, 266–269
prepositions, 268

O

Occurence report, 240–242
Opinions, informed, 152
Order letters, 218–219

P

Paragraphs, 21–47
analyzing data in, 23–24
checking for unity in, 29–30
controlling ideas in, 26
defined, 21
general or specific subject matter, definition of, 25
grouping in, 23
naming groups in, 25
order of details
general to specific, 42–43
by importance, 43–44
by space, 40–42
by time, 36–39
organization of material in, 22–23
pattern for development of, 31–34
assertion and support, 33
general question/specific response, 31–32
topic and illustration, 26, 34
topic sentence in, forming, 26–28
transitions in, 44–46

Paraphrase, 178
Past participles, 309–314
Past tense, 309–314
  converting to -ing form, 295
  forming, 309–310
  of *to be*, 306
Personal pronouns, 166
Persuasion, 11, 149–157
  in communication, 149
  effective, 150
    investigation, 150
    judgment, 150
    taste, 150
  emotional, 162–165
    on bandwagon, 165
    glittering generalities, 164
    name-calling, 164
    sentimentality, 163
    testimonial, 164
    transfer, 165
  logical deduction, 161
  logical induction, 157–159
  personal, 166–168
    identifying with audience, 167–168
    language choice, 166
  subjects of, 151
Persuasion memos, 223–225
  breakdown of problem in, 224
Phrases, 260–261
  defined, 261
  prepositional, 268, 276–277, 278–279, 288–290, 301–302
Physical description, 51
Pitch, 5
Point-by-point method of comparison, 72–74
Possessive agreement, 300–301
Precis, 177
Prepositional groups, flexibility of, 289
Prepositional phrases, 268, 276–277, 301
  agreement problems caused by, 278–279
  combining sentences with, 288–290
  emphasis and, 289
  and subject-verb agreement, 301–302

Prepositions, 268
  frequently used, 288–289
Present tense
  of *to be*, 306
  rules for, 306–308
Procedural analysis, 116, 123–124
Professional journals, 195
Progress reports, 16, 237–240
  defined, 237
  example of, 239
  format of, 237–239
    body, 238
    conclusion, 238–239
    introduction, 238
Progressive tense, 295
Pronouns, 305, 314–320
  agreement of, 314–316
  clear use of, 316–317
  as indefinite references, 316
  vague, 317–318
    it, 318
    they, 317–318
    this, 317
Proposals, 251–255
  format of, 251–252
    abstract, 251, 252
    cost, 252, 254
    need, 252, 253
    objectives, 252–253
    personnel, 252, 254
    procedures, 252, 253–254
  techniques for, 251
Punctuation, 5
  use of, 6
Purpose of writing, 10

Q

Qualifying words, rule for, 291, 293
Quotations, in summaries, 179

R

Recommendations, in reports, 236
Relative clauses, 290–292

Repetition, avoiding in sentences, 291
Reports, 235–256
    evaluative, 242–246
        appendix of, 244
        bibliography of, 244
        body of, 243–244
        example of, 244–246
        summary of, 243
    formal, 236, 243
    informal, 236
    informational, 237–242
        occurence, 240–242
        progress, 237–240
    interpretative, 242–246
    knowledge of audience and, 236–237
    purposes of, 235–236
    recommendations, making, 246–250
        format and strategies, 246–247
        sample of, 247–250
Research, 154
Response, 178
Resumés, 197–201
    cover letter, 201–204
    defined, 197
    elements in
        career objective, 200
        duties and responsibilities, 201
        education, 201
        employment history, 201
        personal data, 200
        summary of experience, 201
    emphases in
        skills, 198–199
        work experience, 199–200
    examples of, 198–200
    rules for, 197
Reviews, critical, writing, 185–192
Run-on sentences, 273, 286

S

Sentence(s), 27–60, 259–298
    avoiding repetition in, 287–288
    basic parts of, 27–28, 262–263
    clarity, 282–283, 293
    clauses in. *See* Clauses
    combining, 281–298
        with coordinating words, 285–287
        with dependent (subordinate) groups, 296–298
        with *-ing* and *-ed* groups, 293–296
        with prepositional phrases, 288–290
        with relative clauses, 290–292
    controlling idea, 28
    defined, 261
    economy in, 282
    emphasis in, 284–285
    nouns in, finding, 266–269
    phrases in, 260–261
    prepositional phrases in. *See* Prepositional phrases
    run-on, 273, 286
    subject in, finding, 275–276
    topic sentence, 26
    transition words, 44
    types of, 31–34
    understanding, 259–280
    unity words, 29
    variety of, 283–284
    verb in, finding, 269–275
    word groups in, 260–265
Sentence fragments, 273, 291–292
    with dependent clause, 297
    with *-ing* and/or *-ed* groups, 294–295
Sentimental persuasion, 162–163
Sequence and causality, 129–130
Skills, basic, 259–320
Space order, in paragraphing, 40–42
Speaking, and writing, 3–7
    two-way communication, 3–4
Stress, 5
Subject, exploring, 15–19
    brainstorming, 18
    details of, 16
    flow charting, 18
    free association, 16
    free writing, 17
    interviewing, 18
    research, 18
    systematic way, 16

Subclasses, 77
Subject groups, 262, 263
Subject of sentence
   compound, 302–303
   locating, 275–276
   prepositional phrases and, 276–277
   problem, 302–305
      either/or, 303–304
      neither/nor, 303–304
      there is/there are, 304–305
      you/I, 305
Subject/verb agreement, 299–308
   in number, 299–300
   and problem subjects, 302–305
      compound, 302–303
      either/or, 303–304
      neither/nor, 303–304
      there is/there are, 304–305
      you/I, 305
   -s and -es endings, 300–301
   and words between subject and verb, 301–302
Subordinate clauses, 261, 273–275, 294, 296–298
Subordinators, 273–274, 296–298
   list of, 274, 296
Summaries, 177–185
   defined, 177
   editing and revising, 180
   vs. evaluation, 185
   length of, 177–178
   vs. paraphrase, 178
   vs. response, 178
   sample, 180–183
   steps in writing, 178–180
Syllogism, 161
Synopsis, summary, 177–178
System of signals, 5

T

Taste, question of, 151
Technical description, 118
Testimonials, 162, 164
Themes, 175
There is/there are, 303–305
Thesis papers, 176
"They," 317
"This," 317
Time reference, in paragraphing, 36–39
To be, forms of, 306
Topic sentence
   defined, 26
   forming, 26–28
Transference, 162, 165
Transition words, 44–45
   in summary, 179

U

Unity
   checking for, 29–30
   defined, 29

V

Variety, sentence, 283–284
Verbs, 269–275, 299–315
   action
      mental or emotional, 269
      physical, 269
   agreement of, 278–279
   choice of, 36
   defining of, 269–270
   in dependent clause, 273–275
   helping, 272
   infinitives, 272–273
   -ing form of, 271–272
      as adjective, 271
      as noun, 271
      as verb, 272
   main verbs, 271–274
   -s and -es endings, 300–301
   tense forms of. *See* Verb tenses
Verb groups, 262–263
Verb tenses, 269–270
   past, 309–314
   present, 306–308
   progressive, 295
   of *to be*, 306

Voice, 150
   appropriate, 11–12
   distant, 13
   formal, 11
   informal, 12
   involved, 12–13

W

Wh- fragments, 291–292
Wh- groups, 290–292
Whole-by-whole method of comparison, 69–70
Word groups, 260–265
   adverbials, 263–264
   clauses. *See* Clauses
   dangling, 295
   -ed, 293–296
   -ing, 293–296
   phrases, 260–261
   subject, 262–263
   verb, 262–263
   wh-, 290–292

Word usage, 44, 56
   improving, 299–320
      pronouns, 314–319
      subject-verb agreement, 299–308
      verbs, 306–314
Writing
   audience and, 7–15
      attitude toward, 8–9
      guidelines for, 7
      identifying, 8
      purpose of, 9–10
   in college, 173–191. *See also* College writing
   free, 17
   importance of, in business, 209–210
   purpose of, 10, 185
   subject of, attitude toward, 8
Writing analysis, 113, 118

Y

You/I, 305

About the Authors

James Kinney is Associate Professor of English and Director of Composition and Rhetoric at Virginia Commonwealth University in Richmond, Virginia. He received his B.A. from St. Bonaventure University in Olean, New York, and his Ph.D. from the University of Tennessee in Knoxville. He has published articles on the teaching of composition in such journals as *College Composition and Communication, The Rhetoric Society Quarterly, College English,* and *Freshman English News.*

David E. Jones is an assistant professor at Los Angeles Valley College. He received his B.A. from California State College at Los Angeles and his Ph.D. from Kent State University. His articles on composition and literature have appeared in a number of journals, including *College Composition and Communication, The James Joyce Quarterly,* and *The Ball State University Forum.*

John Scally is Dean of Continuing Education and Program Development at Lewis-Clark State College, Lewiston, Idaho. He received his B.A. from the University of Portland, Portland, Oregon, and a Doctor of Arts Degree from the University of Oregon. Co-author of *Writing in an Age of Technology* (Macmillan, 1976), he has published articles on teaching liberal arts in a vocational setting in *The Journal of Higher Education* and *The Journal of Remedial and Developmental Education.* Since 1977 he has served as a member of the National Endowment for the Humanities' National Board of Consultants.